Impact of
RICH COUNTRIES' POLICIES on POOR COUNTRIES

Impact of
RICH COUNTRIES' POLICIES on POOR COUNTRIES

Towards a Level Playing Field in Development Cooperation

Robert Picciotto *&* **Rachel Weaving**
editors

Transaction Publishers
New Brunswick (U.S.A.) and London (U.K.)

This book is printed on acid-free paper that meets the American National Standard for Permanence of Paper for Printed Library Materials.

Library of Congress Catalog Number: 2003067188
ISBN: 0-7658-0236-8
Printed in the United States of America

Library of Congress Cataloging-in-Publication Data

Impact of rich countries' policies on poor countries : towards a level playing
    field in development cooperation / Robert Picciotto and Rachel
    Weaving, editors.
        p. cm.
    Includes bibliographical references.
    ISBN 0-7658-0236-8 (cloth : alk. paper)
        1. Economic development—International cooperation. 2. Economic
    assistance—Developing countries. 3. Poverty—Government policy.
    4. Globalization. I. Picciotto, Robert. II. Weaving, Rachel, 1947-

HD82.I295 2004
338.91'09172'4—dc22

                                                    2003067188

Contents

Preface

This volume addresses a curiously neglected area of policy analysis: the impact of rich countries' policies on the global poor. Four-fifths of the world's people subsist on one-fifth of the world's income. One-fifth live in abject poverty on less than one dollar a day. All United Nations heads of state have endorsed Millennium Development Goals that aim at halving the incidence of absolute poverty by 2015. In order to reach these goals, the developing economies will need to grow twice as fast over the next fifteen years as they did in the 1990s.

The main responsibility for poverty reduction rests with developing countries. But in the wake of globalization rich countries must also play their part. At the United Nations Financing for Development Conference in Monterrey in March 2002, when developing countries took on the commitment to enhance their governance and adopt reforms, developed countries undertook to open up their markets, facilitate technological transfers, and increase both the quality and the quantity of aid.

Rich countries exercise control over the institutions that oversee the global economy. Their policies are major determinants of trade, aid, foreign investment, migration, and knowledge transfers. Their consumption patterns contribute to global environmental stress. Aid at current levels cannot deliver adequate progress towards the Millennium Development Goals. Aid to least developed countries has declined from $33 per capita in the 1980s to $10 today. This is a meager 0.07 percent of the per capita income of rich countries. Geopolitical and commercial considerations often override concerns for development effectiveness. And the tying of aid to providers from aid-donor countries adds 20 percent or more to the cost of goods and services that aid procures.

New rules of the game are needed. Policy adjustment by rich countries is as critical as governance reforms in poor countries.

Worldwide, flows of foreign direct investment dwarf the amounts allocated to aid, but they have little impact on the least developed countries, which collectively receive only 0.5 percent of global foreign direct investment. Trade policy reform is even more fundamental: agricultural subsidies in OECD countries are as large as the entire gross domestic product of Sub-Saharan Africa.

Equally, migration has become a pivotal factor for the economic prospects of many developing countries. Latin America and the Caribbean, for example, receive five times more in migrants' remittances than in aid. Last but not least, industrialized countries dominate global environmental management through the heavy ecological footprint of their production and consumption patterns.

Past research on development problems has concentrated on policy adjustment within poor countries and on aid effectiveness and trade reform. Relatively little is known about the economic consequences of migration, intellectual property regimes, and environmental regulations. Even less research has been done on the interaction and combined impact of the full spectrum of rich countries' policies on the economies, societies, and ecologies of poor countries. These knowledge gaps inhibit rational debate, let alone evidence-based policymaking towards sustainable and equitable growth.

The surveys by eminent development analysts and practitioners included in this volume sketch a road map for a better understanding of the mechanics of globalization and the improved design of development policies. They were prepared for a workshop sponsored by the Global Policy Project in January 2003 in Cairo, under the aegis of the Annual Conference of the Global Development Network. The workshop brought together forty development practitioners and analysts from the North and the South. They identified research priorities on the development effectiveness of rich countries' policies and developed initial ideas on how to translate research findings into policy changes.

The workshop was made possible by financial support from the Swiss Agency for Development Cooperation, the Foreign Ministry of the Netherlands, and the United Kingdom Department for International Development.

1

Overview

Robert Picciotto[1]

The central issue of contention is not globalization itself, nor is it the use of the market as an institution, but the inequity in the overall balance of institutional arrangements—which produces very unequal sharing of the benefits of globalization.

—Amartya Sen

Over the past two decades, the development agenda has focused on actions that poor countries need to take to promote growth. Research has probed the structural and social constraints on development in diverse socioeconomic environments. Advisory services have been geared to the adoption of policies that emphasize market friendliness. Aid allocations have emphasized development performance.

Substantial intellectual resources have been mobilized to assess the effectiveness of aid. The development community has adopted common development targets and performance indicators—the Millennium Development Goals. In all low-income countries, country-based poverty reduction strategy papers (PRSPs) have been mandated. They are subject to public disclosure and systematic review by the International Monetary Fund and the World Bank.

No similar effort is underway to monitor the development effectiveness of rich countries' policies. They have escaped scrutiny even though they determine the amount and quality of aid, foreign investment, trade, migration, access to intellectual property, and global environmental trends. Noisy anti-globalization street protests have mobilized the attention of the media and idiosyncratic domestic political considerations have dominated global policymaking.

In March 2002, the United Nations Conference on Financing for Development, held in Monterrey (Mexico), forged a historic development compact between rich and poor countries. The global partnership matched the adoption of improved policies and governance in developing countries with the provision of increased aid, knowledge transfers and trading opportunities by developed countries. Unfortunately, the obligations agreed at Monterrey are asymmetrical: only one of the eight goals addresses rich countries' policies and it does so partially. Performance indicators are pointed south more often than north. More needs to be done to understand, measure, and monitor the impact of rich countries' policies on the poor of the world.

Context

New technology has triggered the integration of national economies. Shipping costs are only 30 percent; air fares 16 percent, and telephone charges 1 percent of what they were seventy to eighty years ago. More than natural forces, policy choices determine the distribution of benefits resulting from globalization. An unprecedented number of business enterprises and civil society actors now exert influence on economic decision-making. But policy choices rest principally with the governments of the industrial democracies and their electorates.

In the pluralistic industrial democracies, policymaking proceeds in fits and starts, under the sway of the civil society, the mass media, and ever-changing coalitions of interests. A bewildering diversity of nongovernmental organizations, interconnected on a global scale, has promoted social and environmental causes. The ascent of market-based policies following the dissolution of the Soviet Union has facilitated trade, investment and unbundling of "value chains" with little regard for national boundaries.

The volume of international merchandise trade today is nearly twenty times greater than it was in 1950. In parallel, foreign direct investment has surged, reaching a peak of $1.3 trillion in 2000. It has since fallen ($725 billion in 2001), but flows to developing countries have been more resilient than flows among developed countries. Policy-based lending by international financial institutions has moved the integration process along.

By now, most developing countries have become enmeshed in the global marketplace for goods, services, people, and ideas. Countries unwilling or unable to connect to the mighty engine of the global economy have fared worse than others. But the early and heady promises of globalization have not been fulfilled. It remains to be seen whether the current transformation will deliver not only economic and social dislocation but also improved living standards for a majority of middle- and low-income countries.

Globalization Has a Long Way to Go

The nation state remains the dominant policymaking institution. Geography, political borders, currency risks, and cultural and legal differences, along with preferential trading arrangements and trade restraints, continue to inhibit global economic integration. Markets for labor and capital were far more integrated at the beginning of the twentieth century than they are today. In the last twenty-five years, only 2 percent of the world's people have changed their permanent country of residence, compared to 10 percent in the twenty-five years before World War I.

While world trade grew twice as fast as world output in the second half of the twentieth century and foreign direct investment three times as fast, the ratio of trade to output has not risen much in Europe and has declined in Japan compared to what it was before World War I. The ratio of U.S. international trade to output would need to grow another six-fold to achieve neutrality between internal and cross-border trade. Thus, the potential of globalization is far from being fulfilled and its future is uncertain. History suggests that the process can be reversed.

Toward a Level Playing Field

Rich countries have dominated the policy agenda, its rules, and the modalities that govern global economic activity—a reflection of disparate economic and political strengths and the unequal access to the specialized skills that are needed to design, negotiate, and monitor the implementation of agreed international standards.

Characterized by volatile market conditions and a secular decline in commodity prices, globalization has had asymmetrical consequences. Developing countries have been vulnerable to financial contagion since their banking sectors and their capital markets usually lack depth and strength. The poorest and smallest countries have fared worst. Between 1970 and 1997, the cumulative terms of trade losses of non-oil exporting African countries amounted to more than half the cumulative net resource flows to the region. These losses, combined with interest payments, profit remittances, capital outflows, and reserve buildup have resulted in a net transfer of resources from Africa to the rest of the world.

Restraints on international trade have been damaging to the developing world. OECD countries provided over $300 billion in agricultural support, three-quarters of which is in the form of direct payments. These subsidies have created gluts of agricultural commodities that have crowded out developing country production. In addition, new trade-related intellectual property regimes have restricted access by poor countries to essential drugs and other knowledge-intensive products and services. Migration rules have been highly restrictive and stacked against the poor and uneducated.

Most developing countries have lacked the domestic institutions, the skills, and the access to capital needed to achieve economic growth on a scale sufficient to match their demographic expansion and generate substantial poverty reduction. At the end of the 1990s, more than eighty countries had per capita incomes lower than they had ten years earlier. To be sure, the international market has promoted efficiency and growth and social indicators have improved. In particular, the large economies of China and, to a lesser extent, India have scored substantial gains. As a result, aggregate poverty levels have declined somewhat and the world's Gini coefficient of income inequality may be declining for the first time in two centuries.

On the other hand, environmental stress, economic volatility, and inequality within countries have grown. The resulting discontent has created doubts about the environmental and social sustainability of the globalization process. There is no mystery about the threats to the world's ecology caused by demography and energy-intensive development, nor about the growing differentiation in economic performance across countries; in a global economy increasingly driven by trade, knowledge, and private capital, the penalties attached to unsound governance and lack of market-based institutions have been prohibitive. Countries already equipped with a favorable environment for private enterprise, a functioning civil service, and supportive economic policies have attracted the lion's share of capital, entrepreneurship, and skills. The others have been marginalized and unable to reap the full benefits of globalization.

Similarly, with knowledge driving economic efficiency, returns on education and entrepreneurship have risen while the unskilled have seen their standards of living erode, and income differentials have widened. Countries and individuals already at the top of the economic ladder have received a disproportionate share of the benefits of increased economic activity while those lacking financial assets and skills have been unable to share equally in the opportunities offered by market activities. Without a level playing field, those already endowed with know-how and access to capital have benefited disproportionately from globalization.

The Governance Gap

The promise of globalization was grounded in the notion that foreign investment would create new incentives for protecting property rights and adopting sound macroeconomic policies and good governance practices. Larger wage gaps would induce more people to acquire skills. Higher returns to entrepreneurship would trigger creativity and innovation. Over the long run, increased inequality in open and competitive global markets would be the price to be paid for growth and poverty reduction.

But as Keynes famously remarked, in the long run we are all dead. Whereas developed countries have gradually evolved an enabling environment combining market orientation with social development and environmental protection, through a combination of fiscal tools, public goods delivery, and regulatory frameworks, only the rudiments of such a structure exist within developing countries and the prospects for a new financial and development architecture appear distant.

Currently, the intergovernmental process governing global rule making is cumbersome and ineffectual. More than 40,000 treaties and international agreements have been registered with the UN Secretariat, and more than 500 multilateral instruments—covering matters such as human rights, disarmament, commodities, refugees, the environment, and the Law of the Sea—have been deposited with the UN Secretary General. But intergovernmental conventions are years in the making and monitoring and enforcement mechanisms are ineffectual.

The private sector and nongovernmental organizations have sought to fill the global policy gap. There has been an explosive growth in formal and informal partnerships between voluntary agencies, governments, and multilateral institutions. They have diverse goals: to improve access by the poor to potable water; to promote the use of renewable energy in rural areas; to bridge the digital gap in developing countries; to protect endangered species in vulnerable forest areas; to harmonize accounting standards, etc. But their record is mixed and recurring questions arise as to their efficacy, legitimacy, and accountability. Thus, global governance remains fractured, inefficient, and unfocused on results. In sharp contrast with economics, politics remains stubbornly local and national.

Over time, a normative shift towards cosmopolitan values may lead to the empowerment of representative global institutions that elicit broad-based public trust. But such an evolution is unlikely to take place without the stalwart support of national governments. For decades to come, progress will hinge on inducing coherent policy reforms through national political processes in the industrial democracies. In turn this will require more recognition by private firms in industrial countries that their interests coincide with those of developing nations, since this is where new markets and new sources of wealth are located. A judicious combination of policy research, shrewd advocacy, and effective coalition building must channel public emotion towards more effective international cooperation, a greater voice for the poor, and policy reform in the industrial democracies.

The Policy Reform Agenda

In sum, human development depends on enhancing the coherence of rich countries' policies. For globalization to work for the poor, the transmission belts of aid, foreign investment, trade, intellectual property, migration, and the environment must be re-engineered. Development is grounded in physical, human, and natural capital. At the global level, trade policy induces efficient resource allocation. Aid and foreign investment matter because they affect the level and quality of physical capital allocations. Similarly, intellectual property and migration policy reforms could help to improve the distribution of human capital (including knowledge). Last but not least, natural capital endowments are heavily affected by the environmental policies of rich countries.

Aid

Aid is at a crossroads. According to ActionAid, "Never has there been such a large or obvious gap between the stated commitments of the rich world (in the form of the MDGs) and the resources and policies supposed to meet them." The quantity of aid is currently inadequate and its quality undermined by geopolitical motivations, policy incoherence, weak donor commitment, poor accountability, and dysfunctional aid practices.

The Monterrey consensus about goals and principles has not been matched by commensurate action. The commitment to double official development assistance has not been fulfilled. Little has been done to moderate global market volatility, protect developing countries from financial crises, achieve debt sustainability, enhance developing countries' access to rich countries' markets, cut the costs imposed by trade-related intellectual property rights, or channel more private investment toward the least developed countries.

Aid works in the right circumstances. Its effectiveness is improving. There is a large reservoir of popular support for the Millennium Development Goals (MDGs). Yet, public perceptions about development assistance remain unfavorable, in large part because of unrealistic expectations about what aid can achieve without concurrent improvements in the key policies that govern globalization.

The public vastly overestimates the share of government budgets allocated to aid. There is very little awareness that official development assistance as a share of national income has declined from about 0.65 percent in 1967 to 0.22 percent in 2001—despite endorsement by numerous UN conferences of a target of 0.7 percent of national income—or that only five out of twenty-two DAC countries have reached this target.

Aid quality matters as much as its quantity. The following reforms in aid policies would greatly enhance development effectiveness: (1) aid allocations based on development considerations rather than geopolitical objectives; (2) greater concentration of aid towards poor countries; (3) untied aid and reduced reliance on expatriates in aid implementation; (4) harmonization of aid practices; and (5) reduced transaction costs for aid recipients.

Foreign Investment

With globalization, improved investment climates have become a frequent focus of aid, and the corporate policies set by multinational companies have become more influential in developing countries. Market-based capital flows to developing countries are now far larger than aid flows, although they peaked at nearly $300 billion in 1997 and have dropped sharply in the wake of the current economic slowdown, reaching $175 billion in 2001 and $140 billion in 2002.

The distribution of foreign direct investment (FDI) is highly skewed. Least developed countries collectively receive only 0.5 percent of global FDI flows. Of this, 86 percent is concentrated in ten countries, of which more than half goes to four oil-producing countries. Africa as a whole is a marginal recipient, receiving less than 2 percent. Within Africa, as elsewhere in the developing world, FDI flows go to only a handful of countries. Yet, FDI (unlike the turbulent flows of short-term capital) is critical to technology transfers, human capital creation, technical and management skills enhancement, and better integration of national economies within the international trading system.

FDI can promote a more competitive business environment and generate domestic and enterprise development. Amar Inamdar's chapter suggests that, beyond promoting a larger quantity and a broader distribution of FDI among developing countries, the quality of investment flows deserves emphasis. Both the quantity and quality of private investment are shaped by the enabling environment —good macroeconomic management, a sound judiciary and legal environment, physical and social infrastructure, resilient financial and other market institutions, and innovative support to micro, small, and medium enterprises.

Corporate behavior matters, too. FDI may not create net benefits to host countries if associated with capital-intensive development, corrupt use of royalties, limited links to the local economy, negative environmental impacts, or deleterious social consequences for local communities. Hence, the rationale of the United Nations Global Compact, a network of private companies dedicated to the observance of human rights, labor standards, and environmental sustainability. In turn, the corporate investment policies and operating practices of multinational companies are responsive to public opinion and the policy stances adopted by rich countries and international institutions.

Competition, financial transparency, and corporate social responsibility could be enhanced by fair and predictable rules for international investment taking account of the lessons learned in the abortive MAI proposals.[2] At the sector level, voluntary standard setting, stakeholder consultations, and independent verification need support and investment risks should be mitigated through long-term credit on favorable terms, risk guarantees, advisory services, and partnerships with development assistance agencies and voluntary organizations.

Trade

Foreign investment and trade are intimately connected. Tariffs in developed countries disproportionately affect developing and least developed countries and hinder investment flows. The efficiency of investment is affected, too, since developing countries suffer from the effects of tariffs precisely where they are most competitive, including cereals, sugar, fish, fruits and vegetables, clothing, and footwear. The social consequences are detrimental since these products are produced largely by subsistence farmers or by small and medium enterprises. Developed-country tariff-rate quotas are another area of concern.

"Food aid" dumps surplus production, with negative effects on production incentives for developing countries. Full agricultural liberalization would generate benefits worth U.S. $20 billion a year for developing countries. A 40 percent reduction in tariffs on manufacturing goods would add U.S. $380 billion to the volume of global trade, with nearly 75 percent of the gains accruing to developing countries. The gains from liberalizing trade in services could be even greater.

As tariff barriers decline, non-tariff restrictions tend to proliferate. In many cases, standards governing trade are justifiable. In others, they create significant distortions. In particular, incompatibilities between standards and methods of conformity assessment may disrupt trade and provide implicit protection for domestic industries. Equally, private voluntary eco-labeling favors processes and technologies that may be unavailable, unsuitable, or prohibitively expensive for developing countries.

Drawing on extensive research evidence, Vangelis Vitalis recommends early action on a comprehensive reform agenda covering (1) across-the-board tariff reductions; (2) removal of agricultural subsidies; (3) reduction of trade restraints on manufactured exports, especially textiles and clothing; (4) liberalization of trade in services; (5) streamlining of rules and standards; and (6) reconsideration of private voluntary eco-labeling practices. Detailed policy design would take account of the environmental impact of rich countries' consumption patterns on the sustainable development of poor countries, for example, through consideration of the embedded carbon component of such imports as cars or the deforestation impact of increased demand for tropical wood and wood products.

Intellectual Property

Knowledge is a key factor in national competitiveness. Hence, the governance of intellectual property rights has become a high-profile development issue. According to the UK Commission on Intellectual Property Rights (IPRs), such rights should be subordinated to human rights. Whereas IPRs are granted by states for limited times, human rights are inalienable and universal. To be sure, IPRs need protection to promote creativity and innovation on a sufficient scale. Unfortunately, the standards embodied in the agreement on Trade-Related Intellectual Property Rights (TRIPs) have not taken adequate consideration of basic human needs in developing countries.

Charles Clift's chapter demonstrates that standards of IP protection suitable for developed countries may produce prohibitive costs for poor countries that are large net importers of technology. Nevertheless, the level, scope, territorial extent, and role of IP protection have expanded at an unprecedented pace and the TRIPs agreement has extended minimum standards for IP protection globally. Furthermore, TRIPs strengthens the protection offered to suppliers of technology, without commensurate strengthening of competition policies. Naturally, companies are wary of transferring technology as well as keen to limit the competition they face. Therefore, affirmative policy action is needed to encourage competition and promote technology transfer. Equally, more aid should be directed towards capacity building in scientific, technological, and information management domains.

Compulsory licensing is needed for generic production of medicines within developing countries, and new ways must be found for procuring medicines at reasonable cost for countries without manufacturing capacity. IP legislation should be crafted to limit the extent of patenting for basic health products and to facilitate the introduction of generic competition. In agriculture, the amount of public resources devoted to research relevant to small farmers in developing countries should be increased and genetic materials relevant to breeding research should be protected.

In sum, a fundamental reconsideration of current practices governing IPRs is required in order to achieve (1) science and technology capacity building; (2) improved access by developing countries to basic medicines; (3) agricultural technology development relevant to the needs of farmers in poor countries; (4) protection of traditional knowledge; and (5) removal of legal obstacles impeding developing countries' access to copyrighted materials and electronic data bases.

Migration

Given that goods, capital, and ideas have become more mobile, migration makes eminent economic sense and it is proceeding apace. Up to one-third of migrants move through illegal channels. Yet, economic theory has established that factor mobility facilitates economic convergence between rich and poor regions. Induced by differentials in salaries, wages, and working conditions across countries, it corrects labor market imbalances arising out of differential growth patterns and demographic factors. Migration also influences the direction of foreign direct investment and encourages cross-border flows of enterprise, ideas, and knowledge.

Kathleen Newland articulates the reasons why, even though only 3 percent of humanity consists of migrants, migration policy is under stress and needs adjustment. First and foremost, an abrupt demographic transition has generated a pent-up demand for net migration in most developed countries. In addition, the cultural tensions involved in the social integration of migrants, the growing economic reliance of developing countries on migrants' remittances, the looming concerns about "human capital" flight, and the higher profile of security considerations since September 11, 2001 have raised the public profile of migration issues.

Some migration is due to war, civil conflict, or political persecution. Cultural considerations also intervene. But the main drivers of primary migration are economic and most of the secondary effects (such as family reunification) flow from it. Reform has been hindered by domestic politics, vested interests, and cultural prejudice. Current immigration policies obstruct the entry of asylum seekers, interdict entry by unskilled migrants, and ration immigration by well-trained professionals and skilled workers. Such policies are cumbersome to implement, favor "brain drain," and create opportunities for smuggling of migrants that enrich criminal groups and divert public resources towards border control needs.

Tacit tolerance of illegal migration meets labor needs in the destination countries but it induces petty corruption, opens up profitable smuggling opportunities for criminal networks, perpetuates unfair treatment of migrants, and discourages their integration into the fabric of the host country. Thus, comprehensive policy reform is called for. Developing countries should move away from self-defeating policies that aim at stopping the "brain drain" to a new approach that takes human capital exports as a given in human resource planning, nurtures diaspora links, encourages remittances, and taps into the knowledge and entrepreneurship of former citizens.

Equally, rich countries need to face up to the requirements of their labor markets while respecting the fundamental rights of migrants from whose labor they benefit, including migrants' rights to family life. They should also revisit unworkable border control systems and sanctions on employers of illegal migrants that are exceedingly cumbersome to implement. They should devote increased resources to the integration of migrants in their societies and, where appropriate, use development assistance to facilitate capital and skills transfers to migrants' countries of origin.

Furthermore, source and destination countries need to work cooperatively to establish arrangements and/or institutions that encourage the repatriation of migrants' earnings and maximize the developmental impact of these remittance flows. They should put in place policies that facilitate circular or return migration and encourage the formation of transnational communities that can serve as channels for foreign direct investment and trade links.

In principle, greater prominence of migration issues in the network of international institutions appears warranted. The topic is lightly institutionalized, reflecting the lack of international consensus. Regional processes, notably in the European Union and with less intensity in SADC, North and Central America (Puebla Process), may produce limited policy changes. In the words of Jagdish Bhagwati, "the world badly needs enlightened immigration policies and best practices to be spread and codified." But in the current authorizing environment, norms and practices governing migration will require hard and patient work geared to policy development, consensus building, piloting of innovative approaches and learning from experience.

Environment

The policies of rich countries (emulated by poor countries) are inducing unprecedented pressure on the physical environment. Industrialized countries dominate global environmental management through the heavy ecological footprint of their production and consumption patterns, and indirectly through their influence over the policy regimes that govern trade, investment, and the global commons. To illustrate how rich countries' policies affect developing countries, Frances Seymour reviews climate change, marine fisheries, environmental regulation and product standards, and governance regimes.

The policies of rich countries have a major influence over natural resources and environmental management in poor countries. Climate change threatens the most severe and widespread impacts, but extraterritorial resource use (for example, sea lanes, fisheries) and environmental regulations in industrialized countries also create significant impacts, while rich country dominance within governance regimes tends to impede the "development friendliness" of policies and programs.

Among industrialized countries, the United States stands out as the country most needing to change its policies related to climate change, while the European Union and Japan are the most dilatory in adjusting their policies related to fisheries in the waters of developing countries. Among developing countries, geographic characteristics strongly cause vulnerability to climate change, while economic characteristics tend to determine the extent of hardship caused by environmental trade restrictions.

Overall, both within and between countries, the poor suffer most from perverse rich country environmental policies. For example, poor countries are least well positioned to adapt to climate change and artisan producers are least well positioned to take advantage of market opportunities created by eco-labeling schemes. Further, the costs of changing policies for industrialized countries tend to be front-loaded and the benefits enjoyed only in the long run. For example, in the marine fisheries sector, withdrawal of subsidies would result in unemployment in the short term, but healthier fish stocks (as well as sustained employment) over the long run. Thus, policy leadership is needed to design reform strategies that provide compensation to the "losers" of policy adjustment while ensuring sound stewardship of the environment and generating large benefits to future generations.

Toward a Global Policy Research Agenda

Too little policy research is being carried out in developing country research institutions. As international rules and standards evolve, their actual and potential consequences for the poor of the world are often ignored. Preconceived dogma and political expediency hold sway over evidence-based policymaking. Hence, the scarcity of research focused on rich countries' policies is both a cause and a consequence of the global authorizing environment.

A reallocation of work priorities among and within policy research institutions of the North (for example toward more precise assessments of the development friendliness and coherence of rich countries' policies) and of the South (for example toward impact assessments of rich countries' policies and judicious policy responses) would facilitate the transition. Collaborative research involving institutions of both the North and the South (for example to probe the interface and the interaction of policies of the North and the South) would improve the quality of both groups of collaborators.

Poor countries are largely "policy takers." Their prospects are influenced by policy shifts in rich countries. The sustainable poverty reduction impact varies depending on the conditions of individual developing countries. Hence, policy reform in developing countries matters as well. Conversely, developed countries are "policy makers" and alternative policy changes in favor of poor countries have differentiated impacts within the society. Interaction between policies (the "coherence" question) may lead to unanticipated outcomes and call for the design of judicious reform coalitions. Finally, research is needed to examine the interactions between rich and poor countries as they reform their policies to accommodate globalization. Winners and losers must be identified to facilitate the design of advocacy campaigns and also to provide for adequate compensation for losers out of the enormous aggregate welfare increments that global policy reform could unlock.

Development Impact of Rich Countries' Policies

While there is broad agreement that sustainable poverty reduction depends on global cooperation between the North and the South, the focus of policy research has been on policy adjustment in poor countries. Complementary research to assess the impact of rich countries' policies on poverty reduction might help explain why so many countries that have adopted wide ranging policy adjustment measures were not able to generate sufficient growth to induce poverty reduction on a substantial scale. Such research would also help in the design of global policy reform.

Research is needed on the impact on developing countries conceived as "policy takers." Most global policy adjustments involve winners and losers as well as incremental transaction costs and economic disruptions not only in the North but also in the South. For example, from a developing country perspective, estimated benefits of migration in terms of reduction of environmental pressure in marginal agricultural areas, increased remittances, tourism, and foreign direct investment need to be compared to the replacement costs of human capital exports in a variety of developing country circumstances.

Equally, the elimination of preferential tariffs for small developing and least developed countries would have positive welfare effects globally, but special consideration may have to be given to the hardships created in small and poor countries dependent on the monoculture of currently protected products. Moreover, while improvements in developing country access to high value markets may deliver social and economic gains, the environmental gains may be less comprehensively understood. For example, what would improved developed-world market access for Uzbek cotton mean for water consumption drawn from the Aral Sea? What would improved access for Chinese steel or textiles mean for global CO_2 emissions or sulfur emissions?

In these and similar cases, evidence-based research would not only help to design and sequence the policy shift, but also offer insights into related social, economic, and environmental actions designed to help improve the sustainability of production techniques, for example through aid policy. Thus, research might help find ways to minimize the negative economic and social impacts of full TRIPs implementation, the harmonization and integration of patent systems, the global implementation of biotechnology patents, and the looming restraints on electronic information sharing by developing countries.

For such impact assessment research to be operationally relevant, participation of policymakers and potentially affected citizens will be critical to ensure that the right issues are addressed, the right performance measures are selected, the likely consequences of policy changes are properly understood, and appropriate remedial measures are designed to minimize the social costs of reforms.

Coherence of Rich Countries' Policies

Greater coherence among rich countries' policy objectives so as to improve the economic and social prospects of developing countries will have to draw on political economy factors as well as purely technical considerations. Assessments of losers and winners within rich countries and identification of remedial measures to mitigate the costs of adjustment within rich countries would be part of the research. In the case of migration, the costs of migrants' social integration would have to be weighed against the net labor market benefits of migration.

Issues of coherence arise in the relationship between debt and environment (does the pressure to service a debt burden discourage sustainability?); aid and the environment (how can donors assist in the mainstreaming of environmental concerns in public expenditures management within developing countries?); environment and trade (what is the impact of production subsidies on the environmental sustainability of agricultural production practices within rich countries?*)*; migration and the environment (how is climate change affecting public health and migration and what are the consequences for rich countries?*)*

To facilitate policy adjustment, the research agenda may also be influenced by the need to produce evidence and analyses that can help unblock political stalemates. This might include the marshalling of evidence to help convince policymakers in rich countries that their societies as well as developing countries would be much better off if agricultural production-based subsidies were withdrawn.

Case studies directed towards donor countries will be needed to bring out interaction among policies. For example, coherence between environment and investment policy would benefit from research on the impact of subsidies on the protection of natural resources (such as fisheries) or on the impact of environmental regulations on the location of pollution-intensive investment towards poor countries, where standards and enforcement are more lax. The operations of export credit agencies may deserve systematic assessment from an economic, social, and environmental perspective so as to achieve policy coherence within the development system.

Interaction between Rich and Poor Countries' Policies

Policy adjustments in rich countries require appropriate policy responses by poor countries in order to tap the full benefits of new opportunities resulting from reform. For example, the extent to which developing countries would benefit from reductions in developed country protection in the agricultural, clothing, and textile sectors hinges on the efficiency and flexibility of their own production structures. Similarly, changes in policy standards and regulations while justified in principle may have unintended economic and social implications for developing countries (for example in terms of costs of compliance or exports forgone).

Time lags in supply responses would be better understood and policy sequencing improved through country case studies, for example regarding the capacity of small, medium-sized, and large exporters in selected developing countries to respond to the removal of trade constraints on, say, sugar. Formidable data problems would also have to be tackled, for example to establish a trans-boundary consumption indicator, as proposed in Vangelis's chapter, requiring detailed breakdowns of trade flows as well as other data, for example for chemicals, fisheries resource use, and so forth.

Even voluntary standards could have unintended costs. Here again, case studies may help shape policy design or implementation, for example by estimating the balance between the value added and the "chilling effect" of World Dams Commission precepts or by tracing the impact on the ground of Forest Stewardship Council and Fair Trade eco-labeling, and identifying appropriate policy responses by developing countries. Equally, the interface between environmental protection policy and intellectual property rights (for example, as it relates to access and benefit sharing of genetic resources) may be illuminated by research. How should genetic resources be shared between developing countries (which harbor much of the genetic material) and industrialized countries (which have the science and technology to use it)? How should the traditional knowledge regarding that material be reflected in intellectual property rights?

Linking Research with Monitoring

Beyond policy adjustment and capacity building in developing countries, it is the aggregate of rich countries' policies (rather than aid alone) that should be judged by results. Unless this is done, poverty reduction shortfalls versus the Millennium Development Goals might be unfairly attributed to poor aid performance and induce reductions in aid levels just at a time when, based on conservative assumptions, they should be doubled to achieve the goals. From this perspective, the initiative of the Center for Global Development aimed at tracking the development friendliness of rich countries' policies is critically important.

In ActionAid's words, "targets are worthless without ideas about how to reach them." Focused monitoring of the direction, magnitude, and environmental impacts of specific commodity flows may have greater relevance for policymaking. So would monitoring devoted to the capture of key features of rich country policies that directly impinge on developing countries, for example indicators in such areas as subsidies to extraterritorial extractive operations. Furthermore, monitoring should extend to "hidden flows" of natural resources that do not enter the market, and capturing the informal (often illegal) exploitation of natural resources such as forests and fisheries. In addition, monitoring geared to the environmental impacts embedded in resource flows, such as carbon and water, would be useful.

Linking Research with Advocacy and Networking

The voices of a quarter of the world's population living in abject poverty on less than one dollar a day are often muted if not silenced within poor countries and still largely absent in the councils of government of rich countries. Policies that have considerable relevance to sustainable development are captured. Narrow interests with political clout prevail over the public interest.

Judicious interactions between research and advocacy are needed. The interface is fraught with dilemmas and tensions. For research to yield reform, it is not enough for research topics to be operationally relevant, for research methods to be rigorous and research findings persuasive. Results also hinge on judicious and timely policy decisions and these in turn depend on the overall governance framework, the quality of leadership, and the resolution of complex political equations.

The integrity of research work rests on its fairness and objectivity. Conversely, advocacy needs reliable evidence to have credibility. Thus, there is room for principled partnerships between research and advocacy, but they are distinct functions. Research cannot be judged strictly in terms of its direct results lest incentives arise to "spin" research results, to subordinate research methods to "what the policy traffic can bear," or to suppress evidence that goes against the predilections of policymakers or powerful stakeholders.

Hence, while research and advocacy need to be connected to ensure that research results have a fighting chance of being acted upon, too close a connection creates conflicts of interest. A fine balance should be practiced and a respectful distance between the two functions observed. Examples of fruitful interactions include the parallel actions of environmental economists and development practitioners that facilitated the incorporation of sustainability principles within development assistance practices and the combination of solid analytics and public opinion campaigning that yielded the Highly Indebted Poor Countries' Initiative. Counter-examples include the extensive research efforts and fruitless campaigns against the chronic agricultural protectionism of rich country governments.

Charles Clift makes clear that the research-policy linkage is far from linear by describing the interplay between industry, governments, and NGOs that has shaped policy debates about TRIPs. Some progress was achieved due to the mobilization of public opinion around the dramatic issue of the HIV/AIDS epidemic. But it has not been sustained, which suggests that there are limits to advocacy by entities—donors, NGOs—that do not bear the consequences of the positions they advocate, that principled compromises are hard to strike within a multilateral decision-making framework, and that without well-grounded political support, sustained policy change is unlikely when faced by determined opposition by powerful vested interests.

Thus, the challenge of public policy formation is far tougher at the global level than it is at the national level. Each global problem is endowed with its distinctive force field, involves different sets of global and local actors, and requires tailor-made solutions. Some global policy issues have received a great deal of public attention and scrutiny. Others have not. The solutions are known in some cases. In others, research and piloting is needed. Agreement on standards may be a realistic goal in some instances, but not in others. Some issues (such as the disposition of large ships at the end of their useful lives) involve relatively few actors and countries. Others such as the protection of biodiversity call for a mixture of global and country/local actions. Still others, particularly trade, are systemic and call for multilateral agreements. Most are not amenable to effective treatment unless governments and multilateral agencies team up with the civil society and the private sector.

General prescriptions are hard to come by and a follow-up process may be needed to probe these issues further, identify relevant actors, and promote a principled dialogue among them on how to improve global policymaking. For each policy issue, knowledge institutions with a track record in the field could join forces in assessing, evaluating, and reporting regularly on progress towards global welfare. This would involve engaging diverse stakeholders in diagnosing constraints, defining remedial measures, mediating among conflicting interests, implementing relevant programs, and creating tailor-made informal networks involving prominent individuals, business firms, voluntary agencies, or international organizations.

Notes

1. The author is managing director of the Global Policy Project and former director general, Operations Evaluation, of the World Bank Group.
2. The proposed Multilateral Agreement on Investment was an attempt to harmonize investment rules; it was rejected in 1998 after a gestation period of more than seven years. For details, see chapter 4.

2

Reducing Poverty in a World of Plenty:
The Crisis of Aid

ActionAid[1]

The message from the Sierra Leone Government that greets visitors at Lungi airport sums up quite well the prevailing cynicism about outside assistance. It reads something like this: "If you can't help us, at least please do not harm us." And if you ask people in Sierra Leone what they think of development assistance you get pretty much the same answer as you will get in most parts of Sub-Saharan Africa and many other poor countries across the world. The dominant image of aid is of government, donor, and NGO Toyota 4x4s rushing around, begging the question whether the means have literally overshadowed the end. Talk to the people who ActionAid works with in remote places—those who are denied what most of us would consider as absolutely fundamental to human existence— and they say they rarely see the benefits of aid actually reach them. Talk to concerned citizens in the run-down capital cities, where most of the aid crowd hang out to discuss poverty in ridiculously over-priced hotels and restaurants. Aid, these people believe, is what keeps unaccountable governments, donors, consultants, and NGOs in business; it's a gravy train. The thousands of abandoned buildings, machinery, dams, hand-pumps, and other failed projects and displaced people across the developing world bear mute testimony to this pessimistic view.

Yet we know that aid can work (Tarp, 2000) and that public spending in most poor countries is hugely aid-dependent. Unfortunate as it is, even the crumbs that poor people get would disappear if aid did not exist. One need only look at the condition of poor countries that are facing United Nations or other sanctions to realize this. The tragedy for poor people is that they are like the ball in the ping-pong blame game between aid donors and their own governments. Governments of rich countries claim they would give more aid if only the money were put to better use than lining the pockets of the elite, and if the recipient countries were likely to become more self-reliant. Governments of poor countries counter-claim that they are doing their best under difficult circumstances and would have done better if they did not have donor consultants and staff with pre-cooked solutions forcing them to design and implement inappropriate policies and projects. They ask where Japan or Europe would be now without their colonial inheritances or significant injections of aid after World War II. As this argument rages, 1.2 billion people are living below the so-called poverty line. Every fifth person in the world suffers from hunger, disease, and illiteracy.

Little wonder then that international aid is suffering a crisis of legitimacy. This crisis is rooted in chronic problems of the aid system at several levels: a lack of coherence between development goals and the wider global policy environment; a crisis of commitment in donor countries; continuing difficulties in disbursement, including allocation, tying, and coordination; and a lack of accountability of both donor and recipient governments.

These underlying problems have been building up for many years. Today they have been thrown into sharp relief by the fact that we now have a clearer set of development objectives than before: poverty reduction in the form of the Millennium Development Goals (MDGs). It is the failure of the current aid system to even come close to delivering these goals that has made the crisis evident.

This chapter lays out the dimensions of the aid crisis and its roots, and suggests an agenda for both action and research. Section 1 reviews what is at stake by looking at aid through a poverty reduction lens. This is the perspective that underpins ActionAid's interpretation of aid effectiveness; it focuses on how aid affects the lives of poor and marginalized people whose basic rights are routinely violated. Section 2 looks at the context for aid and outlines some key areas of policy incoherence. Section 3 focuses on the crisis in aid itself, dealing, in turn, with volume, allocation, and disbursement issues, and Section 4 suggests some research areas that could help illuminate a new aid system focused on meeting the legitimate rights of the world's poor.

The Current Challenge: Poverty and the MDGs

Since the publication of the 1990 *World Development Report,*[2] poverty reduction has emerged as the primary aim of official development policy, including aid. This aim was given greater focus in 1996 by the International Development Targets (IDTs) distilled by the OECD's Development Assistance Committee from various UN conferences, and the subsequent promotion of the IDTs by the UK government in its 1997 White Paper on International Development. After their endorsement by other governments and the Bretton Woods Institutions in the late 1990s, the IDTs became the Millennium Development Goals at the UN Millennium General Assembly in 2000 (Box 2.1).

Despite their limitations, the MDGs have given the development community, especially in the North, a reference point and a rallying point. NGOs, including ActionAid, UNDP, and others are tracking progress or lack of progress on the quantitative goals (ActionAid, 2002c). The Financing for Development summit in Monterrey in 2002 gave the MDGs center stage, and, importantly, produced a rough figure of an additional $50 billion a year needed to meet them.

Clearly, the first seven MDGs rely on the eighth—a global partnership for development—for their realization. Without such a partnership, it will be hard to attain the Goals in a meaningful way for all regions. But the partnership that is proposed—between the rich and the poor world, donors and recipients—is, of course, an unequal one, and the relationship is characterized by tension as well as a need to work together. The so-called Monterrey Consensus recognizes the scale of the problem, the role of aid in reducing poverty, and the need for more and better-allocated development finance. But the participating parties seem unable to agree about the appropriate solution to many of the challenges ahead. There is, for example, no consensus on how to address some of the key issues that are likely to impede the timely realization of the MDGs, including insufficient levels of official development assistance, restricted market access, and unsustainable debt burdens in many developing countries.

Box 2.1
Millennium Development Goals

Millennium Development Goal	Target
Eradicate extreme poverty and hunger	*Halve the proportion of people with less than $1 a day* *Halve the proportion of people who suffer from hunger*
Achieve universal primary education	*Ensure that boys and girls alike complete primary schooling*
Promote gender equality and empower women	*Eliminate gender disparity in primary and secondary schooling, preferably by 2005, and in all levels of education no later than 2015*
Reduce child mortality	*Reduce by two-thirds under-five mortality rate*
Improve maternal health	*Reduce by three-quarters the maternal mortality ratio*
Combat HIV/AIDS, malaria and other diseases	*Have halted and begun to reverse the spread of HIV/AIDS* *Have halted and begun to reverse the incidence of malaria and other major diseases*
Ensure environmental sustainability	*Integrate the principles of sustainable development into country policy and reverse the loss of environmental resources* *Halve the proportion of people without sustainable access to safe drinking water* *Have achieved a significant improvement in the lives of at least 100 million slum dwellers*
Develop a global partnership for development	*Raise official development assistance* *Expand market access* *Encourage debt sustainability*

Never has there been such a large or obvious gap between the stated commitments of the rich world (in the form of the MDGs) and the resources and policies supposed to meet them. It is precisely because the MDGs are so clear, but also so ambitious in relation to the current situation, that there is such skepticism.

Equally, while there is a consensus that we should tackle the manifestations of poverty, there is no consensus that we should address the underlying causes. ActionAid sees these causes as rooted in the unjust distribution of resources and power. Thus, while the MDGs focus on the *material and social* dimensions of poverty, most commentators, from the World Bank to many bilaterals, from UNDP to many NGOs, including ActionAid, also recognize a *political* element to poverty. As both a cause and consequence of their poverty, poor people (and often poor countries) are denied a voice, and frequently also their dignity.

ActionAid explicitly takes a rights-based approach to both analysis and action. To us, ending poverty implies not only reaching the type of targets outlined in the MDGs, but also the informed and meaningful participation of poor people and their representative organizations in processes that affect their lives. It means that the perceptions of poor and marginalized people of well-being and poverty are important and should help guide policy. Finally, it means to us that all development processes should be designed so as to increase the accountability of powerful actors, whether governments or donors or corporations, to poor people.

The rest of this chapter develops these arguments in more detail. The first step is to look at the broader context of aid.

Aid in the Context of Development: The Issue of Coherence

Development assistance is a very small part of the global economy, and even for some of the least developed countries (LDCs), trade and investment patterns are more decisive. Foreign policy also matters a great deal, and is a key part of the context for aid. Given these patterns, and given the supposed poverty reduction objectives of development assistance, one of the key issues we need to address is the degree to which the trade, investment, and foreign policies of donor countries are in keeping with their global poverty reduction goals.

Trade and Intellectual Property Rights

The Doha round of international trade negotiations has been labeled the "development round," as it is supposed to lead to an agreement to scale down agricultural subsidies in the industrialized world, guarantee access to cheap medicines for countries facing AIDS crises, make progress on defining special and differential treatment, and deal with other aspects of the so-called "implementation" agenda.

Almost all of these aspects of the agenda are in trouble. As this chapter is being finalized, the U.S. government has unilaterally stalled the post-Doha negotiations on cheaper access to vital drugs for poor countries. Moreover, the U.S. government has consistently undermined the commitment to multilateral trade agreements through the WTO process by signing several bilateral and regional trade agreements since the 2001 Doha ministerial meeting.

Despite the dominant theoretical orthodoxies of liberalized trade, the present global trading system is far from free. Trade barriers in rich countries cost an estimated $160 billion a year (The Reality of Aid Project, 2002: 5). Barriers to the markets of the rich world are one cause of the economic marginalization of the commodity-producing least developed countries, trapped in the export of non-oil commodities with ever-sliding and erratic value. UNCTAD (2002) reports that whereas LDCs as a group saw their economic performance improve, especially in the latter half of the 1990s, most non-oil commodity producers (including more than half of the LDCs, located mainly in Africa) saw their trade sharply contract between 1997 and 2000, due to a decline in commodity prices. While overall trade flows have increased dramatically over the past four decades, most LDCs have not benefited from the increase in global trade opportunities and have not diversified. The result is the persistent and widespread poverty observed in LDCs (UNCTAD, 2002).

The flip side of limited market access is the domestic subsidization of agriculture by the industrialized world, encouraging both dumping in poor countries and environmental degradation (ActionAid, 2002a). In 1998, industrialized countries spent $353 billion on agricultural subsidies, roughly seven times the amount of official development assistance (The Reality of Aid Project, 2002: 5). Since the late 1980s, the EU has consistently defended its Common Agriculture Policy (CAP), with its elaborate trade-distorting subsidies, tariffs, and quotas. EU agricultural support policies amount to more than €40 billion (just over $40 billion) annually. U.S. direct support to agriculture is also strong and has increased by about 200 percent since 1996 (ActionAid, 2001a). The recent U.S. Farm Bill has made matters worse. Developed countries' export subsidies for agricultural products seriously undermine the competitiveness of domestic industries in developing countries. In Zimbabwe, for example, EU export subsidies for dairy products led to the collapse of butter production, which fell by 92 percent in the latter half of the 1990s. Similar damage is being done in Jamaica (ActionAid, 2001a: 9).

The new EU Common Agriculture Policy (CAP) proposals, published in July 2002 and appearing in the EC paper for the negotiations on the Agreement on Agriculture, do not significantly reduce the overall sum dedicated to subsidies. Without reductions, little will change. ActionAid does not believe the proposals go far enough to truly decouple subsidies from production, and is disappointed that, beyond existing commitments, there are few moves to reduce market price support. If implemented, the proposals will ensure that the majority of EU subsidies will be compliant with WTO rules and not subject to any further reduction requirements (ActionAid, 2002a).

A specific objective of the Doha round is to address concerns of developing countries in relation to patents and trade-related intellectual property rights (TRIPs). Most developing countries see the TRIPs agreement as yet another protectionist measure serving the interests of Northern multinational companies and their home countries. The recently published UK Government Intellectual Property Rights Commission report recognizes the huge costs to developing countries of meeting the requirements of the TRIPs agreement. It recommends various reforms and the postponement of full implementation until 2016 (IPRC, 2002).

In health and pharmaceuticals, the top ten companies control 35 percent of the $297 billion industry worldwide. The largest five pharmaceutical companies have a market capitalization greater than the economies of Mexico or India, and twice the regional GNP of Sub-Saharan Africa (UNDP, 1999: 2). Such disproportionate economic power gives transnational corporations enormous political power. Indications are that lobbying from pharmaceutical companies has scuppered a deal that would allow developed countries to export generic medicines to developing countries that do not have a pharmaceutical industry. Attempts to sort out this issue at the WTO ministerial meeting in Sydney in November 2002 have since run into the ground. As a result of the current approach, life-saving and life-prolonging medicines are out of reach of most people in poor countries, particularly those that face the devastation caused by the HIV/AIDS epidemic.

Similarly, the TRIPs agreement potentially threatens the right to food security by denying poor people access to seeds and genetic resources for food and agriculture. For example, four multinationals currently hold 44 percent of all patents (numbering more than 900) on staple crops (ActionAid, 2001b: 2). At the same time, trade-related patent protection contributes to enormous wealth accumulation and significant global inequalities.

One of the premises of the TRIPs agreement is that the protection of intellectual property rights (IPRs) will facilitate technology transfer and foreign direct investment flows to developing countries. However, most developing countries do not have the technological and industrial base to absorb sophisticated technology (Balasubramaniam, 2001). More importantly, multinational corporations have little incentive to promote technology transfer or to invest in developing countries. Instead, they can extract knowledge and raw materials, including biological resources, from developing countries and subsequently impose high costs on developing countries wanting to purchase the final products (UNDP, 1999). Finally, the internationalization of strong forms of IPRs, such as patents, can actually dampen, not encourage, innovation, and discourage competition (IPRC, 2002: 65).

A final point on trade is that although almost all developed countries used protection in the past to develop their own domestic industries, they are now aggressively pushing developing countries to liberalize in the early stages of development (Chang, 2002). Recent U.S. proposals for universal elimination of all tariffs on non-agricultural products by 2015, presented as a "bold" contribution to multilateral trade liberalization, have been received cautiously by the WTO and the EC, as the cost to developing countries will be particularly severe.[3]

ActionAid's view is that such proposals are inappropriate because they do not recognize structural inequalities in global production and trade. The imperative is to establish a more equitable global trading system, which would by definition recognize different countries' different economic starting points and different levels of vulnerability to global economic shocks and stresses. Without such reforms, aid will continue to play a palliative role, and the debt problem is likely to reappear.[4]

Even if some of the changes discussed materialize, not all developing countries or producers will benefit equally. Much depends on export capacity, on diversification of exports, and on whether the producers in a country are able to compete with those in other developing countries, once protection is removed.

Three sets of countries are likely to need help beyond improved market access and the phase-out of subsidies in the United States, European Union, and Japan: countries that are net food producers; countries that export tropical foods but import temperate foods; and countries that export small volumes of textiles. Most African countries and island states fall into one or more of these three categories, as do poor countries such as Nepal (Morrissey, 2000). Aid has an important potential role to play here. However, ActionAid believes that the current Integrated Framework for trade capacity building—the main product on offer—is badly suited to the task.

Private Capital Flows and Public-Private Partnerships

Private international capital flows, particularly foreign direct investment (FDI), are seen as having a vital role in the development process, especially by participants in the post-Monterrey debates, in NEPAD, and at the 2002 World Summit for Sustainable Development in Johannesburg. However, it is not at all clear how this agenda will work in practice.

Though private financial flows to developing countries have increased, not all countries or regions have benefited; in Sub-Saharan Africa, for example, aid still accounts for 90 percent of total financial inflows (Hjertholm and White, 2000).

UNCTAD (2002) shows that in 2000, the least developed countries collectively received 28 percent of official net resource flows to all developing countries, but only 1.7 percent of private resource flows, and 2.6 percent of net FDI inflows. Moreover, 47 percent of net FDI flows to all LDCs went to the four oil-producing LDCs (Angola, Equatorial Guinea, Sudan, and Yemen) (UNCTAD, 2002: 10).

The poorest countries attract little FDI and cannot borrow on capital markets. They are highly dependent on official flows. Other developing countries (non-IDA countries) attract more FDI and can borrow. What appears to get relatively little attention is how aid might or might not contribute to countries moving between these states. The assumption that aid serves to attract private investment does not hold true for the majority of LDCs (UNCTAD, 2000).

Equally, while foreign flows are important, the role of domestic investment and the development of domestic private sectors still receive relatively little attention. In general, investment policy is currently evolving without much attention to development objectives, shaped by the profusion of bilateral investment treaties, some ad hoc policy pressure from the World Bank, and regional treaties such as NAFTA and the proposed Free Trade Area of the Americas (FTAA). ActionAid believes that an Investment Agreement in the WTO would not meet the needs of developing countries (as indeed recent Working Group papers tabled by China and other countries suggest).

At the project or sector level, the involvement of the private sector is also not straightforward. Crudely put, there are potential problems with the nonprofitable part of the provision of services (such as rural water supply), and in particular the provision of services to the poor; and there are also potential problems of accountability. Vague talk of "partnerships" will not magically solve deep-rooted problems of how to provide high quality services to very poor people.

Foreign Policy and the Security Agenda

Foreign policy objectives have a significant impact on the overall direction of the global development agenda and on global resource flows. For example, the disproportionate allocation of aid to Eastern Europe and North Africa by the European Community suggests that stemming migration, and the accession of Eastern European states to the European Union, are important considerations for donors. Another example concerns the Gulf War, when Jordan and Syria saw a sudden increase in aid allocations followed by a significant decline once the war ended.[5]

Since the 2001 attacks on the United States, some rich countries are once again putting strong emphasis on global security. Past experiences and recent trends suggest that strategic interests and security concerns are likely to increasingly influence bilateral relations, including financial allocations and other forms of support. For example, while the United States has announced that it will limit its official bilateral aid allocations to about fifteen countries—selected for their democratic political systems and sound economic policy environments—it has also set up a special fund in the State Department to aid its allies in the war against terrorism, regardless of their democratic or economic credentials.[6] The United States is also non-apologetic about the fact that its support for Central and South Asian states is largely shaped by their strategic location in relation to the "War on Terrorism" and that it is in the interest of U.S. national security to address development challenges in this region.

Another likely implication of the preeminence of security concerns is that security-related costs will increase in donor countries, and intensify the competition for resources between domestic, foreign policy, and international development interests. For example, in his recent pre-budget report, UK Chancellor Gordon Brown announced that £1 billion had been put aside for "our international defense responsibilities...to be drawn on if necessary."[7] Although there is no indication that the UK intends to reduce its aid allocations as a result, it is worth mentioning that £1 billion is about a third of the UK's current annual aid contributions.

The current downturn in the global economy will aggravate such competition over resources. For example, the Italian Parliament is currently discussing an amendment to a national law regulating debt relief, which would allow Italy to backtrack on quality and quantity targets for debt relief, arguing that current budget constraints demand this.[8] Similar impacts may be felt in developing countries, especially in Central and South Asia, with a renewed emphasis on military spending over development spending.

There are signs, too, that the "War on Terrorism" will have implications for civil society. Several ActionAid offices have pointed to anti-terrorist legislation or measures that are being used by governments to harass legitimate civil society. This is an alarming development, as the suppression of civil society lessens the prospect for increased accountability and, in the long run, risks creating the kinds of resentment that lead to extreme acts.

A closely linked issue is that of humanitarian aid being used with clear political overtones. Afghanistan is the most recent case in point, where more than $1 billion of donor resources have been pledged essentially to pay for war damages that stem directly from the U.S. foreign policy and security agenda. The humanitarian, let alone reconstruction, costs of the attack on Iraq will be much larger.

In a sense, the context for aid *is* more joined-up than it used to be. For a trade round to be labeled a "Development Round" in itself shows that links are being made in people's minds. Now, increasingly, the difficulty lies in translating thinking into action. There is a profound lack of coherence between the current development objectives of the rich world and the objectives it pursues in trade and foreign policies, as revealed not by statements but by actions. This is fairly clear to most observers—which is partly why a crisis of legitimacy of aid has arisen. However, there are also other reasons, to do with aid itself. It is to these reasons that we now turn.

The Crisis of Legitimacy in Aid[9]

The Crisis of Commitment

Between 1960 and 1992, the net official development assistance (ODA) disbursements of DAC countries increased steadily from $5 billion to close to $63 billion (Figure 2.1), but by 2000 they had fallen to $54 billion (DAC, 2002). Reasons for the drop in the 1990s include the end of the Cold War, which eliminated the reason to use aid for geopolitical and security interests; pressures on the national budgets of donor countries (Hjertholm and White, 2000); and the increased faith in markets and the private sector to deliver economic growth.

As a share of donors' gross national income, ODA declined significantly from about 0.65 percent in 1967 to 0.22 percent in 2001 (DAC, 2002). This is despite the agreement between donor countries, repeated at numerous international events (most recently, the International Conference in Monterrey on Financing for Develop-

Figure 2.1
Net ODA Disbursements of DAC Countries, 1960-2000
(Current U.S. $ billion)

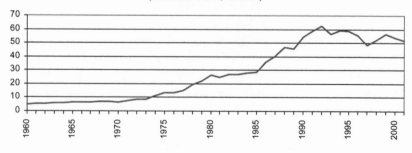

Source: DAC (2002)

ment), that aid should reach 0.7 percent of donors' gross national income (GNI). Only five out of twenty-two DAC countries have reached this target (Denmark, Luxembourg, Norway, the Netherlands, and Sweden) and Ireland is the only country to have set a timetable for reaching 0.7 percent by 2007 (Figure 2.2).

An additional $40-60 billion a year is needed to achieve the Millennium Development Goals (Zedillo, 2002; DFID/HMT, 2002). This figure is far less than the approximately $160 billion that would be available if all countries were to meet the agreed target of 0.7 percent of national income (ActionAid, 2002c).

Figure 2.2
Aid as a Percentage of Donors' Gross National Income, 2001

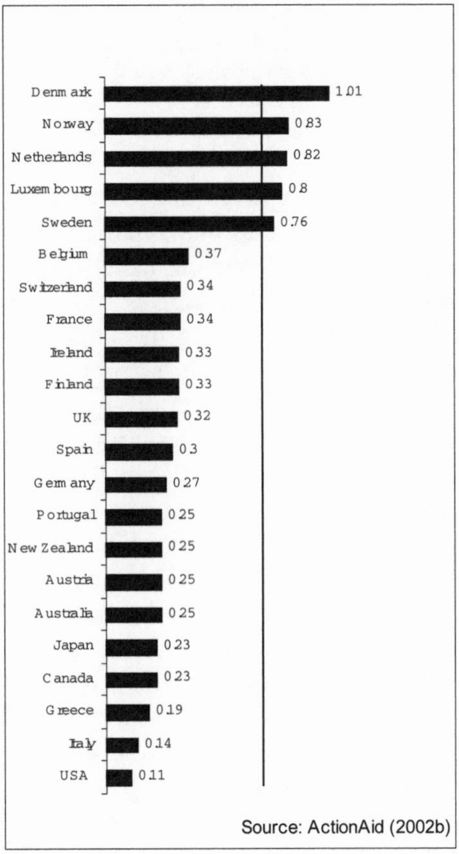

Source: ActionAid (2002b)

Although the United States is the largest contributor to ODA in real terms, it ranks last in share of national income, with a ratio of 0.11 percent in 2001. The UK, after extensive public lobbying and with the greater commitment of the Labor government, has recently announced that it will increase its contribution to 0.4 percent of GNP, up from the current level of 0.32 percent (Box 2.2).

Box 2.2
Successful Campaigning for More Aid Flows

BOND, the network of more than 260 UK NGOs working in international development, has successfully mobilized public and parliamentary support to increase UK ODA allocations. Thousands of cyber-petitions and more than 40,000 letters were sent to HM Treasury in support of increased financing of international development. As a result of intense lobbying, 240 MPs signed an Early Day Motion calling for an intermediate target of 0.4 percent by 2006. On 15 July 2002, the UK Government publicly announced that it had accepted this target. Whereas BOND has commended the UK Government for making this commitment, it underlines that there remains a clear and urgent need for the UK and other donor countries to commit to a timetable for reaching 0.7 percent.

A growing share of ODA takes the form of humanitarian aid. Between 1990 and 2000, official humanitarian aid doubled in real terms, from $2.1 billion to $5.9 billion, increasing its share of ODA from 5.83 percent to 10.5 percent (ODI, 2003). This is often ascribed to the rise in need, reflecting the huge increase since the 1970s in both the number of natural disasters reported and the number of people affected. But with overall aid levels steady in real terms, the result is a squeeze on longer-term development aid. Despite many calls for tighter links between the two types of assistance, this has largely failed to happen.

In many ways, the rise in humanitarian aid is a result of the crisis in commitment: emergency aid is much easier for donor countries to "sell" to their domestic constituencies, and focuses on logistical rather than social or economic tasks. It is easier to lift someone out of a tree with a helicopter during a flood than it is to lift someone out of poverty.

The current system faces a long-run problem of donor fatigue. This is despite the commitments made at Monterrey by the United States and the EU. While George W. Bush's decision to increase U.S. development assistance by $5 billion over the next three years and the EU's commitment to reach an average ODA/GNI ratio of

0.39 percent by 2006 are welcome, there is little evidence that they have prompted a general reversal of the global downward trend in aid spending.

A new approach is needed. One element of such an approach is to identify new and imaginative strategies for financing increased development flows, possibly through the establishment of new taxes, such as the proposed Tobin tax or the carbon tax, both of which have been suggested as a means to fund global public goods. A more recent suggestion is to increase the level of development assistance by bringing aid flows forward in time, as in the International Development Financing Facility (IDFF) put forward by UK Chancellor of the Exchequer Gordon Brown.[10]

However, even with new financing mechanisms, the issue of commitment remains. Currently, outside mainly the Scandinavian group of donors, international aid is based on a charity model, or on a model that seeks to correct for market failures, rather than being based on a right akin to citizenship (FitzGerald, 1996). An aid system based on entitlement, whereby poor people receive assistance by virtue of being members of the global community, would place a social obligation on rich countries and their citizens to meet the rights of citizens from poor countries to live healthy and fulfilling lives. This view differs fundamentally from the perspective that aid stems from the compassion of donor countries, because it regards poor people as "citizens with entitlements to benefits and rights of participation in decisions which affect them" rather than as aid recipients and "beneficiaries" (FitzGerald, 1996: 13).

Such an approach is far from being on the political agenda. But if an entitlement-based approach to aid is not adopted, it is likely that all the problems of commitment, conditionality, and lack of accountability will recur indefinitely.

The Crisis of Allocation

Donor countries often speak of the eradication of poverty as the main goal of development assistance. However, if one compares the geographical distribution of aid with the geographical distribution of poverty, the distribution of aid is highly ineffective:

- Sub-Saharan Africa (the region with the largest number of poor countries and nearly a fourth of the world's poor) has received the lion's share of aid allocations over the past two decades, amounting to an average of 30 percent of total ODA.[11]

- Although most of the world's poor live in South and Central Asia, this region has seen a marked decline in its share of aid flows from an average of 16.9 percent in 1973-80 to an average of 11.7 percent in 1991-96 (Hjertholm and White, 2000: 91).
- Since the mid- to late 1980s, countries in North Africa and the Middle East have also seen their share of aid flows decline. While North Africa received an average of 12.7 percent of aid flows in 1973-80 and the Middle East received 13.8 percent, these figures had decreased to 7.3 percent and 6.7 percent, respectively, by 1991-96 (ibid.). This is largely seen as a result of these regions' loss of geopolitical importance in the post-Cold War era.
- The Far East, which is more economically advanced than most developing regions and has access to private capital, received the second largest share of aid throughout the 1990s, with 21 percent between 1995 and 2000 (Hjertholm and White, 2000).
- South America's share of aid has been relatively small, hovering between 4-7 percent for the past two decades.
- Eastern Europe's share of global ODA disbursements increased from 1 percent in 1975 to 7 percent in 2000.

Using the example of European Community aid, Table 2.1 provides further evidence of the scope for better targeting of aid to where poverty is most severe. In 2001, 34 percent of the European Community's development resources were allocated to Eastern Europe and Central Asia, where only two percent of the world's poor live. The Middle East and North Africa received 15 percent of European Community development assistance, yet they have only one percent of the world's poor.

Table 2.1
Relating EC Aid to the Proportion of Poor People per Region

	% of the world's poor	% of EC development assistance (2001)
South Asia	44	5
Sub-Saharan Africa	24	29
East Asia & Pacific	23	7
Latin America & Caribbean	7	10
Europe & Central Asia	2	34
Middle East & North Africa	1	15

Source: DFID, 2002: 84

It is also important to take account of intra-regional allocations. For example, three countries in Sub-Saharan Africa (Tanzania, Uganda, and Mozambique) accounted for 25 percent of total ODA disbursements to the region in 2000 (DAC, 2002).

The lack of a clear relationship between poverty and the distribution of aid is also evident when we look at the allocation of aid to countries by income group (Figure 2.3). During the 1990s, donors allocated roughly equal shares of ODA to the least developed countries (31 percent), other low-income countries (32 percent), and lower-middle-income countries (33 percent). The overall share of upper-middle-income countries decreased from 10 percent in 1980 to 4 percent in 2000.

Aid to the least developed countries has declined steadily since 1990. Because total ODA has also decreased over time, net ODA to LDCs in 2000 was 22 percent less in nominal terms than in the preceding three years (UNCTAD, 2002: 10). During the 1980s, annual aid per capita to the least developed countries was $33, compared with just $20 today.[12]

Moreover, the fact that the least developed countries currently receive only 29 percent of total ODA contradicts donors' commitment to allocate at least 0.3 percent of their GNI as aid to this group of countries. Only two donors (Norway and Denmark) have met this target, with Sweden, the Netherlands, and Luxembourg allocating just over 0.15 percent of their GNI to least developed countries (ActionAid, 2002b).

Looking at aid allocations by sector, in 2000 the bulk of bilateral aid commitments were for social infrastructure (Figure 2.4). However, spending on basic social services remained far below the tar-

Figure 2.3
Allocation of ODA by Country Income Group, 1970-2000

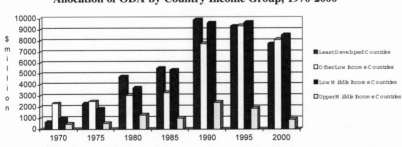

Source: DAC (2002).

Figure 2.4
DAC Bilateral Commitments, by Sector, 2000

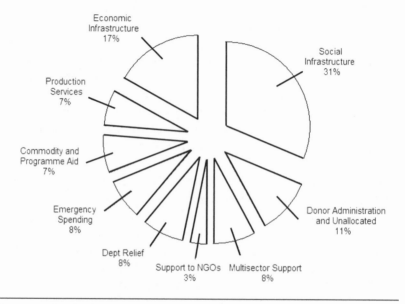

Source: ActionAid (2002b)

get of 20 percent of total ODA that had been agreed in the 20/20 Initiative:[13]

- 6.3 percent of total aid was spent on education and only 1.2 percent on basic education;
- 2.8 percent was allocated to health care, but only 0.9 percent to basic health care;
- 5.1 percent went to water supply and sanitation;
- 1.9 percent went toward population and reproductive health (ActionAid, 2002b).

It is clear that donor countries can significantly improve the effectiveness of aid by better targeting poverty in geographical, economic, and sectoral terms. Few donors adhere to the rhetorical commitments they have made to this effect. It is high time for donors to accept their moral obligation to ensure poor people can attain their basic rights. Some donors are recognizing this and are increasingly concerned that aid should be targeted to countries and regions where poverty is most severe. However, other sources of aid, including the World Bank and the United States, are increasingly driven in their aid allocations by selectivity based on recipient countries' policies. The new U.S. Millennium Challenge Account has heightened concerns about selectivity.

The notion of aid selectivity is informed by the view that aid works, but only in a "good" policy environment. The emphasis on selectivity comes from the realization among donors that aid has limited effect in changing or influencing policy; instead, good policy has become a prerequisite to qualify for aid. The crux of the argument is that for aid to be "poverty-efficient," donors need to allocate aid to countries that meet two criteria: high levels of poverty and the presence of a good policy environment (Collier and Dollar, 2000; Dollar and Kraay, 2002).

The emphasis on selectivity raises a number of questions.[14] Who defines what constitutes a good policy environment? Commonly used indicators such as the World Bank's Country Policy and Institutional Assessment system are not transparent, and bundle together many different policies, not all of which are convincingly related to poverty reduction or pro-poor growth. But the most compelling problem is what to do about countries with high levels of poverty and poorly rated policy environments (Thorbecke, 2000). The selectivity argument does not engage this problem, except to suggest a vague "policy dialogue." This is still a live research issue in agencies such as DFID, the World Bank, and the OECD's DAC.

Like other international NGOs, ActionAid itself exercises a degree of selectivity in choosing partners in the South, based on principles and values. Such selectivity obviously does pose a dilemma for organizations like ActionAid that speak out against the current practice of donor selectivity. However, whilst NGOs can select their partners from among a range of local partners, official donors have only one national government to work with and by choosing not to give aid to a country donors end up denying the population of such a country the benefits of aid all together.

Selectivity as currently practiced by some donors, with an emphasis on a broad post-Washington Consensus set of policy indicators and with no clear answer on how to help poor people in "poorly performing" countries, may be contributing to, rather than solving, the current legitimacy crisis of aid. This is a huge concern for the so-called low-income countries under stress, which are in conflict situations, but also for several other LDCs. In fact, this is a vicious circle where countries with so-called "bad policy environments" are the ones who need support the most and end up getting the least. Betting on the strong simply does not allow the weak to break out of the poverty trap.

The Crisis of Disbursement

Not only is aid chronically misallocated, it is also badly disbursed in several ways. A key problem is aid tying. It is increasingly recognized that tying aid hinders the development process and outcomes in developing countries. In 2001, the debate on aid untying gained new momentum when donors agreed to untie some categories of aid to LDCs.[15] Despite slow progress in implementing the DAC agreement and its limited scope, this remains the only multilateral deal to untie aid. Subsequently, at the Financing for Development Conference in 2002, donors announced they would support efforts to "further untie bilateral aid."[16] In November 2002, EU ministers considered for the first time a European Commission proposal to untie aid across the European Union. The merit of the EC proposal is not just that it unties EC programs, but that it challenges individual member states to follow suit. Approximately €6.2 billion of member states' aid is tied every year and thus far only the UK has untied its aid (DAC, 2002). The debate in the EU is an unprecedented step that could help shape future debates among donors.

Today there is a clear understanding of the negative effects of tying and the gains to be obtained if aid were untied. According to the DAC, half of world aid remains tied and if all aid were untied, an additional $5 billion would be released. The momentum in the untying debate presents an extraordinary opportunity for those concerned with issues of value for money and effectiveness of aid to counteract the legacy of protectionism and commercial pressures. ActionAid's legal complaint to the European Commission that tied aid falls foul of European Competition Policy has resulted in an investigation by the Commission.

The main reasons to untie aid include the following:

- Tying aid reduces value for money, because it prevents competition and the possibility of obtaining lower prices and best quality. OECD studies have shown that tying aid increases the costs of goods and services by 20 percent (ActionAid, 1998) (Box 2.3.)

- Tying aid leads to commercial pressure in donor countries to fund projects that do not match beneficiaries' needs. As such, tied aid compromises the notion of local ownership.
- Tied aid discourages donor coordination and simplification of procedures, as each donor retains its own procedures and favors its own sectors and countries. This imposes additional burdens on recipient countries.
- Tying aid discourages donors from increasing local procurement of goods and services, thereby undermining the possibility of creating commercial opportunities for companies from poor countries.
- Tying aid reduces transparency and can encourage corruption, because governments in donor countries could be prone to the influence of potent lobbies that would gain from the aid conditionality. This may lead to a distortion in aid allocations at the expense of a focus on the poorest countries or on priority sectors to tackle poverty.
- Tied aid discourages donors from using more efficient (untied) forms of aid delivery, such as budgetary support.

Box 2.3
Danish Tied Aid in Bangladesh

In April 2002, Denmark cancelled a $45 million aid contract to repair ferries in Bangladesh. The Danish grant was tied. The repair work was to be carried out in Denmark and sent back to Bangladesh. Some other rehabilitation work was to be undertaken in Bangladesh, but with equipment and capital goods imported from Denmark. The bidding price was four times higher than if all the work had been undertaken and sourced from Bangladesh or within the region. Following a request from the Bangladeshi Minister to increase local supplies to reduce the price, Denmark cancelled the contract. The case is currently being investigated in the Danish Parliament.

Source: Shahidur Rahman, ActionAid Bangladesh

Despite recent recognition among donors of the need to untie aid, ActionAid remains concerned with how "tied aid" is defined. When reporting on levels of tied aid, donors exclude two categories of tied aid: technical cooperation and food aid. For example, whilst DAC figures suggest aid is increasingly untied and that less than 12 percent of aid was tied in 1999, this is partly because the figures exclude technical assistance/technical cooperation. If this were included, the share of tied aid would actually have increased to 53 percent in 1999.

In 1999, technical cooperation accounted for more than 28 percent of total aid, or $16 billion. Some donors make extensive use of technical cooperation as a type of aid. The United States tops the list, with technical cooperation accounting for more than 75 percent of its aid budget. Other keen providers of technical cooperation are Germany (61 percent of total bilateral programs in 2000), Portugal (50 percent), Belgium (46 percent), and France (45 percent). In contrast, Luxembourg and Sweden allocated only 2 percent and 6 percent, respectively, of their total bilateral programs to technical cooperation (ActionAid, 2002d).

If the purpose of technical cooperation is to build sustainable local institutions and to promote local ownership, there should be more emphasis on local procurement. Technical cooperation produces greater dependence on expatriate expertise and can be used to increase donors' influence over policies and projects. In Sub-Saharan Africa, with some 100,000 foreign technical experts at work annually, technical cooperation has probably weakened capacity by displacing local experts, as the World Bank has acknowledged, (quoted in ActionAid, 2002). The key challenge for donor countries is to find ways to manage technical cooperation more effectively.[17] One option may be for donors to make funds available for recipient countries to choose independently which international advisors they would like to engage.[18]

Untying aid will not lead to greater sourcing of local supplies and expertise without changes in current procurement regimes. Donors should ensure that untying is accompanied by measures to provide local firms with a level playing field for access to aid contracts. This will not only produce more relevant goods and services for development projects, but also offer better value for money and enhanced effectiveness.

In addition, ActionAid believes that the purchasing power generated from the procurement of aid contracts can help to promote local growth and yield socioeconomic benefits for local people. Aid contracts could be used to facilitate the introduction of labor, transport, materials, and finance to community-based enterprises in programs and projects. These contracts would permit such enterprises to establish themselves and acquire the necessary skills in respect of supply, materials, and management. They would also promote employment. Some of the measures to promote local firms' ability to tender for aid contracts include promoting local sourcing and building up the capacities of the local supplier community and those of the recipient government to procure.

The relevance of aid procurement as a positive tool for development is greater now than ever. The poorest countries continue to be largely aid-dependent. With the new trend toward decentralization, the need for local, small-scale contractors will grow, as will the need for training and capacity building of local consultants. Moreover, recipient governments will need the skills, capacity, and systems in place to procure, disburse, and account for those financial resources.

New ways of contracting aid need to be devised that go beyond the traditional value-for-money considerations to take into account social and development goals. The procurement process needs to remain competitive, but the challenge is to combine competitive considerations with others, such as social or developmental objectives.

A final aspect of aid disbursement is the need to minimize the administrative burden on both donors and recipient countries. Recipient countries spend much time, energy, and political capital on engaging with external actors. In particular, the separate reporting requirements of the various donor countries impose a significant burden on aid recipients. For example, Tanzania has had to comply with forty donors for 2,000 projects. Likewise, in the mid-1990s the Mozambican Ministry of Health had more than 400 development programs supported by different donors, with administrative costs running to 30-40 percent of total project funds (Kanbur, 2000). In Kenya, fifteen donors are currently active in the education sector, each with its own advisor.[19]

There is an assumption that increased policy coordination *among* donors will make aid more effective. This may be a logical expectation, but in reality little progress has been made toward greater donor coordination. Some donor countries, including Portugal and Spain, have moved to more coherent development frameworks whereas others, like the United States, have shifted to greater policy fragmentation (German and Randel, 2000).

Despite international commitments to development frameworks as provided by the 20/20 Initiative and the MDGs, the parallel practice of continuing to rely heavily on bilateral channels, rather than on multilateral organizations like the UN, allows individual donor countries to exert more discretion over resource allocations and to impose specific reporting requirements. Norway is the only donor country that has channeled more resources through the UN system.

Donors' inclination toward bilateral funding is possibly the result of increased policy coordination *within* donor countries between domestic policies on aid, trade, and foreign affairs. This allows for the geopolitical and commercial interests of donor countries to influence their aid agenda and contributions. It also allows domestic issues, such as concern about refugees and asylum seekers, to take precedence over global development issues.[20]

ActionAid therefore continues to call for improved coordination between donors and progress toward harmonization of procedures.

The Crisis of Accountability: Beyond Poverty Reduction Strategy Papers

For donor countries, the current solution to the problem of how to ensure that aid goes to poverty reduction is the adoption of poverty reduction strategy papers (PRSPs) by recipient countries. Central to this approach, and to the original concept of the PRSP, is the building of local ownership of a development strategy, achieved through the involvement of various stakeholders in the process.

The introduction of PRSPs, while flawed, does look like an attempt to make donors and governments more accountable. But PRSPs face a lot of criticism. In most cases they have been added on to, rather than integrated into, existing planning and political processes. They look increasingly marginalized in mainstream budgetary decisions, and adrift of the old-style conditionality that has re-emerged in PRGF and PRSC documents. They have not, in general, stemmed the crisis in donor-recipient relations that spans the history of conditionality.

The difficult and time-consuming process of stakeholder engagement that underpins the development of a PRSP runs the risk of being fast-tracked or having partial involvement at best, as experiences from Haiti and Pakistan show (Houghton, ActionAid USA, 2002). An ActionAid review of PRSPs in various countries shows that public participation is usually limited to public consultation, which tends to be restricted to the first round of discussions. The actual decision-making about trade-offs, strategies, and instruments happens behind closed doors, with little to no accountability to domestic stakeholders or interest groups. The review further reveals that the IMF and World Bank are able to exert undue influence over the content of PRSPs, because of their dual role as participants/

advisors and decision-makers. And, as in virtually all other aid situations, securing equal participation by women, and ensuring that the impact of decisions on women's rights is articulated and considered, has not been done.

Many of these concerns stem from the fact that for many poor countries, the formulation of a PRSP is linked to stringent conditions on external financing. This need to comply with external policy prescriptions in the International Monetary Fund's Poverty Reduction Growth Facility (PRGF) and the World Bank's Poverty Reduction Support Credit (PRSC) agreements undermines local ownership and local accountability, both of which are supposed to be at the heart of a poverty reduction strategy. In contrast, where countries have developed their own poverty reduction strategies in response to domestic pressures and informed by extensive consultation, as in Uganda's Poverty Eradication Action Plan, government accountability to local citizens is significantly enhanced (The Reality of Aid Project, 2002).

Of particular concern is the fact that the international financial institutions and many donor governments seem to hold that "hard" economic issues (related to macroeconomic adjustment, liberalization, and privatization) are exempt from poverty analysis, despite their direct impact on poverty and inequality and on the poor (The Reality of Aid Project, 2002). As a result, the underlying assumptions of PRGFs and PRSCs are left unchallenged and recipient countries are left with little option but to follow a prescribed development path, regardless of local conditions and the nature of domestic political and social dynamics.

This raises the question of whether aid conditionality and donors' "results-orientation" can be at all compatible with local ownership and domestic accountability. ActionAid's experiences show that although in theory PRSPs aim to reconcile these differing objectives, in practice donors' requirements take precedence over the political process of establishing accountability and ownership, even in those countries where there appears to be more space for public participation in policy formulation.

In ActionAid's view, what is missing from the equation is donor and lender accountability to citizens in poor countries. If this dimension were to be included, PRSPs may look very different indeed and allow for greater flexibility. Clearly, flexibility and respect for a multiplicity of views are essential for effective poverty reduction. Within the Washington Consensus, these aspects are severely lacking. This has led one of the World Bank's former emissaries, Joseph Stiglitz, to suggest that bilateral development agencies should de-link their poverty reduction strategies from the World Bank and the IMF (The Reality of Aid Project, 2002: 11).

The international financial institutions and bilateral donors also need to think about the political impact that their aid programs can have. Aid has political impacts: it can potentially help open up the space for poor people to engage with the development process, or it can foreclose this space. While donors and lenders do support some civil society interaction with governments in PRSP-type dialogue, this direct intervention may, in fact, have less political impact than other aid interventions. They have a responsibility to think about such impacts in advance, possibly through "Political Impact Assessments" analogous to social or environmental assessments.

An obvious strategy for international financial institutions and donors will be to strengthen national citizens' organizations and civil society groups, the media, and parliaments to act as a vital counterbalance to the state and market forces. Given that many of the developing countries are relatively young democracies, such strengthening is essential to ensure the public accountability of governments and corporations.

Beyond mainstream development assistance, donors also need to think about accountability and the dangers of excluding people from humanitarian aid. ActionAid has worked hard to develop a rights-based approach to humanitarian aid, and has seen such an approach yield distinctive results. In the aftermath of the 2001 earthquake in Gujarat, for example, ActionAid focused assistance on the parts of the community that were already marginalized before the disaster, rather than on all affected people. Similarly, social audits in the cyclone rehabilitation work in Orissa were an effective way of increasing local government accountability and enhancing the voice of poor women.

The Crisis of the Global Commons

The new donor frontier is global public goods. Global public goods are usually taken to include the environment/biodiversity and public health, in particular the prevention of contagious diseases. UNDP's list of global public goods also includes access to water, international financial stability, the multilateral trade regime, and corruption-free government (UNDP 2003). Greater interdependence between people, networks, markets, and states has led to a situation where the costs and benefits of using and producing certain goods and services cross boundaries between countries, population groups, and generations. This raises important questions about equity: about who benefits, who is excluded, and who carries the burdens, both now and in the future. Although the distributional effects of international development are not new, the concept of global public goods—which encompasses the notion that the distribution of responsibilities, benefits, and burdens must be equitable—is still relatively new.[21]

The issue of international financing for global public goods was discussed at Monterrey. In particular, the Recommendations of the High-level Panel on Financing for Development (Zedillo 2002) discussed the need for collective action on and dedicated funding for the provision of global public goods. That report estimated that about 15 percent of aid resources (or $5 billion) is currently diverted to the supply of global public goods. It recommended at least a four-fold increase in this figure and that global public goods should be financed from new financial resources provided on a grant basis.

There is no consensus on a global financing mechanism for the provision of global public goods. Clearly, collective action is urgently needed to tackle universal problems and to provide additional and alternative sources of funding. The EU and some individual European countries (in particular France and Sweden) continue to support the quest for appropriate funding mechanisms for the supply of global public goods. However, proposals such as the Tobin tax and the carbon tax are unlikely to get the backing of the G7 that would be needed to make such systems work.

ActionAid's work in developing countries, particularly in Africa, has led us to believe that in principle the Global Fund to Fight AIDS, TB, and Malaria can be an appropriate vehicle for expressing our collective responsibility to respond to the human trauma and devastation caused by HIV/AIDS. The Fund will only be able to live up to its potential if sufficient finance is provided and appropriate procedures and disbursement mechanisms are in place. Current pledges

and allocations are insufficient to respond to the requests for support from affected countries. On 11 October 2002, the Global Fund
indicated that an additional $2 billion is needed in 2003 and that by
2004 this need will increase to $4.6 billion.

In an interconnected world, peace and security can also be
considered a global public good. Given the current preoccupa-
tion with security in global politics, there is clearly an attempt
by world leaders to frame the issue of global security as a global
public good. This raises important questions about how security
is defined; who determines what constitutes a threat to global
security; and what characteristics make a state a rogue state. It
is also important to prevent the security agenda from distorting
aid allocations.

An Agenda for Aid?

In both the North and the South there is undoubtedly a crisis in
the legitimacy of aid. In the North there is donor fatigue; publics
and governments doubt that aid can work. In the South, donors and
governments are often seen as equally distant and unaccountable,
and the experience with PRSPs has made many civil society organizations cynical about claims of accountability, participation, and
ownership.

How do we deal with these problems? One suggestion put forward by Kanbur and Sandler (1999) and endorsed by the UN Panel
on Financing for Development (Zedillo 2002) is the Common Pool
Proposal. Under this proposal donors are expected to cede control
to recipient country governments, only advancing their own perspective on development through genuine dialogue with the countries they assist. The Common Pool Proposal would work as follows:

> The recipient country would first develop its own strategy, programs, and projects,
> primarily in consultation with its own population but also in dialogue with donors. It
> would then present its plans to the donors, who would put unrestricted funding into a
> common pool. The common pool of development assistance, together with the
> government's own resources, would then finance the overall development strategy.
> The level of financing by each donor would depend on their assessment both of the
> strategy and the program, and the recipients' ability to implement the strategy and
> effectively monitor progress and expenditures. The views based on these assessments
> would be made known to the country and to other donors during the dialogue leading
> up to the financing decision; but earmarking of this or that donor's funds to this or that
> item, or specific donor monitoring and control of specific projects or programs, would
> not be permitted.[22]

While this proposal addresses a series of the problems identified in the present chapter it is unlikely to be implemented in the near future. This is because many of the difficult problems—including how to achieve greater coherence between aid objectives and other policies, more poverty-focused allocation of aid, and real accountability—are political rather than technical in nature. A new research agenda is therefore needed that focuses on providing evidence for certain types of change that will move political stalemates.

Research

In the North, one example might be to marshal evidence that would convince countries that currently oppose the reform of the European Common Agricultural Policy (CAP)—such as France, Ireland, and Italy—that their societies would be better off if they agreed to reduce the use of production-based subsidies, because of the global growth effects.

Another would be research investigating more carefully what kind of economic, social, and political policies are most directly linked to poverty reduction, so that influential donors can be convinced to shape selectivity more appropriately.

There is also a case to assess whether countries with strong PRSPs indeed have more effective aid programs and are ultimately better at reducing poverty. Along with this comes the question of the relative effectiveness of budgetary support, program aid, and project aid in relation to poverty reduction.

With increased provisioning of services through NGOs and for-profit private outfits, research on the relative effectiveness of various providers in different sectors and contexts is apposite.

Clearly, all aspects of the crisis in aid, in terms of context and content, quantity and quality, generate significant research needs. For ActionAid, with an emphasis on the rights of poor people, a critical area that warrants further investigation is the accountability of donors, developing country governments, and corporations, and how best to generate and measure it. For example, independent researchers from the Institute of Development Studies, Sussex, have observed that the introduction of a new Accountability Learning and Planning System that emphasizes downward accountability to poor and marginalized people is showing very positive early results in ActionAid programs. At the same time, the System challenges the behaviors and working methods of ActionAid even further.

The discussion on the research agenda for aid has to bear in mind not just the "what" question but equally the "how" question. To be useful, research must engage people and organizations with intimate local knowledge, and put the concerns of poor and marginalized people at the center. The balance between scientific rigor and participatory research poses severe challenges to traditional researchers. Building local research capacity in the poor countries on issues that matter to poor people should therefore be as much a priority as the research itself.

Monitoring and Advocacy

As mentioned earlier, complementing the research agenda and almost more urgent is the task of monitoring existing aid commitments and the policies and practices of donor and recipient governments in the aid chain. The success of the debt campaign in forcing donor attention on this crucial issue has shown the value of public advocacy.

Some have called for performance targets for donors, and various models for measuring donor performance have been proposed. These include the Aid Diamond (Hjertholm and White, 2000) and the proposed Index of Commitment to Development developed by the Center for Global Development (CGD). The Reality of Aid Project, a consortium of NGOs from the North and the South, offers an independent review of aid efforts since 1993, although its efforts are hampered by the lack of transparency in official data. Social Watch is another effort to monitor commitments such as the 20/ 20 Initiative from the Copenhagen World Summit for Social Development.

ActionAid certainly believes that any system to assess donor performance should include measures that encourage greater accountability of donors to recipient countries and their citizens. But targets, including the Millennium Development Goals, are worthless without ideas about how to reach them.

Above all, we need new models for aid financing and delivery, such as that proposed by Helleiner (2000), who outlines core elements of an aid performance monitoring system that would have as its goal the promotion of a true partnership between donor and recipient countries. Such a system would involve greater transparency and accountability in terms of aid commitments, actual disbursements and shortfalls, tying of procurement, and technical cooperation. Importantly, it would imply that donor expenditure supports and recognizes the declared priorities of recipient countries, and ways of reporting on this aspect.

Notes

1. This chapter was written by Mirjam van Donk, Matthew Lockwood, Salil Shetty, Belen Vazquez, and Birgit la Cour Madsen in the UK Advocacy Team of ActionAid, a leading international development and advocacy NGO working in more than thirty of the world's poorest countries. Judith Randall, Robert Picciotto, and John Williamson provided useful comments on earlier drafts of this chapter. Responsibility for any remaining errors rests solely with the authors.
2. World Bank, 1990.
3. The response of Supachai Panitchpakdi, director-general of the WTO, was: "I am not sure that this issue would be the priority on our agenda" (*The Financial Times*, 25 November 2002).
4. Indeed it is already doing so, as the case of Burkina Faso in the Highly Indebted Poor Countries Initiative shows.
5. DAC (2002) data show that ODA from DAC countries to Jordan increased significantly between 1989 ($130 million) and 1991 ($683 million), after which it dropped significantly ($313 million in 1992). Similarly, after Syria lost its strategic importance at the end of the Cold War, ODA levels declined to $69 million in 1990, only to see a threefold increase to $236 in 1991. In 1992, ODA declined drastically to $50 million.
6. *International Herald Tribune*, 25 October 2002.
7. This additional allocation comes on top of the extra £1 billion added to the UK defense budget in mid-2002 as part of the comprehensive spending review (*The Guardian*, 28 November 2002).
8. Information provided by *Azione Aiuto* (ActionAid in Italy).
9. In this chapter we see debt relief very much as part of aid, which we define broadly as development finance. As with conventional aid, debt relief efforts are also facing crises of commitment and disbursement. Multilateral and bilateral debt relief measures introduced since 1999 have resulted in some modest changes. At the end of 2000, the total debt stock of least developed countries (LDCs) stood at more than $143 billion and debt service payments (as a ratio of exports of goods and services) were reduced by more than two percentage points since 1999 to 9.6 percent (UNCTAD, 2002: 12). Yet, the effectiveness and the long-term impacts of debt relief measures have been questioned. For one, the benefits of debt relief have not been shared equally between all LDCs, and some heavily indebted countries do not qualify for debt relief under the Enhanced Highly Indebted Poor Country Initiative (HIPC II). Second, some countries, including Zambia and Niger, will pay more towards debt repayment *after* HIPC II than before, and others are likely to see their debt repayments rise within the first few years (Eurodad, 2001). Third, more than two-thirds of LDCs still have unsustainable levels of external debt, even under HIPC II terms. Out of the twenty-two countries receiving debt relief under HIPC II, three-quarters will still be allocating between 10-27 percent of government revenue to debt servicing, sixteen countries will spend more on debt servicing than on public health care, and ten countries will spend more on debt repayment than on primary

education and health combined (Eurodad, 2001). Such high spending on debt service undermines the capacity of these countries to ensure basic education and basic health care. To conclude, high levels of debt continue to impede economic performance and poverty reduction efforts in many LDCs.

10. The idea behind the IDFF is to establish a temporary fund that can "borrow from the future" in order to spend more at the present. Donor countries would be borrowing money by issuing bonds on private capital markets, which would not have to be paid back until sometime after 2015.

11. Africa's share peaked at 35 percent in 1990 and declined to 29 percent in 2000.

12. In comparison, in 2000 the average income per capita in rich countries was close to $30,000 (The Reality of Aid Project, 2002: 152).

13. The 20/20 Initiative was first adopted at the 1995 World Summit for Social Development, Copenhagen, and is based on an agreement that developing countries will contribute 20 percent of their domestic budget to basic social services and that 20 percent of ODA will be allocated towards these services.

14. See, among others, Beynon (1999), Robinson and Tarp (2000), and Thorbecke (2000) for more detailed critiques of the selective use of data, the partial analysis, and the theoretical assumptions and limitations of the Collier/Dollar models.

15. See DCD/DAC (2001) 12/FINAL at www.oecd/dac.org.

16. See ActionAid (2002d).

17. A study of Tanzania in the early 1990s showed that total donor spending for technical cooperation personnel (excluding spending on external short-term consultancies) by far exceeded Tanzania's own spending on its total civil service (quoted in Anderson, 2000: 186).

18. This option differs from the Tied Trust Funds, which are still based on the understanding that these funds are used to fund consultants from contributing donors, such as the United States, Japan, and Denmark.

19. According to Elimu Yetu, the education network in which ActionAid plays a major role.

20. The Reality of Aid Project (2002: 157) shows that in 1999 two percent of bilateral aid of DAC countries was allocated to asylum seekers and refugees in donor countries.

21. See UNDP (2003) for a more in-depth discussion of the concept and its link with global equity.

22. Kanbur and Sandler (1999: 4).

References

ActionAid. (1998). *Tied Aid Report.* London: ActionAid. (www.actionaid.org.uk)

_____. (2001a). *Food Rights: The Agreement on Agriculture.* London: ActionAid.

_____. (2001b). *Food Rights: TRIPs on Trial.* London: ActionAid.

_____. (2002a). *Farmgate: The Developmental Impact of Agricultural Subsidies.* London: ActionAid.

_____. (2002b). *Trends in the Distribution of Aid.* London: ActionAid.

_____. (2002c). *Halfway There? The G8 and the Millennium Development Goals in 2002.* London: ActionAid.

_____. (2002d). *Making the Case for Untying of European Aid.* Brussels: ActionAid Alliance.

_____. (2002e). *Global Trends in Emergencies and Related Policies.* London: ActionAid.

Anderson, K., et al. (2000). "Potential Gains from Trade Reform in the New Millenium." Paper presented to the Third Annual Conference on Global Economic Analysis, held at Monash University, Melbourne.

Balasubramaniam, K. (2001). *Access to Medicines: Patents, Prices and Public Policy. Consumer Perspectives.* Paper presented at the Oxfam International Seminar on Intellectual Property and Development, "What Future for the WTO TRIPs Agreement?" Brussels (20 March).

Beynon J. (1999). *Assessing Aid and the Collier/Dollar Poverty Efficient Aid Allocations: A Critique.* Discussion Paper, Economic Policy and Research Department. London: UK Department for International Development.

Chang, Ha-Joon. (2002). *Kicking Away the Ladder: Development Strategy in Historical Perspective.* London: Anthem Press.

Collier, P. and D. Dollar. (2000). "Can the World Cut Poverty in Half? How Policy Reform and Effective Aid Can Meet the International Development Goals." Development Research Group, World Bank, Washington DC. Processed.

Development Assistance Committee of OECD. (2002). *International Development Statistics.* Paris: Organization for Economic Cooperation and Development.

Department for International Development (DFID). (2002). *Departmental Report 2002.* London: UK Department for International Development.

DFID/HM Treasury. (2002). *The Case for Aid for the Poorest Countries.* London: HM Treasury and Department for International Development.

Dollar, D., and A. Kraay. (2002). "Growth is Good for the Poor." *Journal of Economic Growth* 7, 3: 195-225.

Eurodad. (2001). *Debt and HIPC Initiative Update.* Brussels: Eurodad. (http://www.eurodad.org)

FitzGerald, E.V.K. (1996). "Rethinking Development Assistance: The Implications of Social Citizenship in a Global Economy." Paper presented at the UNRISD Conference, "Globalization and Citizenship: An International Conference," Geneva (9-11 December).

German T., and J. Randel. (2000). "Trends towards the New Millennium." In *The Reality of Aid: An Independent Review of Poverty Reduction and Development Assistance,* pp. 14-26. The Reality of Aid Project. London: Earthscan.

Goldin I., H. Rogers, and N. Stern. *The Role and Effectiveness of Development Assistance: Lessons from World Bank Experience.* Washington, DC: The World Bank.

Healey and Killick. (2000). "Using Aid to Reduce Poverty." In F. Tarp, ed., *Foreign Aid and Development: Lessons Learnt and Directions for the Future,* pp. 223-246. London: Routledge.

Helleiner, G. (2000). "Towards Balance in Aid Relationships: Donor Performance Monitoring in Low-Income Developing Countries." *Cooperation South* 2: 21-35.

Hjertholm, P., and H. White. (2000). "Foreign Aid in Historical Perspective: Background and Trends." In F. Tarp, ed., *Foreign Aid and Development,* pp. 80-102.

Houghton, I. (ActionAid USA). (2002). "Up Against the Wind: Recent ActionAid Experiences of Engaging the Poverty Reduction Strategies and Other IFI Lending Policies." Paper presented at the Conference "From Engagement to Protest," organized by Structural Adjustment Participatory Review International Network (SAPRIN). Washington DC (19 April).

Intellectual Property Rights Commission. (2002). *Integrating Intellectual Property Rights and Development Policy.* London: UK Department for International Development.

International Federation of Red Cross and Red Crescent Societies. (2002). *World Disasters Report.*

Kanbur, R. (2000). "Aid, Conditionality and Debt in Africa." In F. Tarp, ed., *Foreign Aid and Development,* pp. 409-422.

Kanbur, R., and T. Sandler. (1999). *The Future of Development Assistance: Common Pools and International Public Goods,* Policy Essay No. 25. Washington DC: Overseas Development Council.

Monterrey Consensus of the International Conference on Financing for Development, adopted on 22 March 2002, available at: http://ods-dds-ny.un.org/doc/UNDOC/GEN/N02/392/67/PDF/ N0239267.pdf?OpenElement

Morrissey, O. (2000). "Foreign Aid in the Emerging Global Trade Environment," in F. Tarp, ed., *Foreign Aid and Development*, pp. 375-391.

Overseas Development Institute. (2003). "Uncertain power, the changing role of official donors in humanitarian action," available at: http://www.odi.org.uk/hpg/papers/ hpgreport12.pdf.

Potter, G. A. (2000). *Deeper than Debt: Economic Globalization and the Poor*. London: Latin America Bureau.

Ranis, G., and F. Stewart. (2001). "The Debt-Relief Initiative for Poor Countries: Good News for the Poor?" *World Economics* 2 3: 111-124.

Robinson, S., and F. Tarp. (2000). "Foreign Aid and Development: Summary and Synthesis," in F. Tarp, ed., *Foreign Aid and Development*, pp. 1-14.

Tarp, F., ed. (2000). *Foreign Aid and Development: Lessons Learnt and Directions for the Future*. London: Routledge.

Thorbecke, E. (2000). "The Evolution of the Development Doctrine and the Role of Foreign Aid, 1950-2000." In F. Tarp, ed., *Foreign Aid and Development*, pp. 17-47.

The Reality of Aid Project. (2002). *The Reality of Aid: An Independent Review of Poverty Reduction and Development Assistance*. Manila: IBON Books.

United Nations Conference on Trade and Development (UNCTAD). (2002). *The Least Developed Countries Report 2002: Escaping the Poverty Trap*. Geneva: UNCTAD.

United Nations Development Program (UNDP). (1999). *Human Development Report: Globalization with a Human Face*. Geneva: UNDP.

_____. (2003). *Providing Global Public Goods: Managing Globalization*. Oxford: Oxford University Press.

World Bank. (1990). *World Development Report 1990*. Washington DC: World Bank.

Zedillo, E. (2002). *Recommendations of the High-level Panel on Financing for Development*. New York: United Nations.

Comments on "Reducing Poverty in a World of Plenty: The Crisis of Aid": Is There an Aid Crisis?

John Williamson[1]

Just when some of us thought that aid had acquired a new respectability, as the post-Cold War downward trend in aid appeared to have been halted and perhaps even reversed, along comes ActionAid to tell us that the whole aid enterprise is in crisis: the recipients are cynical about aid, the donors are fatigued and anyway pursue policies in other areas that undercut its impact, questionable selectivity thwarts the allocation of aid to the most needy, the practice of tying creates a crisis in its disbursement, and poverty reduction strategy papers are asserted to create a crisis of accountability.

Are things really this bad, or is this a case of crying "wolf!" that is more likely to impede constructive reform than to promote it?

Recipient Cynicism

Enough development professionals and aid-financed officials of nongovernmental organizations drive around in expensive SUVs and stay in fancy hotels to make one cringe at ActionAid's opening paragraph. Yet their paper goes on immediately to acknowledge that public expenditure in many poor countries is enormously dependent on a continued flow of aid. Moreover, many aid-financed projects have surely been highly beneficial: from my brief three years in the World Bank (working on South Asia) I recall with some pride the construction of the Jamuna Bridge, as it was then called, in Bangladesh; nutrition projects; the restoration of sodic (waterlogged) land; an attempt to clean up the Indian coal industry; efforts to stop the bleeding of fiscal resources into non-merit power subsidies; and so on. Admittedly the true impact of an aid project cannot necessarily be inferred from knowledge of what it formally finances, because of the problem of fungibility—a fundamental issue in assessing the impact of aid, although one would not learn that from reading ActionAid's paper. But even if one assumes complete fungibility, aid will still be of value to the citizens of a recipient country as long as their government is attempting to act in their interests and is not totally incompetent.

Perhaps the most disappointing feature of this paper is that it makes almost[2] no attempt to suggest a solution for the problem of excessive transactions costs that it levels at conventional aid programs. This is strange because, in fact, a proposal intended inter alia to accomplish that objective has been advanced by Ravi Kanbur and Todd Sandler (1999) and was endorsed by the Zedillo Panel. In the words of the latter, under the Common Pool Proposal:

> Each potential aid recipient would elaborate its own development strategy, programs, and projects, primarily in consultation with its own population but also in a dialogue with donors. It would then present its plans to the donors, who would, if the plans meet with their favor, put unrestricted financing into a common pool of development assistance. This, together with the government's own resources, would finance the overall development strategy. The level of financing by each donor would depend on its assessment of both the strategy and the recipient country's ability to implement the strategy and effectively monitor progress and expenditures. Donors' views would be made known to the country and to other donors during the dialogue leading up to the financing decision. However, earmarking of this or that donor's funds to this or that item, or specific donor monitoring and control of specific projects or programs, would not be permitted to those donors that choose to participate.[3]

Under such a proposal there would be little occasion for hordes of donor professionals to mill around in SUVs. More important, the proposal offers a resolution of the problem of fungibility. Perhaps most important of all, it would advance the cause of local ownership of development strategies, which is surely 90 percent of the answer to recipient cynicism.

Donor Fatigue

We heard a lot about donor fatigue in the 1990s, as the end of the stimulus that had been provided by the Cold War led to an erosion of aid programs. But there was another element that reinforced this erosion, and that was a realization that it is possible for aid to immiserize those it is supposed to benefit. This can occur, for example, if the provision of aid permits a predatory ruler to perpetuate his misrule. This concern presumably helped nurture the body of research that eventuated in the suggestion by Craig Burnside and David Dollar (2000) that aid should be steered by two criteria, namely poverty and a good policy environment, because without the latter aid is prone to be at best wasted and at worst perverse.

This proposition seems both intuitively reasonable and to have some solid empirical backing. By providing support for the view that aid can work, and that its poor record is substantially explained by the way in which aid was often driven by strategic or commercial rather than developmental considerations, the analysis helped lay the basis for the recent revival of aid programs. I am thinking here especially of the $5 billion a year that George W. Bush committed the United States at Monterrey to give via the Millennium Challenge Account, and of the UK commitment to raise aid to 0.4 percent of GDP, lauded in the ActionAid paper. It strikes me as behind the curve to be lamenting donor fatigue on the basis of what happened in the 1990s.

ActionAid dreams of a world in which aid would be recognized as an entitlement of poor world citizens rather than regarded as an act of charity. I suggest that post-Monterrey this is a somewhat less far-fetched dream than it was a few years ago. The UN Millennium Summit and subsequently the Monterrey conference declared the Millennium Development Goals to be a global objective. As ActionAid says, it is vacuous to proclaim goals and not to follow through by accepting responsibility for achieving them. If and when the international community takes this next step, it will be compelled to seek an estimate of the cost of achieving the Goals, on the lines first ventured by the Zedillo Panel. It will surely discover that ActionAid is right in arguing that the commitments made to date are inadequate to achieve the desired goals. At that point the minimum level of aid would be set by the needs of the poor, not by the charity of the rich. We are not there yet, but just possibly the thin end of the wedge has already been inserted.[4]

Unfortunately, what ActionAid says about the incoherence of aid policies—which may be inadequate but are at least pro-development—and a number of other developed-country policies, is all too justified. But other authors in this volume discuss trade and TRIPs, so I will not go into those subjects here. Likewise I will not venture into a discussion of global public goods, except to note that I agree with Inge Kaul and her colleagues (2002) that aid and global public goods have different purposes, and mainly serve different constituencies, and therefore merit distinct financing arrangements.

Could donor fatigue be overcome by instituting the Tobin tax? As might be inferred from my sympathy for the idea that aid should be a right of the poor rather than a charitable act by the rich, I have no problems with the concept of an international tax regime to provide the finance to satisfy that right (and to provide global public goods). But I do wish the advocacy community would overcome its infatuation with the naïve idea that the Tobin tax could provide vast amounts of finance for international good causes while mitigating the problems of financial speculation from which so many emerging markets have suffered in recent years. Perhaps such a tax could raise $20 or $30 billion a year, but certainly not the hundreds of billions about which its advocates so often salivate. These estimates rely on the assumption that a tax rate of several hundred percent of value-added would barely reduce the volume of transactions. The tax would do essentially nothing to prevent the large speculative pressures that arise from an overhang of large short-term asset positions and/or the ability to borrow at short term in local currency; pressures that have nothing to do with the "hot potato trading" that is responsible for the large daily turnover in foreign exchange markets.

But at least ActionAid acknowledges the alternative to the Tobin tax that was suggested by the Zedillo Panel—namely a carbon tax, which really would have a desirable byproduct in its impact on relative prices and resource allocation. The problems of designing and operating an international carbon tax would be one of my candidates for the future research agenda.

Aid Allocation

As already noted, the current conventional wisdom holds that if aid is to be effective in reducing poverty it should be allocated to countries according to two criteria: that they have a lot of poor people, and that they have a decent policy regime that holds promise of being able to use the aid effectively. These criteria give promise of at long last getting rid of the traditional dominance of strategic and commercial considerations in guiding the distribution of aid. It is their adoption that explains the concentration of aid on Mozambique, Tanzania, and Uganda about which ActionAid complains. These countries get 25 percent of the aid going to Sub-Saharan African countries because their policy regimes appear to be able to make effective use of aid to relieve poverty, rather than buying votes as is allegedly happening with food aid in Zimbabwe.

The contention that aid is effective in reducing poverty only in a decent policy environment has been challenged in a recent paper by Hansen and Tarp (2001), and in a new paper by Easterly, Levine, and Roodman (2002). But assuming that further research serves to refute this challenge and confirm the intuitively plausible conventional wisdom, I will continue to regard the adoption of these twin criteria as important intellectual progress. I am shocked to learn that ActionAid apparently campaigns against "donor selectivity," by which I assume they mean use of the criterion that the policy environment be favorable. If the adoption of that criterion is what they believe constitutes a crisis, then I am all for this particular crisis.

Of course, use of these two criteria poses several important questions that have not yet been satisfactorily answered. First, how does one trade off the two criteria—the prevalence of poverty, and the good policy environment—one against another? Second (an issue that ActionAid rightly emphasizes), what does one do about a country that has a lousy policy environment? Just let the poor suffer? Can one use an international regime like the Global Health Fund to provide the poor in such a country with benefits in at least some areas? Or should one channel funding through NGOs independent of the government? Third (another issue on which ActionAid focuses), how does one interpret the concept of a "good policy environment"? In practice, this has usually been measured by a country's score on the World Bank's Country Policy and Institutional Assessment (CPIA). Since I was involved in the redesign of the CPIA when I was in the Bank, I happen to think that this is very much on the right lines, though obviously not the last word. Even so, I can understand that those who make a sport of denouncing the Washington Consensus may think otherwise. All three issues strike me as in need of a continuing research effort.

Aid Tying

A large part of aid has for years been tied to the purchase of goods or services from the country that is providing the aid. Donors seeking to persuade their public of the virtues of an aid program have even been known to boast that their aid involves no balance of payments cost but instead generates local demand. We all know that this economic illiteracy is disgracefully costly to the aid recipients, so if ActionAid were to describe the continued existence of tying, especially of technical assistance, as a scandal, I would enthusiastically second their charge.

But a "crisis of disbursement"? Tying is something that has been going on for decades, and on which there has recently been some progress, as the paper recognizes. British aid has been completely untied, to the point where British aid personnel are not allowed to pay more to fly the flag. The EC is proposing to follow suit for European Union programs. The OECD Development Assistance Committee has endorsed untying everything except food aid and technical assistance. I do not understand how progress, even if incomplete, can sensibly be described as a crisis.

Accountability

The delivery of aid has not been a hot political topic in most donor countries in the past. This left the aid bureaucracy free to pursue its own agenda with little political accountability beyond the need to throw occasional sops to pressure groups in donor countries—for example assuring them that aid was tied. And since aid was regarded as charity rather than a right, donors did not feel themselves accountable to the publics of the countries being aided. There has indeed been a lack of accountability.

Poverty reduction strategy papers were not designed to resolve these problems of donor accountability. Their purpose is rather to design a reform program that will enjoy local ownership because it reflects widespread concerns and embodies solutions that command a wide degree of public confidence, on the view that reform programs are unlikely to succeed unless they are endorsed by those most affected.[5] I believe that the PRSP process was inspired by the example of Uganda's Poverty Eradication Action Plan, which is commended by ActionAid. It is surely important to monitor how well the PRSP process succeeds in replicating the Ugandan model. It is not obvious that this is something that can be successfully imposed from the outside; nor is it certain that the staffs of the Bretton Woods institutions will succeed in changing their mindset and really allow local determination of things that they have been used to deciding.[6]

There is a fundamental dilemma involved in seeking to promote national ownership of development programs: whose will prevails when a nation owns a policy that the international financial institutions believe to be misguided? ActionAid discusses this question. I would not want to exempt "hard" issues such as macro adjustment, liberalization, and privatization from poverty analyses, but, of course, I believe that budget discipline, market liberalization, and even privatization are generally good for the poor (that is why I support them). If some demagogues manage to win control of the PRSP process and push for bigger budget deficits to finance more parastatals to employ their poor relatives, does one go along in the interests of "flexibility and respect for a multiplicity of views"? To take a concrete case, Argentina passionately owned the stupid policy of maintaining parity between the peso and the dollar in the years leading up to the crisis of 2001, but the result of the IFIs acquiescing in this locally owned policy was to deepen the ultimate crisis and the poverty it bred. Since I am not much of an enthusiast for national sovereignty, my inclination is to allow national preferences to be overruled, but this implies that ownership rights are to be restricted to what the IFIs think makes some sort of technical sense. It is obviously important to monitor how often this type of clash arises, and to analyze who is right when it does.

I must admit that I find it difficult to see how donors could be made accountable to citizens in poor countries, as ActionAid wants. What is feasible is to make more transparent the net impact of the various actions of donor countries on developing countries. That is the objective of the proposed Index of Commitment to Development that has been constructed by the Center for Global Development.[7] Transparency is, of course, the first requirement for accountability, but for now at least the accountability at stake is likely to remain accountability to the public in donor countries.

A Research Agenda

The preceding discussion has raised a number of suggestions for the direction of future research on aid. Perhaps the most critical need is to further test whether the effectiveness of aid is critically dependent on a good policy environment, given the recent efforts to focus aid on countries where this condition is satisfied.

If that thesis emerges unscathed, then it will be important to research the three unresolved issues that arise in trying to implement an aid program based on it: how one should trade off poverty against the quality of the policy environment; how one should handle countries with poor policy regimes; and how one should measure the quality of the policy environment.

Two other research issues have emerged. One concerns the operation of the Common Pool Proposal. In principle the Common Pool appears to offer a number of important advantages, but more thought is needed about the issues that would arise in operating such a regime. One surely has to worry that the policy environment in many of the poorest countries would not be adequate to justify such a hands-off approach by donors; it is important to ask what sort of conditions would provide the minimum environment to move to this system. The other concerns the proposal for a global carbon tax, where more rigorous thought is needed on the details of a proposal that appears on the face of it to have a number of attractive features.

It is desirable to monitor the operation of two important recent initiatives. One is the PRSP process, which looks highly attractive in principle but whose success will depend importantly on whether the Ugandan model can be successfully replicated. The other concerns the clashes between what countries want to own and what the IFIs think they ought to own. Such clashes are bound to arise, and it is mightily important for someone to keep a reasonably systematic account of them rather than to allow them to be pushed under the rug in a childish pretense that there is complete consensus on what is desirable. Not only should a record of such clashes be established, but some effort should be made to decide who was right.

I am doubtful that research can contribute much to resolving some of the most critical policy failures. One such is the issue of European agricultural policy: I doubt very much whether France and Germany will be convinced to phase out production subsidies by any evidence that could be marshaled by ActionAid or anyone else. Change awaits a political leader prepared to risk the wrath of the agricultural lobby; my guess is that s/he will find that the electoral sway of the agribusiness lobby that benefits from production-based subsidies is, in fact, rather modest, but this thesis remains to be tested. Another is the switch to an aid program based on entitlement, in the sense of a world citizen's right to certain basic services and a minimal standard of living. This may come some day, but if so it will be the result of a statesman's vision and not a technocrat's research program.

Is There an Aid Crisis?

No. There is a case for pushing further the line of thought that has given us PRSPs, to the point where we implement the Common Pool Proposal for countries that have their act together. The recent increases in aid are inadequate to the task of meeting the Millennium Development Goals, but the trend has at least resumed the right direction. The presumption remains that the selectivity that is now being sought is an advance rather than a threat. Aid tying remains a scandal, but a somewhat lesser scandal than formerly. Accountability remains a problem, but PRSPs are a good initiative that may have as a minor byproduct some alleviation of that problem. In sum, there is plenty of room for improvement, but precious few grounds for proclaiming crisis and doom.

Notes

1. The author is senior fellow, Institute for International Economics, and visiting fellow, Center for Global Development, Washington DC.
2. The exception is the timid suggestion that (for managing technical cooperation more effectively), donors "make funds available to recipient countries to choose independently which international advisors they would like to engage."
3. Zedillo (2001: 60).
4. There would still, of course, be an issue of how one would get the money to the poor in countries with bad policy regimes.
5. A natural corollary of local ownership is that it will provide a standard by which to hold the national government accountable, but that is a very different matter from facilitating donor accountability.
6. I do not think it fair to criticize the Interim PRSP in Pakistan (let alone the putative Interim PRSP in Haiti) because of the limited public involvement in its formulation: the whole point of Interim PRSPs is to allow countries to access some of the benefits in a time-frame shorter than is needed for the full consultation process embodied in a PRSP.
7. The aid component of that index is based on a paper by William Easterly (2002).

References

Burnside, Craig, and David Dollar. (2000). "Aid, Policies, and Growth." *American Economic Review* 90, 4 (September): 847-68.

Easterly, William. (2002). "Evaluating Aid Performance of Donors," mimeo. Washington DC: Center for Global Development.

Easterly, William, Ross Levine, and David Roodman. (2002). "More Data, More Doubts: Revisiting Aid, Policies, and Growth," mimeo. Washington DC: Center for Global Development.

Hansen, Henrik, and Finn Tarp. (2001). "Aid and Growth Regressions." *Journal of Development Economics* 64, 547-70.

Kanbur, Ravi, and Todd Sandler. (1999). *The Future of Development Assistance: Common Pools and International Public Goods*. Washington, DC: Overseas Development Council.

Kaul, Inge, Pedro Conceição, Katell Le Goulven, and Ronald U. Mendoza. (2000). *Providing Global Public Goods: Managing Globalization.* New York: Oxford University Press for UNDP.

Zedillo, E. (2001). *Report of the High-Level Panel on Financing for Development.* New York: United Nations.

3

Globalization, Developed Country Policies, and Market Access: Insights from the Bangladesh Experience

Mustafizur Rahman[1]

Not long after the independence of Bangladesh (in 1971), a book titled *Bangladesh: The Test Case for Development*, by Just Faaland and J. R. Parkinson, created quite a stir. The authors noted that the newborn country faced enormous developmental challenges, and concluded:

> If development can be made to succeed in Bangladesh, there can be little doubt that it can be made to succeed anywhere else. It is in this sense that Bangladesh is the test case for development.

The authors maintained that "without aid the economy will collapse" and that only through a joint endeavor with the international community could Bangladesh hope to survive and develop.

Three decades and many reform programs later the report card on Bangladesh's achievements over these past years is at best a mixed one. Compared to some of the other least developed countries, Bangladesh's track record has been good. However, given the challenges and the unfinished development agendas that need to be addressed, the development deficit continues to be enormous.

Bangladesh has indeed made notable progress in attacking poverty, integrating the economy globally through promotion of exports and opening up the domestic market, and through important achievements in social sector development that have led to considerable improvements in basic human development indicators. It has graduated from being a predominantly aid-receiving nation to a trading nation: in the early 1990s annual aid and export receipts were of equal value, but today exports of goods and services are worth four times aid receipts.[2] During the 1990s the degree of openness of the Bangladesh economy almost doubled, from 16.8 to 32.1[3] (Table 3.1). Over the past decade, the percentage of the population in poverty has fallen on average by 1 percent a year.

But today, despite the considerable achievements, about half of the country's population of 130 million continues to live below the poverty line, the absolute numbers of people in poverty are on the rise, as is inequality; and addressing the problems of the hard-core poor remains problematic. In terms of basic human development indicators, both from quantity and quality perspectives, Bangladesh lags behind the fast achievers. In terms of some of the important indicators, the gap is widening.

The developed countries have played an important role in shaping the policies and programs pursued by Bangladesh, through both bilateral aid and multilateral initiatives. The annual Bangladesh Consortium Meeting has been held regularly in Paris, and aid pledges made at those meetings have provided the bulk of the country's resources. With aid came aid conditionalities. The Structural Adjustment Program (SAP), a reform package with support from policy-based sectoral lending of the World Bank and the Structural Adjustment Facility (SAF) of the International Monetary Fund, dominated Bangladesh's reform agendas throughout the 1980s and the first half of the 1990s. The share of aid has been decreasing, but today it still accounts for about half the development budget in Bangladesh. It is no exaggeration to say that through the macro and sectoral reform programs supported by aid, developed country policies shaped Bangladesh's development policies in the 1980s and 1990s.

The premise of this chapter is that under the export-led growth strategy that Bangladesh is now pursuing, the success of the country's macroeconomic performance and efforts to alleviate poverty will depend critically on its capacity for strengthened global integration. Success in this effort will depend largely on Bangladesh's ability to address the challenges and attendant risks—and to seize the opportunities—that are associated with market access for its goods and services, and, no less important, on its capacity to successfully integrate the poor and their interests in this process. Aid and developed country policies are expected to play a crucial role in this.

Section 1 reviews the aid-induced reforms in Bangladesh of the 1980s and 1990s and the transmission channels through which these reforms affected economic performance and poverty levels; section 2 reviews the trends in poverty levels in Bangladesh and their dimensions at a period of accelerated global integration of the country's economy and their broad implications for policy; and section 3 looks at some of the more pressing market access concerns of Bangladesh in the context of the ongoing process of globalization. Section 4 identifies four areas of interface between developed-country policies and market access issues of importance to Bangladesh; it suggests policies that will need to be implemented by the developed countries to address emergent concerns that have important implications in terms of poverty alleviation in the country, and identifies areas for research that would yield insights on how to raise the efficacy of the partnership between developed countries and Bangladesh.

Aid-Supported Adjustment Programs and the Opening of the Economy

The policies pursued by Bangladesh immediately after Independence in 1971 were anchored in a growth strategy led by the public sector and shaped by concerns to protect the domestic market, build an import-substituting industrial base, and maintain a good balance of payments. The need to shift policies was increasingly felt as the negative impact of allocative and productive inefficiencies, and the cost of the anti-export bias, became more pronounced. Early signs of such changes in Bangladesh are evident even in policies pursued in the mid- and late 1970s.

Economic liberalization began in the early 1980s when tentative measures were taken to open up the economy with support from structural and sectoral adjustment loans. Liberalization speeded up in the late 1980s with the implementation of reforms under the Structural Adjustment Program, which was underwritten by the multilateral donor agencies. In 1986-87 the government adopted a medium-term adjustment program administered under a three-year arrangement under the IMF's Structural Adjustment Facility (SAF), and an Extended SAF was in place during 1990-93.

From FY1980-96, adjustment lending accounted for about one-third of the total commitments of the International Development Association to Bangladesh. The lending policies of most of the other bilateral and multilateral donors during the period were also, to a large extent, conditioned by the spirit of adjustment lending. Subsequent lending to Bangladesh by its development partners, especially by the World Bank and IMF, has also been largely influenced by the policies pursued under the Structural Adjustment Program.

The structural reforms resulted in a clear shift towards a more open regime: substantial reduction in effective rates of protection; substantial removal of the anti-export bias in the economy, deregulation, decontrol, and liberalization of the investment and exchange rate regimes; denationalization; gradual withdrawal of the state from a large number of economic activities; and a more prominent role for the private sector. The trade reforms promoted and stimulated imports of intermediate inputs as well as of finished goods. The export sector received a number of incentives in the form of preferential duties, cash compensation schemes, duty drawback facilities, and a reduced interest rate.

The structural reforms played a crucial role in integrating the country's economy with the global economy through outward and inward flows of goods, services, capital, and labor. As Table 3.1

Table 3.1
Growing Importance of External Sector in the Bangladesh Economy (mln US$)

Item	1991	2001
a. Exports (X)	1718.0	6008.0
b. Imports (M)	3472.0	9362.9
c. Remittances (R)	764.0	1882.1
d. FDI	1.0	157.5
Total (a-d)	*5955.0*	*17410.5*
GDP	**30974.8**	**47825.8**
Degree of openness (%)	16.8	32.1
Extent of globalization (%)	19.2	36.4
ODA	1,732.0	1588.0
X as % of ODA	99.2	378.3
(X+R) as % of ODA	143.3	496.9
X as % of M	49.5	64.2
(X+R) as % of M	71.5	84.3
Debt servicing as % of (X+R)	12.8	7.6

Source: Computed from Center for Policy Dialogue Database.

shows, over the 1990s the degree of openness of the economy (measured as the share of exports and imports in GDP) increased from 16.8 percent to 32.1 percent and the extent of globalization of the Bangladesh economy—taken to be the share of exports, imports, FDI, and remittances in GDP—currently stands at 36.4 percent, compared to 19.2 percent in 1991.

Trade as Driver of Macroeconomic Performance

In FY1991-2001, exports grew at more than twice the rate of GDP—at 12.4 percent, compared to 5.6 percent. Export earnings as a share of GDP more than doubled, from 5.5 percent to 13.8 percent, and the share of imports rose from 11.3 percent to 17.3 percent. (Table 3.2.)

The composition of exports and imports also underwent important changes. The export basket shifted gradually from primary exports to processed exports, and from jute to apparel. Unlike many other least developed countries (LDCs), by the end of the 1990s Bangladesh had built a considerable market for its exports of readymade garments, and to a lesser extent shrimp and leather. Within the import basket, the share of export-oriented inputs grew significantly during this period (Table 3.3.).

The export sector now accounts for about 30 percent of manufacturing GDP, about two-fifths of aggregate industrial employment, and about a third of private sector industrial investment. Hence, its growing importance through multiplier impacts.

Because of the structural shifts in the global markets for products originating in rural Bangladesh, and also because of the inability of domestic producers to access the emerging agriculture-based export markets, the share of exports coming from the agriculture sector in Bangladesh has declined in recent years (Table 3.4). Some of the traditional primary exports such as raw jute and tea have seen their share of export earnings fall drastically.

While exports were rising during the 1990s, official development assistance as a share of Bangladesh's GDP almost halved, from 5.6 percent to 2.9 percent (Table 3.2). Aid from the principal donors has gradually shifted from project-based to program-based lending. Very recently it has been made contingent on the preparation of a poverty reduction strategy paper.

Table 3.2

Flows of External Resources into Bangladesh, FY91-01

(million US$)

	Export	as % of GDP	Import	as % of GDP	Remittances	as % of GDP	ODA	as % of GDP	FI	as % of GDP	GDP	GDP Growth Rate (%)
FY92	1993.92	6.36	3526.00	11.25	848.00	2.71	1611.47	5.14	33.66	0.11	31334.73	5.04
FY93	2382.89	7.44	4017.00	12.54	944.00	2.95	1675.01	5.23	38.05	0.12	32031.17	4.57
FY94	2533.90	7.49	4191.00	12.38	1088.80	3.22	1558.64	4.60	106.40	0.31	33853.00	4.08
FY95	3472.56	9.15	5834.00	15.38	1197.63	3.16	1739.00	4.58	102.93	0.27	37939.80	4.93
FY96	3884.00	9.54	6947.00	17.06	1217.06	2.99	1443.75	3.55	16.58	0.04	40725.76	4.62
FY97	4427.00	10.46	7162.00	16.92	1475.42	3.49	1481.23	3.50	-62.12	-0.15	42318.74	5.39
FY98	5172.00	11.75	7524.00	17.09	1525.43	3.46	1251.38	2.84	320.82	0.73	44033.66	5.23
FY99	5324.00	11.65	8018.00	17.54	1705.74	3.73	1536.06	3.36	262.61	0.57	45712.65	4.87
FY00	5752.20	12.21	8403.00	17.83	1949.32	4.14	1587.95	3.37	228.68	0.49	47125.02	5.94
FY01	6467.30	13.78	8130.00	17.32	1882.10	4.01	1368.81	2.92	222.41	0.47	46933.65	5.16

Source: Estimated from Center for Policy Dialogue Database.

Table 3.3
Changing Export Structure of Bangladesh (in percent)

Commodity	FY1991	FY2002
Raw Jute	6.1	1.0
Jute Goods	16.9	4.1
Tea	2.5	0.3
Frozen Food	8.3	4.6
Leather	7.8	3.5
Woven-RMG	42.8	52.2
Knit-RMG	7.6	24.4
Chemical Products	2.3	1.1
Primary Commodities	17.9	6.5
Mfg. Products	82.1	93.5
Total Export	100.0	100.0
Total Export (in million USD)	1718.0	5986.1
Export as % of GDP	5.5	12.0

Table 3.4
Agricultural Exports (mln US$)

Commodities	1990	1995	2000
Raw Jute	125	79	72
Tea	39	33	17
Frozen fish	138	306	344
Agri-commodities	11	13	18
Other primary	10	21	18
Total	323.0	452.0	469
(as % of total exports)	(21.1)	(13.0)	(8.1)

Source: EPB (various years).

Impact of Adjustment Reforms on Poverty: Transmission Channels

The following sections examine the transmission channels through which the adjustment programs have affected poverty, and the extent to which the poor have benefited.

Manufacturing. Trade liberalization has helped Bangladesh successfully expand its apparel exports. The country's export-oriented apparel sector at present includes about 3,400 readymade garments

(RMG) manufacturing units, which employ about 1.7 million workers, 70 percent of whom are women.

However, Bangladesh has not been able to diversify its export base. Demand for its traditional manufactures based on jute has gone down drastically. The share of the manufacturing sector in GDP has tended to stagnate at about 14-15 percent (Table 3.5).

Agriculture. Though its share in GDP has been declining, agriculture still provides about 60 percent of employment in Bangladesh (Table 3.6).

The declared objectives of the agriculture sector reforms pursued by Bangladesh during the 1980s and the 1990s and implemented through a policy of deregulation and reduction of subsidies, were to: (1) stimulate and encourage private sector involvement in

Table 3.5
Sectoral Contributions to Bangladesh's GDP
(percent, at constant 1995-96 prices)

Sector	1991-92	2001-02
Agriculture	23.96	19.21
Manufacturing	13.28	15.58
Tertiary	62.76	65.21
	100.00	100.00

Source: Bangladesh Economic Survey (2002).

Table 3.6
Share of Employed Labor Force, by Sectors, 1995-96 (in percent)

Sector	1995-96
Agriculture, forestry and fisheries	63.2
Mining and quarrying	-
Manufacturing	7.5
Electricity, gas and water	0.2
Construction	1.8
Trade, hotel and restaurant	11.2
Transport, storage and communication	4.2
Finance, commerce and services	0.4
Commodity and personal services	9.3
Others	2.2
Total	*100*

Source: Bangladesh Bureau of Statistics, Labor Force Survey, 1995/96.

markets for both inputs and outputs, (2) gradually reduce the state's institutional involvement in agriculture, (3) infuse competitive behavior in the market and thereby reduce the price level, (4) promote private sector involvement in import of agro-inputs, (5) maintain adequate producer price incentives, and (6) raise efficiency and productivity in the agricultural sector. The reforms included a gradual withdrawal of subsidies from agricultural inputs; dismantling of the system of renting out agricultural equipment (such as irrigation machines) by the state sector in favor of allowing such machines to be imported; and a gradual downsizing of the institutional support that had been channeled through the Bangladesh Agricultural Development Corporation (BADC).

Bangladesh's agricultural sector grew substantially faster in the post-reform era than the 2.6 percent annual rate attained between Independence and the start of reforms. Although causal relationships are difficult to establish, as noted in Murshid (2001), the reforms have had important implications for income, poverty, and food security in rural Bangladesh. Liberalization of imports of irrigation equipment resulted in substantial reduction of their costs and led to a rapid expansion in the proportion of cultivable land under irrigation. Cropping intensity rose from 142 percent in the 1970s to more than 190 percent in 1999. The removal of a government monopoly on fertilizer had some positive impacts on price levels, availability, and timeliness of deliveries. Withdrawal of a ban on private sector imports of rice/food grains helped to reduce shortages and stabilize prices. The National Seed Policy allowed privatization of seed production beyond the foundation stage; this stimulated private sector involvement in seed production and resulted in a greater choice for farmers. Reforms in the public food distribution system discontinued rural rationing in favor of food distribution through safety net programs such as Vulnerable Group Development and the Food for Works program.[4]

Rahman and Shahabuddin (1997) conclude that the agricultural reforms had important implications for all groups of farmers, but they found no clear-cut indication that large farmers benefited more than smaller ones.

During the 1990s an important structural shift took place out of cropping into other agricultural activities (Table 3.7). The contribution of forestry, livestock, and fisheries doubled, from 20 percent to

Table 3.7
Structural Transformation of Agriculture, 1973-74 to 1998-99
(% of agricultural GDP)

Subsectors	1973-74	1989-90	1998-99
Crops	80.0	71.5	57.8
Forestry	4.2	9.8	10.9
Livestock	7.6	9.3	12.9
Fisheries	8.2	9.5	18.4
Total	100	100	100

Source: Bangladesh Bureau of Statistics (various years).

42 percent of agricultural GDP, as a result of higher crop productivity and reallocation of low-yield areas to growing of vegetables and fruits. Micro-credit programs supported a large proportion of such non-crop and non-farm activities. These changes in the rural economy have had important implications for real income in the rural areas. As Hossain (2000) points out, first, high output growth in non-crop activities—unlike in rice and other food crops—can be sustained without depressing prices and farmers' incomes. Second, these shifts can potentially lead to a shift from non-tradable to tradable activities, since products such as fish, fruit, and vegetables have potentially high export opportunities in the global market. Looking ahead, for Bangladesh to make the most of these opportunities would require substantial investments in infrastructure development, quality control, and establishment of marketing channels, as well as improvements in rural credit programs, discussed further below.

Labor Market, Real Wages, and Rural Poverty

Shifts in the rural labor market. The rural labor market has been undergoing important changes related to the overall liberalization of the economy and the opportunities emerging in the informal and non-crop sectors and in rural export-oriented activities, such as shrimp culture in coastal regions.

Labor force dynamics within agriculture are important because agriculture is still the major provider of employment in Bangladesh. The share of households selling agricultural labor declined from 22.6 percent to 16.9 percent between 1983 and 1984 and 1995 and

1996 (Murshid, 2001). This decline can be related to four factors that owe their origin to the rise in labor productivity in crop production, which was strongly correlated with the policy deregulation of agriculture. These are: (1) a shift from crop to non-crop agriculture, (2) a shift from farm to non-farm employment, (3) a shift to self-employment,[5] and (4) out-migration to urban areas.

Within rural areas, capital accumulation and higher labor productivity have led to considerable shifts in both labor and land out of farming to more productive activities. Substitution of capital for the declining labor resources available for crop agriculture has helped to raise labor productivity and improved farmers' capacity to pay higher wages (Hossain, 2000). Meanwhile the relatively high labor-intensity of HYV crop production has positively affected the rural demand for labor.

Real wages. Real wages are a proxy to determine the impact of the policy reforms on poverty correlates. Real wages in both agriculture and manufacturing rose in the post-reform period, though not by enough to have a major impact on poverty in Bangladesh as a whole.

Average real wages rose substantially faster in manufacturing than in agriculture (Table 3.8).[6] Though in Bangladesh at large, trade liberalization is likely to have improved returns on all factors, the welfare gains may be distributed unevenly, with owners of capital and, to some extent, urban workers benefiting more than rural workers (ILO, 1998). Rural workers are often unable to access the job

Table 3.8
Real Wage Rate Indices (1969/70=100)

Year	General	Agriculture	Manufacturing
1985/86	95	82	102
1989/90	110	96	115
1990/91	107	95	114
1991/92	107	98	113
1992/93	113	105	119
1993/94	114	106	121
1994/95	111	103	121
1995/96	114	104	123
1996/97	120	109	130
1997/98	122	107	137

Source: Ministry of Finance, Bangladesh (1999).

opportunities that stem from trade liberalization, because the new jobs tend to be urban and to require skills that rural workers lack. Since the returns to urban jobs are relatively high, rural workers' lack of access to these jobs may widen the rural-urban differential in incomes and poverty rates. The poverty dynamics in Bangladesh appear to corroborate this hypothesis (see section 3 following).

Within rural areas, average daily wage rates registered some increase, to the tune of about 16.5 percent, between 1987/88 and 1996/97. The incidence of poverty was lower among non-agricultural wage laborers than among agricultural laborers (41-50 percent as against 67-71 percent) (CPD, 1996). Average real wages rose more than three times faster in irrigated areas than in non-irrigated areas. In agriculture, real wages have varied depending on access to irrigation facilities; data presented by Murshid (2001) show the wage variance to be between 14 and 30 percent. Demand for labor is higher in Green Revolution areas, where nominal wage rates are relatively high compared to the consumer price index. However, that effect has not been strong enough to pull up the average real wage in rural areas by any significant amount, nor to make a visible dent in rural underemployment (Shahabuddin and Rahman, 1998).

Accessing the global labor market. One of the important avenues by which globalization has affected Bangladesh has been the growing participation of its workers in the international labor market. Over the last decade, more than 1.3 million Bangladeshis have gone abroad to work, mainly in the Middle East and Southeast Asia. Most of them come from rural areas. In FY2000, official figures show, they remitted home nearly US$ 2 billion (Table 3.9)—equivalent to about half the net foreign exchange earnings of Bangladesh from commodity exports in that year. The actual inflow of remittances is probably much higher than officially recorded, given that a sub-

Table 3.9
Bangladesh Workers in the Global Market

Year	FY1990	FY1995	FY2000	Total 1990-2000
No. of migrant workers *(thousands)*	110.0	199.9	248.3	2192.4
Remittances *(mln US$)*	758.3	1197.6	1953.1	13482.7

Source: Bangladesh Bank (*Economic Trends*, various years).

stantial part of the money is transferred through informal channels (known as the *hundi*).

Evidence suggests that remittances are used for consumption as well as for investment and are an important source of income for many rural households. Indeed, in some regions of rural Bangladesh, remittances are the main source of household income. Since a large segment of the migrant labor force comes from rural poor households, it can be inferred that participation in the global labor market has a positive impact on rural income levels and hence on rural poverty.

Most of the Bangladeshi migrant workers participate in the down-market segment of the global demand curve for labor. Their average income is substantially lower than that of workers from countries such as India and Sri Lanka.[7] Here the challenge is to enhance the capacity of the rural poor by creating opportunities for more gainful work abroad.

It needs to be noted here that a large part of the global labor market remains highly restricted. Although the Uruguay Round and current World Trade Organization (WTO) provisions have gone a long way to free up the movement of commodities and capital, the movement of labor—where least developed countries such as Bangladesh enjoy comparative advantage—has tended to remain highly constrained. The General Agreement on Trade in Services (GATS), negotiated during the Uruguay Round, contains little about the movement of natural persons. As HDR (1995) points out, developing countries suffer an estimated loss of US$ 500 billion a year because of restrictions on the movement of their workers to developed countries. Here two types of intervention appear to be needed: adequate measures to enhance the skills of potential migrant labor, and a more flexible regime for movement of labor from developing to developed countries.

Liberalization of the investment regime and poverty. Liberalization of the investment regime (Table 3.10), coupled with global market opportunities, has led to the emergence of a private entrepreneurial class in Bangladesh and also encouraged inflows of foreign capital.

Up to now, however, private investment, domestic or foreign, has been rather limited in Bangladesh. The gross private investment rate is only about 10 percent of GDP, and foreign direct in-

Table 3.10
Current Investment Regime in Bangladesh

Investment regimes	Fiscal/financial incentives
Restricted sectors for FDI	*Fiscal incentives for FDI*
Four sectors are restricted: arms, nuclear energy, forestry and railways; and regulations on drug manufacturing effectively bar foreign corporations from investing in this sector.	Tax holiday, accelerated depreciation allowance, and duty-free importation of capital goods for export-oriented industries.
Foreign ownership restrictions	*Foreign-exchange repatriation*
- foreign private investment could be undertaken either independently or as a joint venture. - 100 percent foreign equity was allowed on all investments including those in special zones.	Full repatriation of invested capital, profits and dividends, easy terms in case of winding up of business.
Licensing/approvals, rules and procedures	*Access to domestic finance*
No formal permission was required to set up a company with foreign investment.	Foreign investment companies can borrow working capital from commercial banks as term loans.
Performance requirements	*Guarantee against nationalization*
For all export items, prior permission of the Bangladesh Bank to open back-to-back letters of credit has been waived as long as exports conform to guidelines for domestic value addition.	Foreign companies have constitutional guarantees that stipulate that they will not be nationalized or expropriated by the state.

Source: Board of Investment, Bangladesh (2002).

vestment, averaging about US$ 250 million in the second half of the 1990s, has been concentrated in sectors such as gas, electricity, and infrastructure development.

The more liberal investment regime has benefited the rural economy most in an indirect way. Most of the 1.7 million workers in the export-oriented readymade garment industry are women and many are from rural areas. This industry has obviously reduced the pressure on rural employment. Such emerging employment opportunities, induced by liberalization policy and strongly connected with rural areas, have been playing an important role in augmenting rural household incomes.

Liberalization of the investment regime and global market opportunities have also encouraged export-oriented shrimp culture, mainly in rural coastal regions. The shrimp industry alone earns about US$ 450 million a year in foreign exchange, and employs about a million workers in direct and indirect ways.[8]

Along with fiscal and financial incentives, the freer investment regime has also stimulated the growth of rural fisheries, livestock, and poultry production, which currently provide most of the incremental job opportunities in rural areas. As noted above, their share of agricultural GDP has more than doubled over the past decade, and since average wage rates in these activities are somewhat higher than in cropping, the structural shift has somewhat improved the incomes of the households involved in them. But it is becoming increasingly clear that extremely poor rural households cannot readily take part in these activities, mainly because they cannot access agricultural supporting services. However, microfinance facilities have helped some rural poor households to participate in activities such as livestock and poultry rearing.

The declining trend in Bangladesh's traditional agricultural exports should be a matter of concern to policymakers. At a time when global opportunities for agricultural exports are likely to expand considerably, because of the agreement on agriculture (AoA) and other market access initiatives, it emphasizes the need to ensure adequate agricultural investment. There is also a need to explore new global opportunities that are emerging because of the renewed interest in sustainable development and fair trade and to connect them to reforms that affect the rural economy of Bangladesh.

Financial sector liberalization and rural poverty. Bangladesh took a number of important steps to liberalize its financial sector, in order to increase competition, stimulate mobilization of funds, and promote better resource allocation. These reforms, initiated under the financial sector reform program of the IMF, included denationalizing a number of commercial banks, granting permission to set up private banks, imparting flexibility in the determination of interest rates on lending and deposits and in the determination of exchange rates, and liberalizing capital markets. The reforms led to considerable deregulation and decontrol of the country's financial sector and introduced a large measure of market-driven elements.

One effect of the reforms was to reduce the access of the rural economy to credit resources. Several factors were at work here: first, removal of interest-rate subsidies raised the cost of borrowing; second, because refinance facilities had been withdrawn, the nationalized commercial banks reduced their lending to rural areas; third, rural savings mobilization suffered since the newly established private banks were not interested in rural banking; and fourth, a number of rural branches of public sector banks were closed down when the government implemented a branch rationalization scheme.

A considerable rural-urban resource transfer has taken place through formal channels in recent years. During the 1990s, credit to rural borrowers fell as a share of total credit, from 23 percent in 1989-90 to 17 percent in 1998 (Table 3.11), while the share of deposits originating in rural areas remained relatively stable. Table 3.12 corroborates this observation: for most of the 1990s, the net flow of credit to rural areas was negative.[9]

Table 3.11
Share of Rural Banking in Bangladesh (%)

Year	Rural (as share of total)		
	Branches	Deposit	Credit
1980	64.03	15.99	11.88
1989	66.29	20.32	23.16
1990	65.98	21.17	23.41
1995	61.69	22.1	19.78
1996	61.26	22.07	19.07
1997	61.04	23.14	17.8
1998	60.66	22.62	17.11

Source: Bangladesh Bank, *Scheduled Banks Statistics*, various issues.

Table 3.12
Net Flow of Agricultural Credit by All Banks (Tk million)

Year	Disbursement	Recovery	Net flow
1989-90	6867.8	7019.4	-151.6
1990-91	5956	6253.2	-297.2
1994-95	14900	11241.1	3658.9
1995-96	14820	12730	2090
1996-97	15173	15942.7	-769.7
1997-98	16428.4	16990.7	-562.3

Source: Bangladesh Bank, *Scheduled Banks Statistics*, various issues.

Even so, informal financial markets are still important sources of credit for rural people, especially the poorer segment of the population, despite the growing presence of the micro-credit institutions. As is corroborated by Choudhury and Raihan (2001), as of now only half of the demand for rural credit is met. The high interest rates charged by money lenders, and their implications for the rural poor, are well documented, and remain a cause for concern—particularly because it is increasingly recognized that NGO micro-credit programs face formidable difficulty in reaching the very poor and meeting their credit needs (Sen, 2000).

If it is accepted that for people without investible resources, credit provides the only opportunity to establish themselves in productive self-employment, then the problems that inhibit the rural credit market are cause for concern. For the poor, the ability to access the opportunities opened by globalization hinges critically on their capacity to access financial resources. Designing adequate mechanisms, instruments, and institutions to ensure that the poor have access to affordable courses of credit is one of the major challenges before the policymakers of Bangladesh.

Reforms and the Dynamics of Poverty in Bangladesh

The adjustment reforms have positioned Bangladesh much better for reducing poverty, but the problems remain enormous.

Even with the relative good performance of exports and GDP growth, poverty as measured by income levels declined by a modest 1 percent a year on average in the 1990s, from 58.8 percent of the population to 49.8 percent (Table 3.13). The decrease was not fast enough to offset the population growth rate, which averaged 2.1 percent over the period, and the result was a significant rise in the absolute number of people living below the poverty line.

Since income poverty levels do not fully capture the well-being of a population, it is also important to review trends in non-income indicators. For Bangladesh in the 1990s, these indicators suggest a better pace of human development than do the income poverty figures above. The proportion of underweight people declined notably in the 1990s, from 71.8 percent in 1991/92 to 66.3 percent in 1995/96, and dropped further to 61.9 percent in 1998, while the level of wasting declined from 17.7 percent to 10 percent between 1996 and 2000 (Sen, 2000). In other human development indicators—such as access to education and health, the infant mortality

Table 3.13
Poverty and Inequality in the 1990s

	1991/92	2000	Change per year (%)
Headcount rate			
National	58.8	49.8	-1.8
Urban	44.9	36.6	-2.2
Rural	61.2	53.0	-1.6
Poverty gap			
National	17.2	12.9	-2.9
Urban	12.0	9.5	-2.5
Rural	18.1	13.8	-2.8
Squared poverty gap			
National	6.8	4.6	-3.8
Urban	4.4	3.4	-2.7
Rural	7.2	4.9	-3.8
Gini Index of Inequality			
National	0.259	0.306	2.1
Urban	0.307	0.368	2.3
Rural	0.243	0.271	1.4

Source: Interim Poverty Reduction Strategy Paper, Government of Bangladesh (2002).

rate, birth rate, and life expectancy—Bangladesh made significant progress in the 1990s (Table 3.14).

However, an urban-rural divide was also becoming increasingly discernible at this time (Table 3.15). In the mid-1990s, the rural-urban income disparity index in Bangladesh was 26 percent, and the comparison with Sri Lanka—a country with a much higher composite index value, 0.710 compared to 0.405 for Bangladesh, and also a much more open economy—is rather instructive. The two countries have very similar index values for the rural-urban income disparity, suggesting that rural-urban disparities may persist even when development indicators show positive trends across sectors and regions.[10] There is a need to study whether increased openness and globalization encourages rural-urban transfer of resources and how the attendant concerns should be addressed through policies.

The Urgent Need to Connect the Poor with Global Markets

At the current pace, poverty in Bangladesh will not be eradicated for fifty years, and estimates by UNCTAD show that with its present

Table 3.14
Movements in Social Indicators in the 1990s

Indicators	Bangladesh	
	1990	2001
Annual population growth rate (%)	2.7 (1960-90)	1.6
Population below income poverty line (%)	49.7	39.8
Adult literacy rate (%, age 15 and above)	35	40.8
Infant mortality rate (per 1,000 live birth)	111	101
Life expectancy at birth (years)	51.8	58.9
Total fertility rate	4.8	3.8
Undernourished people (as % of total population)	—	20 (1996/98)
Population with access to safe water (%)	38	56 (1999)
Population using adequate sanitation facilities (%)	42	61(1999)

Source: Compiled from UNDP *Human Development Reports*, 1993 and 1994, 2002.

Table 3.15
Rural-Urban Disparity Index: Mid-1990s

Country	Composite index value			Rural-urban disparity index value (%)
	Rural	Urban	National	
Bangladesh	0.381	0.516	0.405	26.16
India	0.373	0.612	0.438	39.05
Nepal	0.274	0.511	0.301	46.38
Pakistan	0.356	0.595	0.445	40.17
Sri Lanka	0.658	0.907	0.710	27.45

Source: Mujeri (2000).

economic growth rate, Bangladesh may perhaps graduate from its least developed country status by the year 2040 (UNCTAD 2000). Clearly, adequate strategies need to be designed to eradicate poverty within the shortest possible time. The Interim PRSP document (I-PRSP) of Bangladesh states that globalization has had a significant social and economic impact and has brought both challenges and opportunities for connecting the poor with global market opportunities:

> Exploiting globalization opportunities would require a sound investment climate, affordable access to information and communication technologies, improved efficiency

of trade promoting services, and investments in human capital and skills to exploit new opportunities.

Further global integration of Bangladesh's factor and goods markets will help the cause of poverty alleviation. The challenge will be to connect the rural poor to global markets—both because the overwhelming majority of the poor live in rural areas and also because urban poverty cannot be resolved without addressing its origins in rural areas.

Trade Policies and Market Access Issues

Now that Bangladesh is such an open economy, market access issues are of crucial importance for both growth and poverty alleviation. Of Bangladesh's various concerns with respect to market access, some of the most important are briefly outlined here.

High Tariff Barriers and Domestic Support in Developed Countries

Despite significant reductions in tariff rates during the GATT Uruguay Round, tariff peaks (high tariffs on particular products) and tariff escalation (increases in tariff rates in tandem with the degree of processing) and tariff-rate quotas continue to inhibit the market access of a large number of commodities exported by least developed countries such as Bangladesh. As is well recognized, these countries remain severely constrained by high tariff rates on items they export, including apparel, textiles, leather, and frozen food.

Importing countries' high tariffs on apparel are significant for Bangladesh, for which apparel makes up three-fourths of exports. In the United States, whose average effective import tariff has come down from 3.4 percent in 1991 to 1.6 percent in 2001, the average tariff on apparel and shoes is at 11.4 percent, and tariffs on specific categories are even higher (Table 3.16). For the United States, clothing and shoes account for only 6.7 percent of annual imports, but they supply 47 percent of total tariff revenue. In the EU, the current average tariff rate on apparel is as high as 12.4 percent.

Table 3.17 shows what such high tariffs mean for countries such as Bangladesh. Imports from Bangladesh to the United States, worth $2.3 billion, paid $331 million in tariffs. By contrast, imports to the

Table 3.16
Tariff Rates on Selected Apparel Categories

Bangladesh's exports exceeding $ 30 million		Bangladesh's exports between $10-30 million	
Items	Avg. tariff rate (%)	Items	Avg. tariff rates (%)
Knit-shirts MB	22.2	Dresses	13.5
Non-knit blouses WG	19.8	Coats MB	17.8
Cotton trousers MB	16.6	Cotton Coats WG	8.9
Non-knit shirts M	21.1	Knit Blouse	20.8%

Note: M- Men's; MB- Men's and Boys; WG- Women's and Girls.
Source: Center for Policy Dialogue (2000).

Table 3.17
Bangladesh's Exports Pay More than France's! (figures for 2001)

Country	Per capita GDP	Exports to U.S.	Tariffs paid	As %
Bangladesh	$370	$2.353 billion	$331 million	14.1
France	$24,170	$30.023 billion	$330 million	1.1
Norway	$33,470	$5.173 billion	$24 million	0.5
Singapore	$30,170	$14.899 billion	$96 million	0.6
Pakistan	$460	$2.228 billion	$240 million	10.8
Saudi Arabia	$6,900	$12.359 billion	$65 million	0.5

Source: Gresser (2002).

United States from France, worth 13 times as much, paid $1 million less in tariffs. The effective tariff rate on Bangladesh's exports to the United States is 14.1 percent, compared to a mere 1.1 percent on exports from France. It goes without saying that such high tariff rates undermine Bangladesh's competitive strength in the U.S. market.

In agriculture, continuing high subsidies and market-support measures in developed countries constrain the market access of countries such as Bangladesh. Farm support and subsidies in the OECD countries currently stand at almost a billion dollars a day.

Deteriorating Terms of Trade

Bangladesh's terms of trade have been declining since 1996 (Table 3.18). As Figure 3.1 shows, in recent years the country's

Table 3.18
Bangladesh's Falling Terms of Trade, 1996-2000 (1979/80=100)

Year	Export index	Import index	Terms of trade
1995/96	128.9	129.5	99.5
	(6.7)	(7.3)	(-0.6)
1996/97	135.0	133.4	101.2
	(4.8)	(3.0)	(-1.7)
1997/98	140.2	137.9	101.7
	(3.8)	(3.4)	(0.5)
1998/99	140.6	145.0	97.0
	(0.3)	(5.1)	(-4.6)
1999/2000	141.3	158.0	89.4
	(0.5)	(9.0)	(-7.8)

Source: Compiled from Bangladesh Economic Survey 2002.

Figure 3.1
Decomposition of Export Growth, FY1998-2003

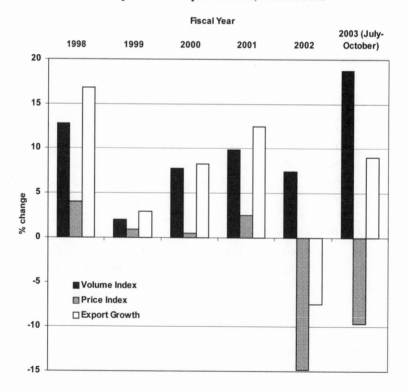

export growth has been driven mainly by increases in volume, not prices, so that Bangladesh has had to export more in volume terms to earn the same amount of foreign exchange. Bangladesh's weak competitive strength, limited capacity to diversify its exports and markets, and inability to move up-market, are matters of major concern.

Inability to Benefit from Market Access Initiatives

A welcome development in recent years was the offer of zero-tariff, quota-free access to the EU market for virtually all products from the LDCs (except rice, sugar, and bananas) under the Everything but Arms initiative. This initiative opened about 919 tariff lines in agriculture.

Unfortunately, Bangladesh does not stand to gain much from this initiative, at least in the short term. Its export base is narrow and it lacks the capacity to produce most of the products for which market access has been accorded under this initiative. Besides, the rules of origin (RoO), which need to be complied with to access preferential market access under the various Generalized System of Preferences Schemes (GSPs), are often found to be too stringent.[11] In major exportable product groups such as apparel, the RoO severely constrain Bangladesh's market access, particularly in the European market.

The negative effects of the RoO on Bangladesh's exports are clearly visible from Table 3.19. The findings of an ongoing study at the Center for Policy Dialogue (CPD) show that if the rules of origin requirements do not change, the incremental exports in response to this initiative will be worth only about $60 million dollars annually, or less than 3 percent of the value of Bangladesh's current exports to the EU.

By contrast, with a change in RoO, incremental exports would be worth $150 million in the apparel sector alone (Table 3.20).

Canada and Japan have recently revised their preferential schemes to provide enhanced market access for LDCs. Bangladesh stands to gain significantly in terms of market access for apparel in these markets. However, because of lack of supply-side capacities potential market access opportunities for some of the other products are likely to remain unrealized, at least in the short to medium term.

As shown by a recent study conducted at the Center for Policy Dialogue, a U.S. initiative similar to the EU-EBA would substan-

Table 3.19
Rules of Origin for Preferential Treatment under EU
Generalized System of Preferences

Year	1980-96	1996-98	1998-2000	October 2000 till Date	2002
Woven-RMG	2 Stage Conversion	2 Stage Conversion	2 Stage Conversion	2 Stage	Offered 2 Stage Under RC
Knit-RMG	3 Stage Conversion	Derogation to 1 Stage Conversion (Under Quota)	2 Stage Conversion	2 Stage	Offered 2 Stage Under RC
GSP Utilization Rate		41.2%	19.9%	39.9%	

Note: Stages are: Stage 1: Cotton-Yarn (Spinning); Stage 2: Yarn-Fabrics (Weaving);
Stage 3: Fabrics-RMG (Cutting and Making).
Source: Rahman (2002).

Table 3.20
Everything but Arms (EBA) Initiative: Impact on Bangladesh's Exports to the
EU with and without Rules of Origin

	Exports	Post-EBA Impact	
	Amount in mln US$	With RoO	Without RoO
Apparel	1,013.3	8.03	100.2
Textiles	577.1	52.7	45.4

Source: Bhattacharya, Rahman and Raihan (2002).

tially enhance market access opportunities for Bangladesh's goods in the U.S. market. Such an initiative is likely to lead to incremental exports of about $850 million to the U.S. market (equivalent to about 30 percent of Bangladesh's current exports to the United States). Although a proposal to accord quota and duty free market access to all the LDCs has been on the table for quite some time, and in 2000 the U.S. Government did come up with a similar initiative (under the Africa Growth and Development Act and the Caribbean Basin Initiative), unfortunately Bangladesh and a few other LDCs remained excluded from it.[12] As the aforementioned study shows, the sector in Bangladesh that would benefit most from such a U.S. initiative would be apparel, in which Bangladesh has substantial supply capacity and a demonstrated capability to access the U.S. market.

Impact of NTBs on Market Access

Many non-tariff barriers in the developed economies inhibit the market access of countries such as Bangladesh. They take various forms: export-import quotas, quantitative restrictions, anti-dumping and countervailing duties, sanitary and phytosanitary standards (SPS), and technical barriers to trade (TBT).

Compliance with agreements on Trade-related Intellectual Property Rights (TRIPs), SPS and TBT, among others, is becoming a major constraining factor for Bangladesh's export performance. Bangladesh is unable to access many of the newly opening markets because it cannot comply with the required standards. And in the recent past, Bangladesh's exports have faced sanctions or threats of sanctions in developed country markets on account of anti-dumping duties, SPS, and technical barriers to trade. For example, in 1997, the EU banned imports of shrimp from Bangladesh because they did not comply with the EU's Hazard Analysis Critical Point (HACCP) standards. Bangladesh suffered an immediate loss of about $60 million, with subsequent major disruptions in marketing of the products. In 1999, Bangladesh was threatened with sanctions on exports on the grounds that fishermen were not using turtle-extruding machines in open-catch fishing.

Some developed countries are trying to impose environmental standards through such measures as eco-labeling and compliance stickers. Some would like to impose more stringent standards on exporters for safety, human rights, and labor conditions. Along with the trade authorities in the developed countries, various consumer groups and nongovernment consumer watchdogs are coming up with their own demands, especially with regard to social standards. Under pressure from consumer groups in developed countries, importers and retail chains in practice often enforce standards that are more stringent than those required under WTO Agreements or national government regulations. And sometimes national standards are more stringent than required by the WTO.[13]

For example, a draft plan called the Apparel Industry Partnership was recently introduced in the U.S. Senate. It stipulates that U.S. importing companies will "voluntarily" monitor workplace codes of conduct in exporting units (in terms of working hours, minimum wage, safety standards, work environment, overtime schedules etc.). Under certification tools such as SA 8000—an accord between major U.S. clothing and footwear makers and human rights activists—production practices in apparel and footwear factories in LDCs will be closely scrutinized and sanctions will be imposed on firms that appear not to conform to the stipulated code of conduct. Compliance with stringent demands in the context of ISO-9000 and ISO-14000 is becoming an important factor in Bangladesh's ability to access markets in developed countries.

Some of the standards policies pursued by different developed countries contradict one another. For example, while the United States is demanding trade union rights in Bangladesh's export processing zones (EPZs), Japanese and Korean investors, who are major players in these EPZs, are starting to show reluctance to make further investments in anticipation of labor unrest in the EPZs. And while the EU was banning Bangladesh's shrimp exports, export of the same products to the United States, Japan, and some other developed counties registered significant growth. Such contrasting signals make it very difficult for poor countries to know what are appropriate priorities for reforming their practices.

If Bangladesh and other poor countries are to successfully integrate with the global economy, there is a strong case for the developed countries to give priority attention in their various policies to addressing the concerns associated with standards, including assisting poor countries with compliance. Otherwise, poor countries stand to be further marginalized as globalization proceeds.

Developed Countries' Policies and Their Interfaces with Market Access Issues

Bangladesh's increased integration with the world economy, and its increased dependence on access to export markets, has critical implications for its relations with developed countries as development partners. Developed countries' policies affect Bangladesh's market access interests through four groups of interfaces: global trade negotiations; regional trading arrangements; domestic policies in developed countries; and bilateral relations; especially through aid. Decisions taken at these interfaces will have a big influence on how much integration with the global economy Bangladesh is able to achieve in the coming years, and consequently on its ability to reduce poverty. More appropriate policies need to be identified and pursued in each of the four interface areas:

- to relate the policies pursued by developed countries in global forums such as the WTO to the market access concerns of poor countries;
- to keep in perspective the implications of regional trading arrangements that have market access significance for poor countries outside the arrangements;
- to recognize the impact of developed countries' domestic economic policies and initiatives on poor countries' market access;
- to tighten the nexus between aid and trading capacity.

The following sections discuss policy issues at these four levels and highlight needs for research.

Policy Stance in Global Negotiations

The developing world will gain substantially if developed countries pursue a more accommodating and supportive strategy in global forums that deal with market access issues. Of particular interest to Bangladesh are the ongoing discussions in the WTO. The Doha ministerial meeting did call for supportive developed-country policies to address the emerging market access concerns of the LDCs.[14] The Doha Ministerial Meeting set up a Negotiating Group on Market Access to discuss the relevant issues in the WTO. In the Negotiating Committees and Working Groups, LDCs such as Bangladesh have either come up with their own proposals or supported proposals submitted by other countries or groups of countries.

In the market access negotiations, developed countries may extend support in various forms:

- support for proposals submitted by the LDCs;
- effective derogations in support of LDCs;
- firm commitments to open their domestic markets to goods and services of interest to LDCs;
- flexibility in imposing trade-related sanctions (for example, Bangladesh has been asking for non-imposition of anti-dumping and countervailing duties on exports from LDCs, particularly for exports of apparel, for a ten-year period to follow the expiration of the Multifiber Agreement); and
- effective technical assistance under the Integrated Framework Initiative.

For example, to assist with the further integration of poor countries into the global economy, the developed countries will need to be ready to consider proposals submitted by the LDCs and developing countries that aim at opening up trade in the services sector—from which they stand to gain substantially. The ongoing negotiations in the WTO on the General Agreement on Trade in Services (GATS) are a case in point. To make sure that the market opening under GATS is balanced, developing and least developed countries are pushing for enhanced access to the labor markets of the developed world under Mode-4 of GATS, which relates to the movement of natural persons.[15] They are also arguing against developed countries' use of the economic needs test (ENT) and local needs test (LNT), which are tests that constrain the movement of labor. Until now, the focus of the developed countries has been mainly on the movement of professionals in the context of Mode-3, relating to commercial presence. If countries such as Bangladesh are to access the benefits under GATS Mode-4, developed countries will need to consider flexibility in granting visas, and in applying ENT and LNT to facilitate temporary movement of labor from the LDCs.

LDC proposals in the WTO often relate to modalities, derogation, and technical assistance needs, and in general reflect their specific market access concerns. The developed countries should carefully study these LDC concerns, to see how they can be addressed in the negotiations (to be continued till 2005), as well as through their direct assistance policies for LDCs. The latter are all the more important when the LDCs are unable to achieve their desired outcomes within the complex multilateral setting of the WTO.

Research needs. Research is needed to respond to the following questions:

- In which professions do LDCs such as Bangladesh stand to gain the most from any market opening in GATS Mode-4?
- What type of skills do the LDCs require to access those market openings?
- What type of assistance can developed countries provide to en-hance Bangladesh's capacity to access such market openings?
- LDCs do enjoy preferential treatment in the WTO under the various Special and Differential (S&D) provisions, but these provisions have been criticized as being merely good intentions (on the part of the

developed countries) and unenforceable. A pertinent need here is a good estimate of the amount and nature of financial and technical support that would be required to implement the S&D clauses in the WTO. As is known, in the second WTO Ministerial Meeting of the WTO held in Singapore in 1999, the participating ministers unanimously endorsed a proposal to support LDC efforts towards strengthened integration into the ongoing process of globalization through technical and financial support.[16]

Regional Trade Policies

Along with the current fast pace of globalization there is also a growing tendency now for countries to promote and strengthen regional integration by setting up regional trade agreements (RTAs). In many instances such RTAs negatively affect the market access interests of countries that remain outside such arrangements. Agreements such as NAFTA, the EU-Turkey Free Trade Agreement, U.S.-Vietnam Free Trade Agreement, and U.S. initiatives such as the Caribbean Basin Initiative and the Africa Growth and Opportunity Act often provide preferential access to developed country markets for goods from RTA member countries. The comparative advantage thus far enjoyed by many LDCs in developed country markets has eroded considerably in recent times as a result of such preferential arrangements.

Research needs. There is a need to find out to what extent RTAs undermine the competitive strength of countries such as Bangladesh and identify the mechanisms which need to be put in place in developed country policies to address the attendant concerns.

Domestic Policies

Provision of preferential access to LDCs. As noted above, most of the developed countries provide preferential market access to LDCs such as Bangladesh, but without a similar initiative from the United States, the incremental gains will be insignificant, at least in the short term. There is thus a need to press for such a global initiative by all the developed countries—since this is likely to have an enormous impact on market access for exports from countries such as Bangladesh. LDCs have been calling for global duty-free, quota-free market access for LDCs, in a proposal that has been on the WTO negotiating table for some time.

Research needs: A relevant research area is to quantify the cost to the developed countries of providing such preferential access and to identify supportive measures for domestic producers in developed countries to offset production dislocation, if any. Canada carried out such a study before taking the initiative to provide zero-tariff access for imports from Bangladesh. This research helped substantially to swing Canadian public opinion in favor of the proposal.

Often rules of origin do not permit LDCs to take full advantage of market access initiatives by developed countries. Here several issues could usefully be taken up:

- To what extent do rules of origin undermine Bangladesh's capacity to access market access initiatives?
- What changes and flexibility in the RoO would best help countries such as Bangladesh to take advantage of the market access initiatives?
- What are the costs and benefits of changes in RoO for the economy of the recipient countries (since changes in RoO may also undermine efforts to develop domestic capacities)?

In the markets of developed countries, the competitiveness of products from countries such as Bangladesh is often constrained by high tariff rates and by domestic support measures in the form of subsidies. Developed countries will need to carefully monitor and evaluate the potential impact of their policies on market access for goods from the LDCs. In-depth research is needed to understand the possible impact of the changes in developed country policies for particular LDCs. For example, while phasing out of subsidies in the agricultural sectors of developed countries could open up export opportunities for some countries, it could also push up prices of agricultural goods in the global market to the detriment of the net food importing countries. There is thus a need to study the attendant costs and benefits and to come up with concrete measures to address the negative fallouts of the developed country policies. In-depth study is also required to identify measures that would stimulate the private sectors in the LDCs to respond appropriately to market access opportunities. Such studies will allow countries such as Bangladesh to benefit from the promised market openings in some erstwhile protected markets, for example if the ongoing negotiations in the WTO on the Agreement on Agriculture are successfully completed.

Coherence of policy toward poor countries. To take advantage of global market opportunities and address the attendant risks Bangladesh, like other poor countries, needs to have adequate trade-related capacities in place. Developed country policies play a crucially important role in capacity building. In view of the critical importance of the market access issues, it is increasingly felt in countries such as Bangladesh that there is an urgent need to strengthen the nexus between aid and trade, and to raise the efficacy of aid and technical assistance to help strengthen trade-related supply-side capacities.

Research needs: A pertinent research issue here would be to identify what supportive measures need to be put in place to enhance supply-side capacities in Bangladesh for accessing the potential benefits of such market access initiatives as the EU's Everything but Arms agreement.

As to standards, it is increasingly felt that the new generation of aid policies must give more attention to the emerging issues, including assistance for compliance. One research area here could be to quantify the costs of compliance with standards requirements and the expected benefits (or losses from non-compliance) in terms of enhanced (or forgone) market access opportunities and also to identify effective ways to support these concerns through technical assistance. If it is convincingly shown that the benefits to be accrued from compliance outweigh the costs, producers, governments, and development partners will be more inclined to respond to the emerging concerns with appropriate initiatives.

Opportunities arising from special treatment. Under the WTO's Special and Differential Treatment provisions, LDCs have been given a number of derogations that may create market access opportunities. The Doha Declaration on TRIPs and Public Health may be cited as an example here: LDCs such as Bangladesh were granted an additional ten years (up to 2016) to comply with the provisions of the TRIPs Agreement. The Doha Declaration promises to provide important market access opportunities for the pharmaceuticals sector in the LDCs, where Bangladesh has considerable domestic capacity. It is important that Bangladesh is able to take the fullest advantage of the promised market access opportunities.

Research needs: Pertinent research issues here may be:

- What are the potential benefits to Bangladesh's pharmaceutical sector?
- Which policies should Bangladesh pursue to maximize the country's benefits and to stimulate and promote private sector interest?
- Which supportive policies (including encouraging foreign direct investment into the sector) should be pursued by the development partners to help Bangladesh realize the potential benefits?

Implementing commitments. There is also a need to relate developed country policies to the Integrated Framework Initiative of the WTO, as part of which developed countries have committed to provide trade-supportive technical assistance to the LDCs. Concrete measures are also needed to implement the positive agenda in support of the LDCs. Concrete initiatives are still to be taken in this regard, though implementation of these commitments is likely to substantially enhance market access for goods exported by countries such as Bangladesh.

Research needs: Studies are needed to identify concrete initiatives and measures that developed country policies could support and promote to service their respective commitments in the WTO in support of the LDCs.

Concluding Remarks

Reforms pursued in Bangladesh over the past decade have gone a long way to create a conducive environment for connecting domestic market forces with global market opportunities. Better progress in poverty alleviation will largely depend on the efficacy of the developed and home country policies in opening up opportunities for the poor to be able to take advantage of these potential opportunities. Attainment of the Millennium Development Goals (MDG), which has set the objective of halving global poverty by 2015, will critically hinge on this.

Both aid and trade policies in the developed countries now need to be refocused, integrated, and sequenced in a coherent manner to respond to the structural changes that have taken place, and address the market access concerns that have consequently emerged, in LDCs such as Bangladesh. To enable countries such as Bangladesh to raise their competitive strength, translate comparative advantage into competitive advantage, and competitive advantage into revealed comparative advantage in the global marketplace, will require that the developed countries pursue a comprehensive supportive strategy at the global, regional, and bilateral levels.

Bangladesh will need to substantially improve the quality of its macroeconomic management and will have to ensure that its economic governance is geared to poverty alleviation. Bangladesh's ability to reach the targets set in the PRSP of the Government of Bangladesh and the Millennium Development Goal of halving global poverty agreed upon by the global community of nations, will to a large extent hinge on whether it is able to make developed country assistance work towards strengthened global integration of its economy and whether, in turn, the developed country aid is able to address effectively Bangladesh's concerns and interests with respect to the ongoing process of globalization. Addressing the challenge of making aid work for poverty alleviation is thus a shared responsibility of both the government and other stakeholders in Bangladesh, and the country's development partners.

Notes

1. The author is research director, Center for Policy Dialogue, Bangladesh, and a professor at the University of Dhaka, Bangladesh. He is very grateful to Robert Picciotto for his helpful comments on an earlier draft of the present paper.
2. The estimates used here are based on disbursed aid.
3. The degree of openness is defined here as the share of export and import of goods in GDP (while the degree of globalization takes into cognizance also export and import of services and investment flows).
4. Subsidized sales from the public food distribution system do not at present play as significant a role as they used to in the past; programs to ensure price stability through open market sales are still in place, albeit on a limited scale.
5. There was a large increase in rural self-employment through increased economic activities in the trade and transport sectors, which was facilitated by large-scale expansion of rural roads and communication network. For example, Hossain (2000) informs that households reporting ownership of rickshaws and rickshaw vans, popular means of rural transport, increased from 55,000 in 1983-84 to 500,000 in 1995-96.
6. If the wage rates indices presented in Table 3.8 are recomputed with 1991-92 as the base year, this observation is reinforced.
7. Although a large part of the income of migrant workers is remitted through *hundi* (informal channels), and hence estimates about average remittance may be misleading, an analysis of the average amount of remittances per worker received by migrant workers from South Asian countries testifies to the abovementioned observation.
8. Export-oriented shrimp culture funded and managed by private entrepreneurs has often resulted in displacement of land and labor from traditional agriculture, leading to social stress in local communities. Many commentators have also raised questions about the environmental costs of shrimp culture and there is an ongoing debate in Bangladesh as regards the overall impact of the shrimp culture on environment, long-term income, and livelihood practices in the cultivation areas. A few studies

have suggested that it is possible, at least in some regions of Bangladesh, to have environmentally sustainable shrimp culture provided appropriate economic and policy instruments are put in place to address the attendant problems (Center for Policy Dialogue, 2000).

9. See Choudhury and Raihan (2001) for a detailed discussion of the relevant issues.
10. The composite index takes into account both income and non-income factors. A discussion on the methodology of estimating the relevant indices is available in Mujeri (2001).
11. The RoO under the various GSP Schemes could be in the form of minimum local value addition requirement or stages of conversion the inputs would need to undergo within the exporting country. Preferential treatment accorded to the exports from developing countries and the LDCs are contingent upon compliance with the relevant RoO criteria. Often LDCs such as Bangladesh are unable to access such preferential treatment because of lack of backward linkage supply-side capacities.
12. As matter of fact, in recent years several countries, including Canada (for most of the goods), Japan (for apparel/textiles), New Zealand and Australia, have come up with similar market access initiatives in support of the LDCs.
13. For example, compliance requirements under EU's HACCP standard are more stringent than provisions of the Sanitary and Phytosanitary Measures (SPSM) in the WTO.
14. Thus, the Doha Mandate commits members to "reduce, or as appropriate, eliminate tariffs, including reduction or elimination of tariff peaks, high tariffs, and tariff escalation, as well as non-tariff barriers, in particular on products of interest to developing countries," and goes on to mention that the forthcoming negotiations "shall take fully into account the special needs and interests of developing and least-developed country participants, including through less than full reciprocity in reduction commitments."
15. India has proposed an occupational approach to identify skills of interest to developing countries from the perspective of market access.
16. This proposal, which came to be known as the *positive agenda in support of the LDCs* committed the rich nations to allocate adequate funds to enhance the capacity of the LDCs to ensure compliance with WTO rules and address the attendant risks, to put in place the required supplyside capacities in the LDCs and enable these countries to take advantage of the emerging market access opportunities.

References

Asaduzzaman, M. (2000)."Bangladesh Agriculture in the Era of Globalization: Constraints and Opportunities." In Abu Abdullah, ed., *Bangladesh Economy 2000: Selected Issues.* Dhaka: Bangladesh Institute of Development Studies.

_____. (2000). "Livestock Sector, Economic Development and Poverty Alleviation in Bangladesh." In M. A. Sattar Mandal, ed., *Changing Rural Economy of Bangladesh.* Dhaka: Bangladesh Economic Association.

Bhattacharya, Debapriya, and Rashed A. M. Titumir. (1999). "Towards Demystifying a Process: The Structural Adjustment Policies in Bangladesh." In Mahbubul Karim, ed., *Discourse—A Journal of Policy Studies.* Dhaka: Institute for Development Policy Analysis and Advocacy, Proshika.

Bhattacharya, Debapriya, Mustafizur Rahman, and Ananya Raihan. (2002). "Implications of EU's Everything But Arms and Japan's Recent Market Access Initiatives for Bangladesh's Export Sector"; Draft Report of the ongoing study conducted at the Center for Policy Dialogue for the Ministry of Commerce, Government of Bangladesh.

Board of Investment. (2002). "Investment Opportunities in Bangladesh." Board of Investment, Bangladesh (mimeo).

Center for Policy Dialogue. (1996). "Experiences with Economic Reforms: A Review of Bangladesh's Development 1995." University Press Limited, Dhaka, Bangladesh.

_____. (2001). "Dynamics of Labor Market: A Review of Bangladesh's Development 2002." Dhaka: University Press Limited.

Choudhury, Toufic Ahmad, and Ananya Raihan. (2001). "Structural Adjustment Participatory Review Initiative, Bangladesh: Implications of Financial Sector Reforms." In *Structural Adjustment Participatory Review Initiative*, Bangladesh. Report prepared for presentation in the Second National Forum of Bangladesh, held on March 13-15, 2000. Dhaka: Center for Policy Dialogue.

Faaland, Just, and J. R Parkinson. (1976). *Bangladesh: The Test Case for Development.* London: C. Hurst and Company.

Government of Bangladesh. (2002). *Bangladesh: A National Strategy for Economic Growth and Poverty Reduction (Draft)*, Economic Relations Division, Ministry of Finance, Government of the People's Republic of Bangladesh. November 2002.

Gresser, Edward. (2002). "America's Hidden Tax on the Poor: The Case for Reforming US Tariff Policy." Washington DC: Progressive Policy Institute.

Hossain, Mahabub. (2000). "Recent Development and Structural Changes in Bangladesh Agriculture: Issues for Reviewing Strategies and Policies." In Rehman Sobhan, ed., *Changes and Challenges: A Review of Bangladesh's Development 2000*. Dhaka: Center for Policy Dialogue and University Press Limited.

Hossain, Mahabub, and Manik Lal Bose. (2000). "Growth and Structural Changes in Bangladesh Agriculture: Implications for Strategies and Policies for Sustainable Development." In M. A. Sattar Mandal, ed., *Changing Rural Economy of Bangladesh*. Dhaka: Bangladesh Economic Association.

International Labor Organization (ILO). (1998). *Yearbook of Labor Statistics*. Geneva: ILO.

Khan, Azizur Rahman. (2000). "Economic Development: From Independence to the End of the Millennium." In Rounaq Jahan, ed., *Bangladesh: Promise and Performance*. Dhaka: The University Press Limited.

Mandal, M. A. Sattar. (2000). "Dynamics of Irrigation Water Market in Bangladesh." In M. A. Sattar Mandal, ed., *Changing Rural Economy of Bangladesh*. Dhaka: Bangladesh Economic Association.

Mujeri, Mustafa K. (2000). " Macroeconomic Developments in the 1990s." In Abu Abdullah, ed., *Bangladesh Economy 2000: Selected Issues*. Dhaka: Bangladesh Institute of Development Studies.

_____. (2002). "Poverty-Poverty Links in Bangladesh: Some Broad Observations." In *Bangladesh Facing the Challenges of Globalization: A Review of Bangladesh's Development 2001*. Dhaka: Center for Policy Dialogue and the University Press Ltd.

Murshid, K.A.S. (2001). "Implications of Agricultural Policy Reforms on Rural Food Security and Poverty." In *Structural Adjustment Participatory Review Initiative, Bangladesh*. Report prepared for presentation in the Second National Forum of Bangladesh, held on March 13-15, 2000. Dhaka: Center for Policy Dialogue.

Quasem, Md. Abul. (2000). "Quality of Agricultural Inputs: The Role of the Government." In Abu Abdullah, ed., *Bangladesh Economy 2000: Selected Issues*. Dhaka: Bangladesh Institute of Development Studies.

Rahman, Mustafizur. (2000). " Bangladesh Country Paper." In *Liberalization and Poverty: Is There a Virtuous Circle?* Jaipur: Center for International Trade, Economics and Environment.

Rahman, Mustafizur, and Quazi Shahbuddin (1997). *Crisis in Governance: A Review of Bangladesh's Development*, 1997-98. Dhaka: Center for Policy Dialogue and Vedams Books.

Rahman, Rushidan Islam. (2001). "Consequences of Structural Adjustment Policies on the Poor." In *Structural Adjustment Participatory Review Initiative, Bangladesh*. Report prepared for presentation in the Second National Forum of Bangladesh, held on March 13-15, 2000. Dhaka: Center for Policy Dialogue and Vedams Books.

Rashid, Mohammed Ali. (2001). "Impact of Trade Policy Reforms on Industrial Capacity and Employment in Bangladesh." In *Structural Adjustment Participatory Review Initiative, Bangladesh*. Report prepared for presentation in the Second National Forum of Bangladesh, held on March 13-15, 2000. Dhaka: Center for Policy Dialogue.

Sen, Binayak. (2000). "Growth, Poverty and Human Development." In Rounaq Jahan, ed., *Bangladesh: Promise and Performance*. Dhaka: The University Press Limited.

Shahabuddin, Quazi. (2000). "Review of Food Sector and Policy Options for Food Security." In Abu Abdullah, ed., *Bangladesh Economy 2000: Selected Issues*. Dhaka: Bangladesh Institute of Development Studies.

Sobhan, Rehman. (1996). *Aid Dependence and Donor Policy: The Case of Tanzania with Lessons from Bangladesh's Experience*. Dhaka: Center for Policy Dialogue and the University Press Ltd.

UNDP. (2002). *Human Development Report 2002*, United Nations Development Program.

Zohir, Sajjad. (2000). "Recent Evidence on the Rural Economy: Findings from a BIDS Survey." In Abu Abdullah, ed., *Bangladesh Economy 2000: Selected Issues*. Dhaka: Bangladesh Institute of Development Studies.

Comments on "Globalization, Developed Country Policies, and Market Access: Some Insights from the Bangladesh Experience"

Sara Castellanos[1]

Professor Rahman's analysis of Bangladesh's experience under the export-led growth model clearly illustrates the relevance of developed country policies as a complement to developing countries' own domestic efforts to grow and to alleviate poverty. It provides some compelling data about the complex interaction of developed country policies on a developing country's trade, foreign direct investment, foreign aid, intellectual property rights, migration, and environment, and on the potential role of these policies in determining a developing country's conditions of access into the markets of the global economy.

The findings raise some questions on market access that have broad relevance for developing countries. Decisions are needed on which of these issues may require more research, and which may need just a thorough compilation and presentation of existing results. Also, given the opportunities presented by the Doha negotiations and other global forums, decisions are needed on which issues should have priority over others and how studies would need to be timed.

Rahman's analysis also raises the question of whether agricultural policies and their effects should not be analyzed separately from trade or investment policies. His findings suggest the answer is yes, because the rural sector makes up a large share of total employment in the less developed countries and because it is vulnerable to impoverishment as a result of greater market openness.

This chapter exemplifies the benefits of the case study approach to development analysis. Some past disappointments with the policy-relevance of cross-country regression analysis suggest that development researchers should place more emphasis on case studies, but cases need to be selected systematically. For example, Bangladesh shares common concerns about market access conditions and domestic poverty with India, Mexico, or Chile, but Bangladesh's case differs in several respects from those of the other three countries (and their cases differ from one another). After all, we should remember that it is the emphasis on country differences that has produced such an unequal policy treatment of the developing economies by the developed ones.

Note

1.   Researcher, Economic Studies Division, Bank of Mexico. The views expressed here are hers and do not necessarily represent those of the Bank of Mexico.

4

Rich Country Policies and the Poor: Harnessing Foreign Direct Investment for Pro-Poor Development

Amar Inamdar[1]

Introduction

Transnational corporations (TNCs) are expanding their role in the global economy. UNCTAD (2002) estimates that worldwide there are now 65,000 TNCs, with 850,000 foreign affiliates. In 2001, these affiliates had 54 million employees; they accounted for 10 percent of world GDP and one-third of world exports.

Foreign direct investment—a measure of the financial flows controlled by TNCs—stood at US$735 billion in 2001. Despite a decline during the year 2000, it still dwarfs OECD development aid by almost a factor of four.

Dollar & Kraay (2000) found that "growth is good for the poor." Business is the engine that creates growth, so it follows that encouraging investment by business should reduce poverty. Of course, the overall equation is more complex, especially as we try to understand the conditions that promote sustainable growth. Investment is only one of a complement of building blocks that contribute to sustainable development. Opportunity, equity, and security are all important, especially to the poor, and business investment can influence access to each in different ways.

This chapter explores the relationship between foreign investment and pro-poor development, with an emphasis on understanding how rich countries' policies shape the effects of investments on the poor. The chapter is principally concerned with the role of transnational corporations rather than with broader private investment, which includes portfolio flows, private lending, and bonds. This is partly because of the overall magnitude of foreign direct investment and because of the lasting and powerful impact on development that TNCs exert through their presence in developing countries. In contrast, portfolio flows tend to be more ephemeral.

The Pattern and Distribution of Global FDI

The distribution of (FDI) is highly skewed towards the developed world and a handful of developing countries (Figure 4.1). Of the US$735 billion of FDI in 2001, $503 billion (68 percent) was investment between developed countries. Of the FDI flows to developing countries, 80 percent went to the top ten countries, led by China, Mexico, Hong Kong, and Brazil, and only half of 1 percent went to the least developed countries.

Much has been written about why FDI is distributed the way it is. Held et al. (2000) provide an instructive and exhaustive review and conclude that FDI flows to where the conditions for business are good.[2] Good business conditions tend to depend on a range of indicators including macroeconomic stability, openness to foreign investment, and good infrastructure.[3] Where, as among textile and clothing TNCs, subcontracting rather than direct involvement in production is the norm, the availability of low-cost labor is more of a determinant. And among the poorest countries, particularly in Africa, FDI flows are influenced strongly by the presence of resources that are the basis for extractive industries.

In general, FDI inflows to developing countries are significant in relation to these countries' economies—and proportionately larger than FDI inflows to developed countries. Their size creates a strong rationale to leverage these flows to promote social and economic development, as has been recognized by a number of development agencies including the World Bank and the UK Department for International Development.

The 1990s saw a substantial, if gradual, trend towards the liberalization of FDI regimes in more than 100 countries around the world. A total of 1,513 bilateral investment agreements, clarifying tax and other regulations, had been signed by 1998. In that same

Figure 4.1
World FDI Inflows, by Country Group, 2001

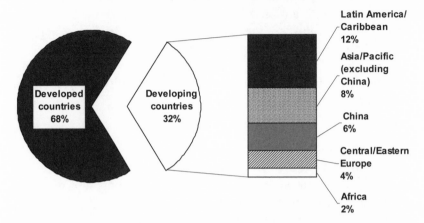

year, a global Multilateral Agreement on Investment, which proposed the elimination of virtually all national controls on FDI, was
effectively aborted in the face of severe nongovernmental protest.
We discuss the lessons learned from this experience later in the
chapter.

The Relationship between FDI and Pro-Poor Development

Analysis of the relationship between business investment and
poverty needs to capture more than just the contribution that businesses make to economic growth. Opportunity, equity, and security
are important in combination. Access by the poor to each of these is
critical, and investment by TNCs can have important influences on
that access.

FDI influence whether or not development is pro-poor through:·

- its contribution to growth and whether that growth is more or less pro-
  poor
- its interaction with local societies and impact on environmental resources
- its influence on governments and political decision-making.

This section discusses each of these influences in turn. Measuring the impact that business has on the poor is extremely difficult.
Agencies that have experience in this type of analysis (especially
governmental and nongovernmental development organizations)

increasingly look to quantitative and qualitative analyses of measures of power, participation, risk, health, and wealth. The "livelihoods approach" adopted by DFID, CARE, and UNDP, among others, reflects this broader focus. Of course, the broad application of these approaches is made difficult by the lack of baselines against which to compare changes in data, by the onerous data colltion required, and by the lack of comparability between interventions.

FDI and Growth

According to the *World Development Report 2000-2001*, economic growth can be pro-poor if it provides semi- and unskilled jobs that are accessible to the poor or if it creates opportunities in sectors, such as agriculture, from which poor people are more likely to derive their income. The Asian Development Bank defines growth as pro-poor "when it is labor-absorbing and accompanied by policies and programs that mitigate inequalities and facilitate income and employment generation for the poor, particularly women and other traditionally excluded groups."[4]

To what extent has FDI demonstrably contributed to pro-poor outcomes?

FDI, like domestic investment, creates benefits through taxes, fees, and royalties; through employment of labor; and through the purchase of goods and services. A recent OECD report[5] summarizes the principal additional benefits of FDI within host countries. These include: technology transfers; human capital and skills enhancement; better integration with international trade; more competitive business environment; and enterprise development. "All of these contribute to higher economic growth, which is the most potent tool for alleviating poverty in developing countries." Additional, non-economic influences are often cited, including social and environmental improvements that result from transfers of cleaner technology and socially responsible practices.

Whether or not these benefits of FDI are able to have a positive influence on the host economy depends on two factors:

- the type of FDI; and
- the enabling environment that already exists in the host country.

A Typology of FDI

Typically, while FDI contributes to growth, only a small proportion is directly invested in micro and small enterprises, which are often the main source of new jobs and income for the poor. In the extractive sector, most of the benefits that accrue to the host country come in the form of taxes, fees, and royalties. Historically, many developing countries that have reaped windfall gains from mineral extraction (most notably in oil and gas[6]) have suffered what Sachs and Warner (2001) refer to as the "curse of natural resources." New-found mineral wealth creates domestic price inflation, reducing the international competitiveness of local businesses and reducing the incentives for entrepreneurial wealth creation. Outside the OECD, economies with large mineral endowments do appear to perform less well than their peers. One way to escape the resource curse is to increase transparency over resource rents and the payments made to governments by extractive industry companies.

Tariffs also play a role in influencing the type of FDI that flows to developing countries. In the extractive industries, for example, OECD countries' tariffs are higher on processed than on unprocessed products, creating a bias towards raw material exports. Data presented by Oxfam America[7] show that, for example, mean OECD tariffs on unprocessed copper, aluminum, zinc, and petroleum are zero, while those on processed copper products are close to 4 percent; on processed aluminum, 5 percent; on processed zinc, 3 percent; and on refined petroleum products, 7 percent. Such tariffs discourage developing countries from creating competitive processing industries, with or without FDI.

The Domestic Enabling Environment

In an analysis of the relationship between FDI and the domestic enabling environment, Held et al. (2000) conclude from a review of wide-ranging sources that "FDI generally only plays a significantly positive role in those countries that have already achieved a prior level of development and have the infrastructure and skills base to sustain growth."[8] The reasoning behind this argument is straightforward. Without preexisting capacity, entrepreneurial culture, and a domestic environment that promotes business, the likely spillovers from FDI—in the form of technology transfer and supply chain opportunities—cannot be taken up and turned into viable businesses. This is a significant finding. It means that in and of itself, FDI is unlikely to yield sustainable benefits for the poor in the poorest countries. More is not necessarily better.

What are the key components of an enabling environment? The UK government White Paper, *Making Globalization Work for the Poor*[9] identifies three basic characteristics: the structure and regulation of capital markets; the capacity of these markets; and supporting infrastructure. The first of these characteristics includes important governance fundamentals: transparency, lack of corruption, rule of law, and efficacy of regulations. Market capacity refers to the diversity and depth of business activity and its ability to absorb new investment. Supporting infrastructure refers primarily to connectedness: the physical channels that enable businesses to communicate, trade, and supply themselves and their markets.

In conclusion, whether or not FDI is good for the poor depends primarily on the enabling environment within host countries. OECD countries' import tariffs play a role in limiting the diversity of FDI and reducing the integration of developing countries into the global economy.

Although research is growing and making available more indicators on the geographical and temporal distribution of FDI, few systematic data are being collected on aspects of FDI that reflect its impact on the poor.

The Environmental and Social Impact of FDI

FDI directly affects environmental quality and the availability of land and other resources to local people. TNCs impact local cultures by bringing with them foreign norms that affect local business partners, employees, neighbors, and host country governments. In rural parts of the developing world, TNCs can play a significant role in monetizing local society and changing the power relationships among local groups.

Some of these impacts can be positive. TNCs generally have higher social and environmental operating standards than domestic firms. They can improve domestic productivity by encouraging local firms to perform more competitively. They can play a significant role in encouraging the improvement of national regulations and raising expectations for increased standards. One clear example where this is happening is at Kelian in Indonesia, where Rio Tinto has involved local and national government in a process for agreeing on a variety of waste discharge standards during and after the closure of a major gold mine.[10]

By contrast, the mining sector in Papua New Guinea illustrates some of the more negative social and environmental consequences of FDI. TNCs exploiting mineral wealth have undoubtedly created economic growth and currently contribute to about 20 percent of the economy. But from a local perspective, little of this growth has been converted into tangible or lasting social benefits. Instead, the perception is that mineral exploitation has exacerbated conflict.[11] Mining operations are routinely disrupted by local community and employee disputes. Gold has long been mined by artisanal workers in Papua New Guinea, but little of it will remain available to future generations. And at one mine, the national government has legislated major dispensations for waste emissions rather than enforce the costs of meeting existing environmental standards.

These examples show that FDI can have positive or negative social and environmental consequences for host countries depending on how the governments of those countries manage the activities of TNCs and the revenues that result. In part, this is an issue of capacity—the ability of national regulators and administrators to achieve socially and environmentally sustainable development. Much depends on the mechanisms they have available to ensure effective and appropriate allocation of the costs and benefits of investment between local, provincial, and national levels in a country. In turn, this ability can be distorted by the powerful incentives for governments to attract FDI to their shores, and by what they are prepared to do to avoid losing it. This brings us to the third aspect of FDI: the political implications of investment.

The Political Implications of FDI

Business investment can strongly influence government decisions, especially when a government is poor and business is rich. At local as well as national levels, governments in the developed as well as the developing world often work hard to attract investment, and in the process sometimes go against the interests of the weak, the poor, or the environment. As noted above, they do this by turning a blind eye to environmental standards (or awarding dispensations). lowering previously agreed labor or safety standards, or providing tax concessions or outright subsidies.

In their quest for FDI, governments sometimes disadvantage domestic firms. Free trade zones, where domestic regulatory requirements do not apply and tax holidays are awarded to foreign investors, clearly fall into this category. Governments that take an active interest in the domestic regulations and policies of their perceived competitor nations can create innovative responses and increase the productivity of their public services. Equally, however, they can create a "race to the bottom," by incremental undercutting of standards and taxes, which erodes the benefits to society and lowers the likelihood that environmental or social externalities can be mitigated.

FDI and Pro-Poor Outcomes: Opportunities for Research

Ultimately, the responsibility for promoting pro-poor growth through FDI rests mainly with the governments of developing countries themselves. Reforms to attract financial flows should ideally be complemented by reforms to increase the availability of FDI to the poor.

Policies of rich countries have focused on increasing investment rather than on improving its impact on the poor. Drawing on the findings outlined above, this section returns to the question of the role that rich countries can play in improving the developmental impact of FDI.

Governments of rich countries can use four basic levers of influence:

- International investment policy;
- Official development assistance, to promote pro-poor investment;
- Domestic legislation and regulation of capital markets, to promote corporate responsibility; and
- Reductions in subsidies and tariffs that limit international and domestic competition.

International Investment Policy

NGOs are not arguing against the need for rules on international investment flows, only against the basis of rules under the Multilateral Agreement on Investment.[12]

At least some of the problems associated with international investment arise because there are no enforced international standards that protect investors as well as the host countries that they are invested in. The rationale for an international agreement is that it could be used to simplify the large number of investment rules in existence and ensure a level and competitive playing field between companies and countries. The risk of a race to the bottom, where countries compete to lower their standards, could be mitigated.

The Multilateral Agreement on Investment (MAI) was one attempt to harmonize investment rules, and was rejected in 1998 after a gestation period of more than seven years. The principal reason for its rejection was that it was seen to be loaded in favor of investors and against governments and others in civil society. The proposed agreement contained no measures to promote transparency or reduce corruption, and lacked provisions for the consideration of developing country or social and environmental concerns.

In essence though, it was the way that the MAI was negotiated, almost as much as its content, that proved to be its undoing. By the time formal negotiations were launched in May 1995, the main elements of an agreement had already been established: liberalization of restrictions on foreign investment, protection for foreign investors from discrimination and expropriation, and a dispute-settlement mechanism that allowed investors to challenge non-conforming government laws in an international tribunal. Perhaps the most significant problem with the initial negotiation process was the secrecy and lack of inclusion of developing countries, or elements of civil society.

Moreover, finding an institutional home for the MAI was difficult. Neither the UN nor WTO initially appeared favorable and as a result the agreement was lodged with the OECD. Combined with the lack of emphasis on the responsibilities of foreign capitalists, this placement reinforced a perception that the MAI was an initiative to promote the interests of developed country TNCs above that of developing countries.

The MAI's negative reputation is unlikely to change. There is already considerable opposition to its re-emergence in the Doha round of the WTO. Civil society groups, under the banner of the World Development Movement, have proposed an alternative International Investment Agreement (Box 4.1).[13] Perhaps it is time to seriously consider this contender?

Box 4.1
World Development Movement's Provisions for an
International Investment Agreement

Enable governments to attract high quality investment as part of a sustainable development strategy. A rules-based system that provides sufficient stability so that foreign direct investment is attracted to developing countries, while at the same time maintaining sufficient flexibility so developing country governments can attract high quality investment and ensure that the investment contributes to pro-poor growth.

Protect basic rights through global standards for the operations of foreign investors. Corporations, rather than governments, would be responsible for complying with standards to protect the rights of individuals and communities, all based on existing UN agreements.

Using ODA to Promote Pro-Poor Investment

Insufficient domestic enterprise capacity, education, technology, infrastructure, and health prevent the poorest countries from benefiting from inward foreign investment. Imperfect and underdeveloped financial markets have a similar effect. Countries that cross these thresholds create increased opportunities for domestic firms, especially in the small and medium-size enterprises that typically employ people from poorer backgrounds.

In this context, the most helpful role of rich countries may be to leverage ODA together with FDI to promote the development of adequate infrastructure, build skills, and create conditions for businesses to thrive. The UK's Department for International Development (DFID) has pioneered innovative uses of aid to promote major infrastructure projects in the developing world. For example, the Africa Private Infrastructure Financing Facility (APIFF) aims to reduce perceptions of risk that leave potentially productive investments unfunded; it uses grant money to leverage loans from participating banks. The U.S. Department of Commerce pursues specific initiatives to strengthen governance and judicial institutions in other countries in order to improve their business environment.

Promoting Corporate Responsibility and Investment Quality

Two components are critical.

First is transparency—the timely release of critical information that enables an engaged public to make informed decisions about matters that affect them. Transparency over payments to, or revenues received by, government from the extractive sector falls into this category. Transparency, and analysis of the diverse social, environmental, and economic impacts of new investment, will increase the likelihood that more beneficial investments are selected. A major challenge here is to develop indicators that show whether investment is more or less pro-poor.

Here a helpful role for rich countries may be to mandate companies to take better account of, and to disclose, their social and environmental risks. Broader responsibility for good corporate conduct might be promoted through requiring better governance provisions in company law. Transparency of payments to governments could also be mandated through regulations that govern listing on stock exchanges. Interestingly, major TNCs are currently supporting calls for increased regulation in this area. Research might usefully focus on the costs to business of additional reporting burdens, and on how these costs are distributed between TNCs in the developed as well as the less developed world.

Transparency will be of benefit if the standards of developed countries' export credit guarantee agencies can be harmonized around agreed principles of sustainable development and business responsibility. The United States has been a leader in ensuring that safeguards are incorporated into the Overseas Private Investment Corporation and the Export-Import Bank.[14] Initiatives to do this are already underway at the OECD. Targeted research on the variation in these standards across countries, their efficacy, and whether or not they actually lead to declines in investment (as claimed by skeptics). should be a high priority.

Second, people affected by investment decisions need better access to power. Rules-based institutions such as the courts provide one avenue for people to challenge decisions made by firms and governments and to negotiate outcomes on an equal basis. Independent arbitration, mediation, or ombudsman processes are others. Here the role of rich countries might be to promote domestic legislation that allows people in developing countries to challenge companies that are domiciled in rich countries. The U.S. Foreign Corrupt Practices Act is one example, as is the OECD Convention on Bribery and Corruption.[15] The International Finance Corporation and the Multilateral Investment Guarantee Agency each have an ombudsman function, which offers citizens of any country affected by the investments of these agencies an opportunity to raise and resolve legitimate disputes. This is a model that rich country governments might consider for major project finance or investments supported by their national export credit guarantee agencies.

Reducing Subsidies and Tariffs That Limit Competition

The attractions of FDI can distort government policy and result in perverse incentives. Among rich and poor countries alike, comparative research that increases public awareness of the types of inducements offered, and the distribution of their costs and benefits—both between and within countries—would help to promote pro-poor outcomes.

Liberalizing trade relationships will likely increase the capacity of developing countries to make the most of FDI. Deeper analysis of how rich countries' tariffs on manufactured imports affect the destinations of FDI would yield useful indicators of development friendliness.

Concluding Remarks

This chapter has explored the relationship between FDI, poverty, and rich country policies. FDI, like domestic investment, can distort governance, as well as government policy and the use of resources. Inducements to attract FDI may leave the poor even more marginalized. Greater transparency over investment quality and quantity, and the decisions of government, combined with access to power, are fundamental to improving the developmental impact of FDI. Much of the onus for promoting pro-poor outcomes from investment lies with developing country governments themselves.

Among rich countries, a small number of factors distinguish those that actively promote pro-poor FDI targeted to the developing world from those that do not. These factors are:

- domestic legislation that promotes improved corporate governance, especially in relation to disclosure of social and environmental risk;
- safeguard measures on export credit and guarantee agencies that promote social and environmental diligence;
- domestic legislation that gives foreign nationals access to rich country judicial processes to contest international investment; and

- the level of subsidies and tariffs that limit international competition.

A comparative evaluation of rich country policies to investment along these four parameters—and the extent to which they resonate with international development goals—must be a high priority. The basic question of FDI quality is still contentious and requires further research. Understanding whether higher standards for investment will reduce the competitiveness of rich country companies is a thorn that must be plucked in order to move this agenda forward.

Notes

1. The author is director at Synergy, Oxford, UK.
2. They conclude that in most sectors, "access to major markets is both an important constraint on location and a major incentive for multinational production. The skills and infrastructure base of national economies constrain the capacity of firms to switch production from one country to another." Further, they note that "the advantages of familiarity, agglomeration and economies of scale generate a geographical concentration."
3. Franklin (2002).
4. Asian Development Bank (1999).
5. Organization for Economic Cooperation and Development (2002: 5).
6. Examples include the oil states in the Gulf, Venezuela, Nigeria, and Mexico.
7. Ross (2001).
8. Ibid., 280.
9. UK Government (2000).
10. See www.kelianmineclosure.org for details of decisions taken by the Mine Closure Steering Committee.
11. Toft (1997).
12. World Development Movement, December 1998.
13. http://www.wdm.org.uk/cambriefs/Wto/TNCs.htm, viewed on 10 December 2002.
14. Seymour et al. (2002).
15. http://www.oecd.org/oecd/pages/home/displaygeneral/0,3380,EN-document-88-nodirectorate-no-no-7198-31,00.html viewed on 22 May 2003.

References

Asian Development Bank. (1999). *Fighting Poverty in Asia and the Pacific: The Poverty Reduction Strategy*, ADB, Philippines.

Dollar, D., and Kraay, A. (2000). *Growth is Good for the Poor*. Working Paper, Development Research Group, World Bank.

Franklin, S. (2002). "Globalisation's New Boom." *The World in 2003. The Economist* Newspaper Ltd.

Held, D., A. McGrew, D. Goldblatt, and J. Perraton. (2000). *Global Transformations*. Cambridge: Polity Press.

Organization for Economic Cooperation and Development. (2002). *Foreign Direct Investment for Development*. Paris: OECD.

Ross, M. (2001). *Extractive Sectors and the Poor*. Boston, MA: Oxfam America.

Sachs, J. D., and A. M. Warner. (2001). "The Curse of Natural Resources." *European Economic Review* 45: 827-838.

Seymour, Frances, Lisa Dreier, and Lily Donge. 2002. "Private Finance." In John C. Dernbach, ed, *Stumbling Toward Sustainability*. Washington, DC: Environment Law Institute.

Toft, S. (1997). *Compensation for Resource Development in Papua New Guinea.* Monograph No 6. Law Reform Commission of Papua New Guinea, Australian National University.

World Bank. (2001). *World Development Report 2000/2001: Attacking Poverty*. New York: World Bank and Oxford University Press.

UK Government. (2000). *Eliminating World Poverty: Making Globalisation Work for the Poor*. Government White Paper, UK.

UNCTAD. (2002). *World Investment Report 2002.*

5

The Development Impact of Developed-World Policies on Developing Countries: The Case of Trade

Vangelis Vitalis[1]

Trade is a major engine of world economic growth. Reflecting the removal of many import and export barriers, the volume of international merchandise trade today is nearly twenty times greater than it was in 1950. Aside from being the source of unprecedented wealth for many countries, trade has also led to wider and deeper forms of international economic interdependence.

This chapter briefly delineates the relationship between trade and economic growth and then reviews the state of knowledge on the impact of developed countries' trade policies on developing countries.[2] Particular reference is made to five areas of trade policy which appear to have the most negative effects on developing countries' economic prospects: tariff policies; agricultural protection; restrictions on trade in manufactured goods, particularly textiles and clothing; barriers to trade in services; and the distorting impact of some developed-world regulations and standards, including voluntary measures. It is argued that these five areas should form the core of any putative agenda for developed-world trade-policy reform. Potential areas of research to help fill knowledge gaps in these areas are also identified.

In the context of this agenda it is argued that a focus on the economic effects alone is insufficient to inform trade policymaking in an age where it is acknowledged that economic, environmental, and social effects have interrelated impacts. The call for greater policy coherence that came out of the World Summit on Sustainable Development (WSSD) underlines the point. In short, trade policy can no longer be developed without reference to other policy settings. What is needed is a policy framework that moves beyond the conventional methodologies in a way that improves trade policymakers' understanding of the wider effects on developing countries. Future research should therefore focus on how to assist policymakers to better understand the effects of trade policies across the environmental, social, and economic dimensions of sustainable development.

Trade and Economic Growth

Numerous cross-sectional analyses have shown the positive effect of trade on per capita income growth in developing countries.[3] It is estimated, for instance, that those developing countries that have experienced the fastest growth in exports of non-energy products have experienced annual growth in real GDP 1 percent higher than countries with slower export growth.[4]

Developing countries receive considerably more foreign exchange revenue from trade than from almost any other source. One study concluded that, on a per capita annual basis, developing country exports generate more than thirty times as much revenue (US $322) as aid disbursements ($10). Similarly, the least developed countries generate 12 times as much from exports ($113 per capita) as from aid ($9).[5] Moreover, a 1 percent rise in exports of the developing country group has the capacity to raise annual per capita income in South Asia by 12 percent, 4 percent in Latin America and East Asia, and up to 20 percent in Sub-Saharan Africa.[6] This could reduce the number of people living in poverty by nearly 130 million, or 12 percent of the world total, with the greatest gains likely in Sub-Saharan Africa.[7] In short, even relatively modest improvements in developing countries' levels of access to developed-world markets are likely to generate expanded exports and thus improved revenues.[8]

The negative effects of the trade-related policies in force in developed countries are well known. Essentially, the theory is that barriers to trade raise the prices of both imports and domestic goods. Aside from limiting consumer choices in developed countries, protection also implies higher consumer prices, because it eases competitive pressures. More specifically, developed-world protection fragments markets, limiting exporters' ability and incentives to lower production costs from specialization and access to cheaper inputs. By raising prices, higher trade barriers act like a tax hike with attendant income effects. The burden of these kinds of policies falls particularly heavily on developing countries and has a negative impact on economic growth and poverty reduction.

There is a growing consensus that freer access to international markets would in most cases benefit both developed and developing countries. Depending on the models used, estimates of the annual static welfare gains from the elimination of all barriers to goods and services trade range from $250 billion to $620 billion, of which at least a third to a half (depending on the model one favors) would accrue to developing countries.[9] Table A5.1 summarizes the estimated welfare effects of liberalization.

Against the background of the "win-win" argument, it is useful to consider the product composition of OECD imports from developing countries. This has diversified over the past decade and the share of manufactured products has increased, counterbalancing the weaker growth in imports of raw materials and agricultural products.

Meanwhile, the proportion of OECD imports coming from developing countries has increased only modestly, and the share of least developed countries in OECD imports over the same period has barely changed at all. Overall, developing countries supplied roughly a quarter of OECD imports in 2000, but low-income developing countries supplied less than 5 percent of the total, and least-developed economies supplied only a meager 1 percent.[10]

Although there is broad agreement about the wider welfare effects of trade liberalization, there is still disagreement about the direction of causality between trade and growth. The evidence is such that one should not assume that any single economic policy tool (such as the lowering of trade barriers) would accelerate economic development or poverty reduction.[11] If a country is to reduce poverty, many domestic reforms[12] are required in tandem with international (and domestic) trade policy improvements. In short, trade policy is only one element of any successful growth and development strategy.[13]

While many developing countries are benefiting from changes in the international trading regime and are likely to enjoy further positive gains, some may not. Countries of Sub-Saharan Africa, in particular, appear to have been unable to capitalize on the modest reductions in developed-world protection of, for instance, agricultural markets. There seem to be two reasons why. First is the ongoing conflicts in the region. Second, while agriculture is an important part of many Sub-Saharan African economies, much of it is of the subsistence type, not readily convertible to tradable commodities. Further, the commodities (for example coffee and cocoa) that these countries have traded internationally have generally suffered reductions in world prices in the past ten years with negative effects on poverty reduction.

It is also worth emphasizing that developed-world trade reforms may affect the poor in developing countries, particularly in the short term, in complex ways, some of them negative. Poor urban workers and farmers, for instance, may stand to benefit from the reduction of developed-world barriers as a consequence of faster export growth, higher producer prices, increased wages, and greater demand for labor. But in the short term, some of the effects of such changes may not be so positive, for two reasons. First, the removal or reduction of developed-world agricultural subsidies (for instance) may raise the prices of internationally traded goods compared with non-traded products. Second, wage levels and employment in developing countries may not move in the expected direction. If, for instance, a developing country protects certain sectors that employ significant numbers of poor people and these are suddenly exposed to more efficient external competition, there is a risk of adverse impacts.[14]

Five aspects of developed-world trade policies require reform to maximize benefits for developing countries. For each of these, the following sections outline the impact that the current policy settings have on developing countries, with particular reference to poverty alleviation.

Tariff Policies

There is growing support for the proposition that one of the most effective ways to raise per capita income growth in developing countries is to permit their goods free access to markets in OECD countries. In 2001, for instance, New Zealand implemented duty-free access for all products from least developed countries. The European Union has its "Everything but Arms" initiative.[15] Japan has adjusted its Generalized System of Preferences to allow tariff-free access for least developed countries. And the United States has offered unrestricted access to its markets for exporters from selected African countries, with a particular focus on those whose per capita incomes are below $1,500.[16]

Preferential arrangements are very valuable to those fortunate enough to benefit. UNCTAD has estimated that full preferential access for *all* of the least-developed countries simply to the Quad economies is likely to raise the LDCs' annual per capita income levels by 4 percent (resulting in a small global welfare gain of around US$1 billion).[17]

But nonsymmetrical market access programs have several potential difficulties.[18] First, critics have noted that the consequence of preferential arrangements may be to increase the least-developed countries' exports at the expense of other developing countries' exports, though there is some debate as to the magnitude of such a change.[19] Second, preferential trade mechanisms are often associated with uncertainty about whether the preferential access will be maintained, and for how long. This may inhibit or at least distort investment and decision-making for export industries. Third, a country's growth in incomes as a consequence of improved access may propel it above the threshold of eligibility. This has been a perverse feature, commonly criticized, of the preferential access scheme applied for selected African countries by the United States. Fourth, the structure of these mechanisms is such that they may distort least developed countries' export profiles toward the improved access, away from areas of actual comparative advantage.[20]

More generally, tariffs in developed countries still disproportionately affect exports from developing and least-developed countries. Between a sixth and a third of the tariff peaks extant in Quad economies, for instance, exceed 30 percent, and some tariffs exceed 200 percent.[21] Tariff peaks in the Quad economies affect about 5 percent of all exports from developing countries, and 11 percent of exports from least-developed countries.[22]

The tariff rates applied by OECD countries vary considerably. Those applying to agricultural goods, for instance, are generally higher than others; indeed, this has effectively ensured that imports from developing countries are absent over wide ranges of added-value items in the food industry, and sometimes even for major agricultural export products in individual developed markets. Developing countries also suffer from the effects of tariffs precisely in those areas where they appear to be most competitive, including sugar, fish, cereals, fruits and vegetables, clothing, and footwear.[23] Export producers in developing countries tend to be small and medium-sized enterprises, and these producers find the higher rates particularly difficult to absorb into their operating margins.

The poor performance of developed-country tariff-rate quotas (TRQs) is also a cause for concern. In theory, this mechanism allows better market access for a selected group of developing countries. In reality, the average fill rates of TRQs have been low. This reflects discriminatory administrative systems[24] and high "in-quota" rates that in some cases exceed the Quad's average for agricultural products. The out-of-quota rates are astronomical—including for instance a 130 percent tariff on above-quota bananas, effectively closing the out-of-quota market for developing countries in this subsector. In agricultural and food industry products, there is little if any developing-country trade exceeding the tariff-rate quota levels.[25]

OECD tariffs on tropical products are of particular interest to many developing countries. These tariffs are, for the most part, low or nonexistent because such goods do not compete with local products, but there are some small significant exceptions. The EU maintains several tariff peaks to shield from external competition those of its regions that can produce tropical goods. EU tariff structures are also designed to protect output margins and market access for the members of the African, Caribbean, and Pacific Group of States (APC) countries.[26] Tariffs on bananas are the most egregious example, but tobacco and sugar are two other commodities where exporters not benefiting from preferential schemes have been shut out of the market.[27]

Tariff peaks are also a significant problem for processed tropical goods. Processed coffee and cocoa, for instance, both attract substantially higher tariffs than their raw and unprocessed equivalents.

Tariff Policies: Knowledge Gaps

Further research is needed on several aspects of the impact of tariffs on developing countries.

One is the costs and benefits of changing the current preferential arrangements that developed countries provide to developing countries. For instance, many exporters in the Caribbean and in the South Pacific depend heavily on the preferential access provided by the EU and have developed their export-producing sectors to respond to these artificially created incentives. This makes these countries particularly vulnerable to any changes in developed-world trade policies on preferential agreements, use of the Generalized System of Preferences, and so on.[28] A useful area of research would therefore be to assess the implications of any changes in preferential access for small country exporters and to consider how to address difficulties that may emerge as a consequence.

Another area of particular significance for many developing countries is the concept of "special and differential treatment." This concept is a component of the World Trade Organization Agreements and specifically referenced in the Doha Declaration,[29] but the difficulty has been to give it substance. Research could usefully focus on defining what exactly special and differential treatment might mean in the context of each of the WTO Agreements, and on outlining the costs and benefits of various approaches to the concept.

Agricultural Protection

Agriculture is a key sector for most developing countries. In the least-developed countries it contributes nearly a third of GDP, compared with less than 3 percent in developed countries. The poor in most developing countries are heavily engaged in subsistence farming, and food accounts for a significant proportion of all poor people's expenditure. A high proportion of the poor are rural—more than 60 percent worldwide, nearly 90 percent in China and Bangladesh, and between 65 percent and 90 percent in Sub-Saharan Africa.[30] In theory, therefore, trade policies that reduce rural poverty will also reduce global poverty levels. And the evidence suggests that those developing countries that have enjoyed the fastest agricultural export growth have also tended to achieve faster agricultural GDP growth, with accompanying increases in rural incomes and poverty reduction.[31]

The key international commitment on agricultural trade is contained in the Doha WTO Ministerial Declaration, which identifies a shortlist of areas for negotiation in agriculture. The Declaration notes that countries will work toward "reductions of, with a view to phasing out, all forms of export subsidies; and substantial reductions in trade-distorting domestic support."[32] The following paragraphs outline the current situation in these areas.

Export Subsidies

Export subsidies have a significant impact on world markets, through their ability to increase exports from subsidizing countries and to depress world prices. In this way, they depress the returns to non-subsidized exporters. It is interesting to note that only twenty-five of the current WTO members have export subsidy reduction commitments in their ACC/4 schedules, and that only fourteen of these members are actually using export subsidies. The overwhelming majority of the export subsidy commitments are concentrated in the EU countries, Switzerland, and the United States.

Modeling work suggests that a complete elimination of export subsidies would raise global incomes by $3.6 billion a year by 2010.[33] The greatest beneficiaries would be taxpayers in the European Union.[34] Developing countries would benefit too: world market prices for agricultural products would rise and lead to higher returns for producers. In theory, this should benefit net exporters and farmers in importing countries, though it may add to import costs for economies that are net importers of agricultural goods.

Some have argued that countries that are net importers of food may lose as a consequence of the elimination of export subsidies. This argument is overstated, however. The most significant export subsidies are provided when supplies in exporting countries are at their highest and world prices are therefore already low. Much smaller subsidies are provided when prices are high. Thus, export subsidies may benefit low-income food importers the least precisely during their times of greatest need and the most during their times of least need.[35,36]

Food Aid

It can be argued that the use of food aid—assistance in kind (as distinct from famine relief) to developing and least-developed countries—is a way of concealing export subsidization. Food aid has been used to dump surplus production in a way that negatively affects commercial markets by depressing prices.[37] Deliveries of milk powder, poultry, and beef under the guise of food aid by the European Union to Russia in 1998 and 1999 are cases in point. EU members overproduced these products in the years running up to 1998-99 and consequently, many non-EU traders with Russia suspected that the shipments were designed less to meet the needs of the Russian poor than to help offload the oversupply created by the Common Agricultural Policy (CAP).[38] Food aid can also negatively affect commercial distribution systems in developing countries. Displacement of domestic production is another likely byproduct of food aid. An alternative to food aid would be for developed countries to give countries financial assistance to purchase products at the going world prices.

Domestic Support

Since the Doha commitments, subsidy policies in developed economies have barely been dented and in some cases have worsened.[39] Despite the Doha commitment to "substantial reductions in trade-distorting" domestic support for agriculture, subsidies for farmers in the United States will rise by 70 percent (some $173.5 billion) over the coming decade.[40] European Union and Japanese support for farmers will still be greater than that of the United States, even after these significant increases. Figure 5.1 emphasizes the predominance of the three wealthiest OECD members/groupings (EU, Japan, United States) in providing such assistance to their farmers.

The net effect of domestic support policies in developed countries is to increase production levels and, by inflating consumer prices, to discourage demand. The significant surpluses that result have to be sold (or "given away") on world markets, often with the assistance of export subsidies or via food aid with an attendant depressing effect on prices. Moreover, the range of mechanisms used to deliver support to the sector prevents consumers and farmers from responding to realistic price information. In this way, a larger share of the burden of adjusting to shocks is passed on to other participants in the market, widening the fluctuations in world prices.

Farm support in OECD member countries absorbs more than $300 billion a year, or about 1.2 percent of those countries' GNP, and more than five times what these countries spend on development assistance to developing countries. The individual statistics

Figure 5.1
Developed-World Domestic Support, by Country

1986-88

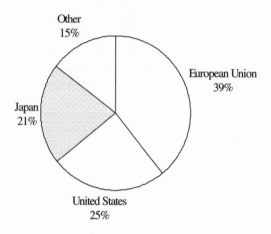

1995-97

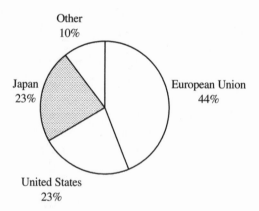

Sources: OECD (2001), *The Uruguay Round Agreement on Agriculture: An Evaluation of Its Implementation in OECD Countries*, OECD, Paris.

are sobering. Annually, for instance, the EU spends nearly €$2 billion on subsidizing its sugar farmers to produce a product that can be produced more efficiently and cheaply in the developing world. In the United States, oilseed farmers receive nearly $12,000 a year each in income support.[41] Compare this to the modest aim of achieving the Millennium Development Goal of raising developing world incomes above $1 a day.

The costs to consumers of such assistance are similarly significant. The Common Agricultural Policy has been estimated to cost an average family of four around €1,450 a year in artificially supported prices and direct costs of €100 per head as taxpayers to subsidies farmers directly.[42] More lightheartedly, the New Zealand Government has estimated that EU consumers and taxpayers transferred sufficient funds, through a variety of border measures and domestic price support policies, to pay for each of the OECD's 41 million dairy cows to fly first class around the world one and a half times.[43] A similar more up-to-date calculation concluded that, not only could the cows fly around the world, they would have nearly €1,000 spending money as well![44]

It is difficult to quantify the impact on developing countries of developed countries' agricultural protection. This is partly because the specific costs of policies depend on very precise information about implementation and flow-on effects. Another problem is that not enough is known about how the distribution of assets like land, capital, and labor might affect any welfare gains accruing to developing countries. Nor is enough known about how much rural prices and wages might change as a result of multiplier effects of improvements in agricultural trade. While aggregate data are available on income effects, not enough is known at a disaggregated level, for instance about the multiplier effects of market access changes on domestic agricultural wages and prices. Moreover, much of the modeling work is underpinned by assumptions about supply responses. Though the calculations tend to be sophisticated and are based on available data, we still do not know precisely how producers will react to market access improvements effected via changes in domestic support for agriculture.

Bearing in mind these caveats, the international modeling work on the likely effects of the liberalization of agricultural trade does suggest significant global welfare gains. From a full agricultural liberalization, these may be as high as $20 billion a year for developing countries.[45] Other estimates indicate gains of $15 billion a year to developing countries from a partial liberalization.[46]

More recent modeling work, summarized in Table 5.1, amplifies these results. It shows that reducing direct and indirect agricultural subsidies in the developed world would produce potentially significant gains for agricultural producers in low- and middle-income developing countries and for developed-country consumers (and taxpayers). These figures should not be accepted uncritically, but they do suggest that substantial overall welfare gains are likely to developing countries.

Declines in developed-country domestic support (and indeed export subsidies), coupled with reductions in border protection, should affect prices by reducing the global supply of many agricultural products. The price rises are likely to be significant—the price of wheat, for instance, is expected to increase over the 1993 level by 6.2 percent, prices of dairy products by 12.2 percent, and prices of beef and veal by 7.2 percent[47]—and to have a positive effect on profits and incomes in developing countries.

The gains from a decline in developed-country agricultural protection are expected to accrue mainly to middle- and upper-income developing countries. These are countries that have reformed their agricultural sectors and therefore stand to benefit most from improvements in global trade access. The likely losers from liberalization are expected to be a small number of least-developed countries, specifically those whose agricultural reform has lagged and which are net importers of food. Potential improvements in

Table 5.1
Enlightened Self-Interest-Gains from Agricultural Reform for Developing
Countries *and* Gains for the Developed World

	(US $1997 bn)	
Countries/regions	Removal of border protection	Removal of all protection
Low and middle income countries	22.3	26.0
Western Europe	21.4	17.0
United States	4.3	5.0

Source: Table abbreviated from J. Beghin, D. Roland-Holst, and D. van der Mensbrugge (2002), *Global Agricultural Trade and the Doha Round, What are the Implications for North and South?* Paper presented to the OECD/World Bank Global Forum on Agriculture, 23-24 May, Paris, OECD. Caveats to the results cited in the original paper (p. 9), apply equally to this version.

welfare may be negatively affected by distortions in domestic economies.[48]

The principal divide between winners and losers from developed-country agricultural trade reform is likely to be between the urban and rural poor in developing countries. Given that the urban poor buy their food, rather than producing it, they are likely to be particularly hard hit by food price rises. Nevertheless, it is worth remembering that poor households can vary greatly in their composition and structure, so that changes in the international trading regime for agriculture may have important second-round spillovers, many of which can reasonably be assumed to be beneficial.

Finally, while there is no doubt that some individual economies would suffer from increases in world prices for agricultural goods, for most of the least-developed economies any losses are likely to be relatively small. In only a handful of countries, for instance, do the estimated welfare changes represent more than 1 percent of GDP.[49]

Agricultural Protection: Knowledge Gaps

An area of growing concern to agricultural traders is the expanding monopsonistic power of developed-world distributors and wholesalers, who purchase a range of developing country goods, including food products. Supermarket chains in particular are believed to have an increasingly central position in purchasing. Indeed, many such chains in Germany, France, the United States, and the UK in particular are believed to be price makers for many agricultural products. Much of the evidence on this kind of monopsonistic behavior to date is anecdotal; it would be useful to put some figures on the size of the problem.

Better insights are also needed into the policy tradeoffs that may need to be made as a consequence of improvements in access to developed-world markets for agricultural products. Policymakers will need to assess not only the economic and social benefits of the potential of increased revenue as a consequence of market access improvements) but also the environmental effects.[50] What, for instance, would better access for Uzbek cotton to developed-world markets mean for water use and the Aral Sea in Uzbekistan? The water supply of Uzbek cotton farmers is dwindling. Currently, more than 40 percent of the water taken from the Aral Sea to irrigate the cotton fields of Uzbekistan evaporates before it even reaches those fields (Uzbek farmers use open channels, not pipes, for irrigation).[51] What would a 5 percent market improvement for the Uzbeks really mean for the country's water supplies and its long-term development? Policymakers need to know whether there is a risk that as Uzbek farmers seek to meet the new demand for cotton, they may destroy their agricultural system altogether, leaving a lasting problem with catastrophic effects on poverty alleviation.

This research suggestion is not intended to suggest that market access should be limited or calibrated simply because it may harm the environment. Rather, the argument is that policies to improve market access need to consider natural resource effects. Without flanking policies, they may trigger lasting damage to the economic growth prospects of developing countries. In short, developed-world policymakers need more comprehensive information to help them minimize negative environmental effects and maximize economic benefits. If market access is improved for Uzbek cotton, for instance, developed country policymakers should be in a position to assess the wider effects of such an improvement in a way that offers an opportunity to think about flanking measures (such as enhanced technical assistance for improved irrigation techniques).

Trade in Manufactured Goods

While reform of developed-country support for agriculture is likely to have the greatest impact on the rural poor in developing countries, similar reductions in trade-distorting support for manufacturing, specifically in the clothing and textiles sectors, could have substantial positive effects on the urban poor.[52]

Manufacturing is of growing economic importance to almost every developing country, though to varying degrees. In Sub-Saharan African countries, for instance, manufacturing accounts for 17 percent of GDP, compared with 21 percent in a range of high-income developing countries and 29 percent in middle-income developing countries. Manufactures also make up a significant share of exports, albeit for a smaller group of developing countries: nearly three fourths of exports (72 percent) for East Asian countries, and just under half (46 percent) for Latin American and Caribbean countries; for developed countries, the share is nearly 81 percent.[53]

Given this level of concentration, it is perhaps not surprising that developed countries have sought to protect their industries, particularly those perceived to be most vulnerable to third-country competition. Thus, while 90 percent of manufacturing tariffs in developed countries are below 10 percent, only about half of textile and clothing tariffs are so low. Moreover, OECD country tariffs on imports of textiles and clothing rise to more than 28 percent, down only slightly from 35 percent in the pre-Uruguay Round period.[54] Aside from tariffs, manufactured products face a range of non-tariff barriers, most significantly on textiles and clothing.

Textiles and Clothing

The WTO provides the framework for international trade in these industries through the Uruguay Round Agreement on Textiles and Clothing (ATC). The ATC represents an attempt to move away from the 1974 Multi-Fiber Arrangement (MFA) through the progressive abolition of quantitative restrictions on the basis of a multifactor formula to be implemented over ten years, with full quota elimination by the end of 2004.[55]

The ATC has significantly improved the prospects for developing countries to access OECD members' markets. It restricts the right of importers to introduce new quotas and outlaws voluntary export restraints (which had functioned in a manner akin to MFA quotas). Developing countries have nonetheless expressed considerable skepticism about its benefits. Products integrated into the WTO to date have been concentrated in the relatively low-value-added range and the phase-out process has been backloaded, so that nearly half of all the quantitative restrictions to be eliminated remain in force until the very end of the implementation period. Although a schedule for the elimination of many quotas is in place, most of these restrictions are still there. It is also feared that the political will in OECD countries to dismantle protection is weakening in the face of vocal domestic lobbies.

Meanwhile, many efficient developing country producers are concerned about the increasing dominance of China—already the world's largest clothing exporter and the second-largest textile exporter—whose presence is expected to significantly alter the distribution of gains from textile and clothing liberalization. Table A5.2

Figure 5.2
Share of Developing and OECD Country Services in Total Trade, 1980-2000

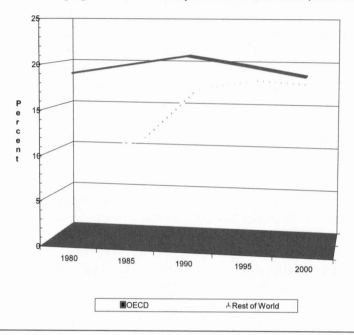

Source: OECD (2002), *The Case for Open Services Markets*, OECD, Paris.

Figure 5.3
Significance of Services in Selected Countries' Exports: Commercial Services
Exports as a Share of Total Exports, 1999

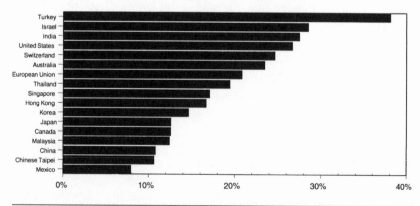

Source: OECD (2002), *The Case for Open Services Markets*, OECD, Paris.

shows the growing dominance of China in textiles and clothing trade.

Quotas and preferential arrangements on textiles and clothing affect developing countries in several ways, particularly production transfers from low-cost to higher-cost suppliers, through the reallocation from constrained exporters to domestic suppliers and from the same exporters to unrestricted exporters. Other permutations have similar effects; for instance, the system establishes and perpetuates property rights to export the permitted amounts of these products, and the rights remain entrenched even after the exporting country has become too economically advanced to justify them. These inefficiencies reduce exports and output by efficient producers, with corresponding declines in incomes and employment. Given that in developing countries, textiles and clothing tend to be produced by urban unskilled workers, the poverty implications can be significant.

Benefits from Reduced Protection

The costs of protection have been substantial. Throughout the 1980s, consumers in the United States, for instance, paid 58 percent higher prices for textiles and clothing because of U.S. import restrictions. Moreover, the costs that quotas, high tariffs, or both impose on U.S. households for clothing alone have been estimated at between $8.5 billion and $18 billion, while for textiles and clothing combined the bill exceeded $27 billion.[56]

Eliminating developed-world protection on manufactured products would have positive price and income effects for developing countries. It has been estimated, for instance, that a 40 percent reduction in tariffs on manufactured goods would expand the volume of global trade by $380 billion, with nearly 75 percent of the gains accruing to developing countries.[57]

It is important to acknowledge, however, that the likely welfare benefits would be unevenly distributed among developing countries. East and South Asian countries are expected to enjoy the greatest benefits, with sizeable gains for China (and Hong Kong), Vietnam, the Philippines, and Singapore in particular.[58] Interestingly, the models suggest that these economies benefit the most because of the sharp reductions (and attendant efficiencies) they have achieved in their industries. In short, harvesting the greatest benefits from international liberalization of trade in manufactured goods may depend, in part, on developing countries' own domestic reform processes and attendant improvements in the efficiency of resource allocations.

In clothing and textiles in particular, liberalization of developed-country restrictions will benefit those developing countries that liberalize their own industries and have the most significant factor endowments, thus multiplying existing comparative advantages. Countries with large and relatively well-educated urban workforces are expected to benefit the most. Given that China and India fall into this category and that their populations comprise a significant proportion of the world's poor, liberalization of the trade in textiles and clothing is likely to have significant positive effects on overall levels of global poverty.

Certainly, for a favored few developing countries, the allocation of quotas under the prevailing system provides rents and removes the negative impact on the terms of trade. For them, the impending abolition of restrictions presents something of a problem because they will no longer enjoy guaranteed market access. The counterargument to this is that such distortional measures have stifled growth in these sectors and that the long-run effects of reform will be positive for these countries.

Manufactured Goods: Knowledge Gaps

A growing problem for developing countries is the increased willingness of many OECD members to apply contingent measures as an adjunct to tariffs. Use of these measures has risen faster in textiles and clothing than in any other sector; in 1990, anti-dumping investigations for textiles, for instance, accounted for barely 5 percent of the total, but a decade later they accounted for more than 11 percent.[59] Contingent measures are a serious concern for developing countries, particularly as the transition to the post-ATC phase is likely to be rather bumpy, with attendant pressures (via domestic lobby groups) on OECD members to either slow the pace of reform or impose countervailing measures. One area of potentially fruitful research would therefore be to examine the economic costs of such measures for developing countries.

As in agriculture, more information would be useful on the wider impacts of improvements in the international trading environment for manufactured goods. Again, the idea would be to help policymakers make sense of potential tradeoffs toward Pareto-optimal decisions. For example, do developed-world trade policymakers sufficiently understand what is happening to global CO_2 emissions and domestic pollution as production in developing countries responds to market access improvements? In China, sharp rises in production, partly as the consequence of improvements in international market access levels, have markedly worsened urban air quality. The cost of the resulting health problems and property damage has been conservatively estimated at more than $20 billion a year.[60]

As with the Uzbek example cited earlier, the point of seeking information about the wider effects of improved market access is not to deter policy reform but to improve policymakers' awareness, in developing and developed countries, of its broader impacts. In this way, when market access improvements are initiated they can be developed in tandem with (for instance) focused technical assistance and technology transfer to mitigate spillovers such as air pollution.

Trade in Services

Trade in services is rapidly becoming more important for developing countries. The share of services in global GDP rose by five percentage points between 1980 and 1998, with the rise for developing countries even greater at nine percentage points. The share of services in some developing countries' exports is increasingly comparable to that of many developed countries (Figure 5.2 and Figure 5.3). [61,62] In India, Malaysia, Thailand, and Singapore, for instance, the shares are comparable to or higher than those of G-7 economies such as Japan and Canada. Indeed, India's share of commercial services exports as a proportion of total exports is greater even than that of the EU and the United States.

The main international agreement governing trade in services is the General Agreement on Trade in Services (GATS). This entered into force on 1 January 1995 and covers all trade in services, except bilateral aviation rights and services purchased or supplied in the exercise of governmental authority. Relatively few liberalizing commitments have been made under GATS. Developed countries, for instance, made commitments in only 47 percent of the 620 sector-mode pairs, while developing countries made commitments in less than 16 percent. Furthermore, many of the so-called commitments amount to little more than an agreement not to add more barriers.[63]

The case for liberalizing global trade in services is broadly the same as that in goods trade; the benefits from enhanced competition combine efficiency gains by local producers with lower prices and greater diversity for consumers.

The gains from liberalizing services trade may in fact be substantially greater than those from liberalizing trade in goods: first, levels of protection are higher in the services sector, and second, liberalization is likely to create additional positive spillovers derived from the associated movement of labor and capital. In this context, the global welfare effects of services trade liberalization are believed to be roughly as large as those associated with full liberalization of goods trade, or around $130 billion annually.[64]

It is also argued that developing countries may gain the most (in aggregate) from liberalizing their services trade. One study indicates that a 25 percent reduction in services protection would yield a 1 percent increase in GDP annually for the EU, 1.2 percent for Japan and the United States, at least 1.4 percent for India,[65] and more than 2.5 percent for ASEAN countries.[66]

Some developing countries are net exporters of services and they therefore have a substantial stake in improvements in services trade. South Africa, for instance, is a growing force in telecommunications,[67] and India is one of the most significant players in the burgeoning supply of call centers and information technology services in general.[68] More generally, studies suggest that the potential market for developing country exports of long-distance services may be worth up to 5 percent of the total employment in services in the G7 countries, implying export revenues of up to $120 billion.[69] There is little doubt therefore that improvements in international services-related market access will deliver significant gains for developing countries.[70]

Trade in Services: Knowledge Gaps

There is enormous potential scope for research on trade in services, but the key to establishing a research agenda relevant to developing countries is to focus specifically on areas that have the greatest potential to deliver economic gains to them in the short to

Box 5.1
Developed-World Regulations and Impacts on
Developing Countries: The Case of IFCO[71]

The International Fruit Container Organization (IFCO) was established in response to a German Government regulatory requirement stipulating that retailers should meet all the costs of recycling or disposing of packaging materials. The IFCO system offers retailers returnable plastic crates, as opposed to the standard wooden crates used by many developing-world exporters. With more than 70 million crates in circulation and German Government support, IFCO has emerged as the single largest packaging supplier for fresh produce globally. This has reduced the market share of developing country producers of crates favoring simpler materials and more intensive use of local labor, causing a decline in production with attendant implications for employment and incomes. Some developing countries see this initiative and its explicit German Government support as an example of how developed countries can manipulate technical regulations to increase market share.

For more information about the IFCO, see http://www.ifcosystems.com

gains for exporting developing countries.[76] Similarly, an examination of the effect of pesticide regulations concluded that a 10 percent increase in stringency levels would depress banana exports from developing countries by nearly 15 percent.[77]

While these studies have established that there is a problem, the costs associated with particular mandatory standards are not known, globally or at a disaggregated level, nor in terms of their effects on income in developing countries. Given countries' increasing recourse to standards and regulations, this is an important knowledge gap.

Voluntary Environmental Labels

Over the past decade, consumers have shown growing interest in how their purchasing decisions may affect the environment. One of the responses to this green consumerism has been the establishment of government-backed and private voluntary eco-labels. The appeal of this market-oriented mechanism for sustainable development is clear: it simultaneously informs consumers about the environmental impact of their consumption and provides producers with a way to extract a price premium by accurately translating the mood of consumers into environmentally friendly product development.

One of the main trade-related risks presented by voluntary eco-labeling programs is that they may act as a kind of non-tariff barrier, favoring particular process and production technologies. Such technologies may be unavailable, unsuitable, or prohibitively expensive for trading partners and there is a suspicion that voluntary eco-labels may therefore have the potential to reduce market access for third countries.[78] Box 5.2 gives an example of the kind of market access restrictions that developing countries may face as a consequence of private voluntary eco-labels.[79]

Box 5.2
Organic Tomatoes from Uzbekistan[80]

Following the collapse of the Soviet Union, domestic support to the Uzbek fruit and vegetable sector collapsed. This led to the "forced organization" of the industry, which turned to natural crop protection agents (etc.) in place of synthetic pesticides and nitrogen fertilizers. Sensing an opportunity, an Uzbek producer (UzbekOboshFruktoviProm) sought to have its tomatoes certified by the Dutch industry-led voluntary eco-label Milieuwuste Voedingstuinbouw (Environmentally Conscious Cultivation), which uses a butterfly as its logo.[81] This is one of the main eco-labels for goods sold through the lucrative Dutch auction system. The Uzbeks found that the butterfly logo can only be awarded to growers registered with a Dutch fruit and vegetable auction *and* that only Dutch growers and traders are eligible to register.

Feeding this suspicion is the phenomenon that the (WTO-driven) downward trend in tariff measures for certain goods in developed countries in the 1990s has been offset by a rise in the use of private and governmental voluntary eco-labels for the same products. In the late 1990s, for instance, tariffs on certain textiles (garments) and cut flowers in the European Union were progressively reduced in line with WTO commitments, but there was a simultaneous rise in the use of private and government voluntary eco-labels for these goods. There may be many reasons for this rise, but it is a phenomenon worthy of further examination, not least to see whether the use of voluntary eco-labels gave developed-country producers a modest marketing edge to help alleviate the impact of tariff reductions.[82]

Some of the main concerns about voluntary eco-labels rest on three interrelated points. First, some of these programs may have the potential to become a de facto market standard against which consumers assess all products. Second, many of these schemes apply a "one-size-fits-all" approach, which fails to reflect the possibility of differing circumstances, whereby one process or production method may be appropriate in one part of the world, but quite inappropriate in another. Third, many voluntary eco-labels are developed with significant input from domestic producers who, in theory at least, may have protectionist interests in establishing particular standards.

Labor Standards

The issue of establishing minimum national standards for the protection of workers' fundamental rights is of growing significance for both developed and developing countries. The focus of recent attention has been on whether to use the multilateral trading system to enforce labor standards.

Proponents of the use of trade measures argue that a failure to include core labor standards in WTO agreements is not only immoral, but may provide an unfair boost to competitiveness and cause a "race to the bottom." Indeed, they emphasize that the strength of the WTO mechanism is such that core standards can be more effectively imposed through this body than through the International Labor Organization (ILO), which uses peer review and "naming and shaming" to effect changes.[83] Opponents argue that the imposition of labor standards on developing countries through the WTO may undermine one of their fundamental areas of competitiveness, as well as result in discrimination with attendant negative effects on employment, output, and poverty reduction.[84] They argue that ILO remains the appropriate forum to pursue this issue.

More specifically, proponents of the use of trade measures have argued that there are benefits available to those developing countries able to meet specially stipulated standards. In support of this, they note the apparent effectiveness of some voluntary labeling schemes. The Fair Trade label for coffee, for instance, incorporates social concerns. It is frequently cited as a voluntary labeling program that can deliver significant gains for developing countries by providing cachet for a product in high value niche markets. In Berkeley, California, for instance, students successfully lobbied more than 80 percent of local cafes to stock only Fair Trade branded coffee. Supporters of the scheme argue that the label has helped considerably to improve market share in a high value segment of the U.S. coffee market for some smaller developing country producers, including several small Central American countries. The initiative even became the subject of a formal ballot ("Measure O") in Berkeley's November 2002 elections.[85] A similar label for chocolate (under the "Divine" label[86]) also produced according to the Fair Trade standard, is believed to have had a similarly positive effect on market share for small African cocoa producers, with attendant positive income effects.

The Coffee Organization, a group of 40 major U.S. importers and developing country exporters, has strongly criticized the Fair Trade label. It argues that the measure supports prices artificially; favors Central American producers; distorts market signals affecting growing practices by encouraging inefficient producers to stay with coffee, rather than other crops; and has had a negative impact on the larger and more efficient coffee producers, including Brazil, Colombia, and Indonesia. These three countries also have large numbers of rural poor. It appears that some developing countries may be in the curious position of being punished by a voluntary labeling program for being too competitive and too efficient.[87]

The rationale for the use of trade measures to enforce labor standards is not particularly robust. The admittedly few case studies on the subject suggest that using such measures to affect/impose labor standards can indeed, as the Coffee Organization argues, have negative effects on developing countries. Such programs can cause the rigging of competition rules, distort domestic production patterns by concealing market signals, and in this way divert and otherwise distort trade. Other problems may also arise. Arguably the most notorious instance occurred in 1995, when the garment industry in Bangladesh attracted considerable opprobrium in the U.S. media for using child labor. Consumer pressure led to the prompt dismissal of thousands of the child laborers and many ended up working in lower paying and more exploitative jobs, including prostitution.[88]

Carefully calibrated labor standards, however, can have significant positive effects on poverty reduction in developing countries. The key success factor appears to be to align the standards with the country's level of development. Setting an overly ambitious target by, for instance, setting minimum wage levels akin to those in developed countries, and enforcing this through trade sanctions, may negatively affect the very people the measure is designed to support.[89] Instead of a focus on punishment, the answer may lie in enhanced technical assistance and resources, as well as improved access to developed-country markets.

Regulations and Standards: Knowledge Gaps

One way to quantify the impact of regulations and standards has been to use price gaps to shed further light on the economic effects. This can be done most directly by measuring the costs of compliance that developing country exporters incur as a result of developed-world standards and regulations.

In principle such calculations could be enhanced by an indirect assessment of costs, made by calculating a tariff equivalent for the difference between the domestic and world prices of the exported product. The direct approach could also be made more sophisticated by focusing on two types of costs: the cost of adapting process and production methods to new standards/regulations, and the recurrent cost of maintaining compliance.[90]

In practice, both direct and indirect approaches are hindered by measurement difficulties. The direct approach is highly data intensive. To prove its utility it would need to be buttressed by case studies illuminating the impact of developed-country policies through quite specific information on costs. The indicator would also need to take into account different levels of compliance, including compliance with standards of limited relevance to domestic circumstances.[91] The indirect approach may run into difficulties because the impact of the standard/regulation needs to be clearly distinguished from those of other potential causes of the price gap between domestic and world prices. Adjusting for the quality differences between domestic and imported products is also likely to be problematic.

Many developing countries have a negative perception of the impact that private voluntary environmental labels have on their trade flows. On the other hand, many proponents of the schemes argue that these offer cachet to exporters in the form of access to niche markets and thus allow them to charge a price premium. Little research, however, has been undertaken to support either view. Research attention could profitably be devoted therefore to assembling hard evidence with which to test these arguments. Research could also usefully focus on the actual economic costs of such schemes, including costs of compliance (direct, indirect, one-off, and recurring).

Doing More: An Indicator of the Trans-Boundary Impact of Consumption

Conventional trade-related knowledge about the areas outlined in this chapter is extremely useful, insofar as it shows policymakers the areas of greatest potential economic gains for developing countries. Information about the negative effects of tariffs in developed countries can, for instance, help analysts understand the extent and concentration of developed-country border protection. Similarly, measures of the levels of domestic agricultural support provide important insights into how developed-world protection may distort developing country trade flows and therefore economic growth opportunities.

Useful as it is, such conventional information may not meet the needs of policymakers seeking to design an integrated approach to policies affecting developing countries. It cannot, for instance, help policymakers understand the environmental externalities that a country's economic growth and increased consumption impose beyond its national borders.

To pursue an integrated approach that offers insights into policy settings for global impacts, policymakers would need information about the pressure of human consumption patterns on the global biophysical environment. Ideally, this information would indicate whether such pressures place us at risk of crossing thresholds beyond which lie very significant environmental perturbations with high economic, social, and environmental costs. It should also trace the impact of consumption patterns and their resource use regardless of the location of recorded economic activity.

There is a good reason to focus work in this area. At its core, trade is about consumption, and to derive a more complete picture of the impacts of developed countries' trade, it is important to understand the effects of their consumption. A more complete picture of the impact of developed-world consumption patterns, as expressed by trade flows, may enable policymakers to make good on the oft-quoted but under-applied term, "policy coherence." This has become something of a buzzword, particularly for OECD country policymakers,[92] but little has been done to apply the concept in any meaningful way. A major problem remains a lack of relevant information and hard data. Without sufficient data, attempts to achieve policy coherence and integration of policies that have effects across national borders will remain largely meaningless.

Another important reason to focus research attention in this regard is the Plan of Implementation that was agreed by heads of governments at the World Summit on Sustainable Development (WSSD) in Johannesburg in September 2002. In this document, countries not only affirmed their determination to ensure "policy coherence for sustainable development"[93] but also made specific and detailed reference to the urgent need to change unsustainable patterns of production and consumption.[94] Some work has already been undertaken in this area, particularly by OECD countries,[95] but it is relatively narrowly focused (for example on household consumption and on measuring consumption patterns behind political borders). No work to date has addressed the wider and more ambitious question posed by WSSD, that is, what are the trans-boundary effects of developed-world consumption patterns?

Only by having such a clear understanding of the trans-boundary effects of developed-world consumption patterns can developed-world policymakers ensure the design of improved instruments to overcome market and policy failures.[96] Generating the data needed for this task is difficult but not impossible. Trans-boundary human impacts may be charted through consumption patterns, and these are reflected in trade flows. The use of trade data to identify associated environmental effects will measurably assist in setting policies that can better take account of the wider externalities generated by developed-world consumption patterns.

An Example: Measuring Embedded Carbon Flows

An example of what might be done in this regard is to examine embedded carbon flows. CO_2 emissions are an area where we have some reasonably sound scientific knowledge about the impact of human consumption on the global atmosphere. Carbon emissions have a range of negative effects, including on developing countries. Not surprisingly, almost every indicator project underway internationally includes a country's carbon emissions (measured by production output) in its set of indicators of sustainability. And it is precisely the global nature of the issue that has prompted many countries to participate in a multilateral arrangement to address the impact of carbon emissions on climate change.

Yet the current focus on country carbon emission levels alone may tell only part of the story. Conclusions about a country's sustainable development and its impact in a global sense may be distorted by a failure of current measures to take into account the carbon intensity of trade flows. A country's measured emission levels, for instance, may be misleadingly low if it imports significant quantities of carbon embedded in non-energy products (i.e., carbon generated in the production of these goods). A national-level indicator that fails to take into account trade flows can easily underestimate the emissions caused by a country's consumption habits.[97] The magnitude of this problem is underlined by the rapid expansion of international trade.

The problem has already received some analysis, as have ways of measuring it. One (1994) study, for the G7 countries other than Italy, found that significant amounts of carbon were embedded in these countries' imports.[98] For the six countries on average, the embedded carbon in imports added another 13 percent to the total carbon emissions generated domestically. The figure for France exceeded 40 percent, and those for both Canada and the UK exceeded 20 percent. Other analysts have reported similar results.[99] Not surprisingly, the carbon embedded in a country's imports of manufactured products tends to reflect the country's patterns of trade. Indeed, many fossil-fuel-rich developing countries generated more emissions in producing goods for export than they generated overseas in producing goods for import. The reverse is true for many fossil-fuel-poor countries (among them many OECD members). The extent of carbon-intensive trade underlines how misleading and arbitrary is an indicator that measures only the carbon generated in domestic production processes.[100]

These findings highlight the challenges created by trade flows, particularly between developed and developing countries, that need to be addressed in a way that can inform policymaking. Mapping the impact of developed-world consumption decisions through trade flows would make possible a more accurate picture for policymakers of the global effects of such decisions.

Knowledge Gaps

Prioritizing Future Research

The following is a summary list of areas for further research of arguably the greatest value to developing countries:

Tariffs: What are the costs and benefits of eliminating preferential tariffs for small developing and least developed countries? Can elimination be justified given the monoculture production processes that prevail in some smaller African, Caribbean, and South Pacific countries?

How can one define special and differential treatment in the context of each of the WTO Agreements, as well as more generally in terms of multilateral trade negotiations?

Agriculture and manufacturing: Is the phenomenon of monopsonistic purchasing power by developed world distributors and supermarket chains real? What are the costs to developing country traders of this behavior?

What is the real cost of the application by developed countries of contingent measures to developing countries?

What are the wider effects of improved access to developed world markets and the consequences of increased production levels in response to these opportunities? At the national level? At the regional level? And at the global level? What developed-world policy adjustments (technology transfer, technical assistance, etc.), in addition to improved market access, could help mitigate some of the potential difficulties caused by increased production?

Services: What is the impact of anti-competitive practices in the tourism sector? Research could focus on the economic effects on developing country service industries of the discriminatory use of information networks, ancillary services to air transport, and the abuse of dominance through exclusivity clauses, tied sales, and quantitative restrictions.

What are the economic effects of a range of maritime transport-related restrictions extant in developed countries?

Standards and regulations: Is there a price premium associated with private voluntary environmental standards? How significant is this and does it outweigh the costs of certification and compliance? (Case studies would be worthwhile, for example on eco-labels such as the Forest Stewardship Council and the Fair Trade label.)

What is the economic impact on developing countries of developed-world private voluntary environmental labels?

Consumption impacts: Databases should be established to measure the contribution of developed countries' consumption patterns to global deforestation, depletion of the world's fishery resource, the overuse of chemicals for farming, and ocean warming (via CO_2 emissions and changes in ocean biodiversity).

Conclusion

Any meaningful agenda for reform of developed-world policies must urgently address five trade policy areas that have the greatest impact on the development prospects of developing countries. These are: tariff policies; agricultural protection; restrictions on trade in manufactured goods, particularly textiles and clothing; barriers to trade in services; and the distorting impact of some developed-world standards and regulations, including voluntary measures.

In an age where sustainable development has become an increasingly significant concept to inform policymaking, such a conventional interpretation of the scope of trade policy effects is insufficient in and of itself. Future research needs to begin to identify some of the wider impacts of developed-world improvements in market access. A practical application of such work would be to highlight for developed-world policymakers how and whether more technical assistance or even enhanced technology transfer to developing countries could be used to mitigate some of the negative externalities generated by trade policies.

Finally, serious statistical work is urgently needed to measure the impact of developed-world consumption patterns on developing countries. This work needs to be shaped in part by data on trade flows and could usefully supplement conventional measures of trade policy effects. In this way, enhancing understanding about some of the less well-understood effects of trade flows would help to provide a basis for implementing the concept of "policy coherence" in an international context. Importantly, such an approach would increase policymakers' understanding of the wider impacts of developed-world trade policies on developing countries' social, economic, and environmental development—or sustainable development for short.

Appendix

Table A5.1
Estimated Welfare Effects of Liberalization: Summary of Recent Studies

		Developing countries	Industrial countries	Total
		Complete liberalization		
Dessus et al. (1999)	Total	64	18	82
Billion 1995 US$ in 2010	Total with productivity growth	757	455	1212
Anderson et al. (2001)	Agriculture	43	122	165
Billion 1995 US$ in 2005	Manufacturing	63	24	87
	Total	108	146	254
Dee and Hanslow (2000)	Primary and secondary	69	65	134
Billion 1995 US$ in 1995	Tertiary	134	-1	133
	Total	203	65	267
World Bank (2002)	Agriculture	142	106	248
Dynamic	Manufacturing	42	65	107
Billion 1997 US$ in 2015	Total	184	171	355
DFAT (1999)	Total			750
Billion 1995 US$				
World Bank (2002)	Agriculture	390	196	587
Dynamic with productivity growth	Manufacturing	149	97	245
Billion 1997 US$ in 2015	Total	539	293	832
World Bank (2002)[a]	Merchandise trade			
Static	Services	1073		
Billion 1997 US$ in 2015	Total			
		Partial liberalization		
Brown et al. (2001)	Agriculture	8	3	11
33 percent reductions	Manufacturing	43	168	211
Billion US$	Services	50	340	390
	Total	101	511	613
DFAT (1999)	Total			380
50 percent reductions				
Billion 1995 US$				
Dessus et al. (1999)	Total	43	30	73
Full OECD liberalization and				
50 percent developing country				
reduction	Total, with productivity gains	292	620	912
Billion 1995 US$ in 2010				

Notes: Definitions of developing countries vary across the models.

a. This scenario relates to developing country liberalization only.

Dessus et al. use a dynamic linkage model and trade elasticities for a relatively short period of three to five years. The dynamic estimation allows trade openness to influence total factor productivity. The liberalization is from the situation in 1995.

Anderson et al. use a steady state GTAP model, with longer-term trade elasticities. Liberalization is following the implementation of Uruguay Round agreements in 2005. They also assume no improvements in agricultural liberalization between 1995 and 2005.

Dee and Hanslow use a static modified GTAP model with foreign direct investment (FTAP). The model incorporates monopolistic competition and imperfect capital mobility. Liberalization is following the implementation of Uruguay Round agreements in 2005.

The World Bank uses a model related to GTAP and a later version of the GTAP database than the other studies. The dynamic estimation allows productivity growth to be a constant function of the export-output ratio. Liberalization is from the situation in 1997.

DFAT uses both static GTAP and dynamic APC-cubed models.

Brown et al. use the static Michigan model of World Production and Trade, with monopolistic competition.

Source: OECD (2002), *Sustainable Development: A Framework for Peer Reviews and Related Indicators*, OECD, Paris (SG/SD (2002) 3).

Table A5.2
Major Traders in Textiles and Clothing, 2000

Clothing			Textiles		
(Billion $US and percentage)			(Billion $US and percentage)		
Countries	**Exports**	**Imports**	**Exports**	**Imports**	**Countries**
USA	8.7	66.4	22.3	18.2	EU
EU	15.0	51.1	16.1	12.8	China
China	36.1	1.2	10.9	15.7	USA
Japan	0.5	19.7	12.8	3.0	Korea
Hong Kong, China	14.3	1.7	11.7	1.5	Chinese Taipei
Mexico	8.7	3.4	7.0	4.9	Japan
Turkey	6.5	0.2	2.6	6.1	Mexico
Korea	5.0	0.8	2.2	4.1	Canada
Canada	2.1	3.7	3.7	2.1	Turkey
Chinese Taipei	3.0	1.1	5.1	0.5	India
Switzerland	0.6	3.2	4.5	0.1	Pakistan
Total above	100.5	152.5	98.9	69	Total above
World	165.5	165.5	126.1	126.1	World
Total above / World	60.7%	92.1%	78.4%	54.7%	Total above / World

Source: OECD (2002), WTO/TMB, Background Statistical Information with Respect to Trade in Textiles and Clothing, September 2001.

Notes

1. Vangelis Vitalis is currently the chief adviser at the Round Table on Sustainable Development at the OECD. He is on secondment from the New Zealand Ministry of Foreign Affairs and Trade. The views expressed in this chapter do not necessarily reflect those of the OECD or the New Zealand Ministry of Foreign Affairs and Trade. The comments provided by Anne Harrison, Ron Steenblik, Robert Picciotto, Sheila Page, Alan Winters, and the participants at the January 2003 Cairo Workshop of the Global Policy Network, particularly those of Bernard Hoekman, are gratefully acknowledged. All errors and omissions are the sole responsibility of the author.
2. For the purposes of this chapter, developed countries are defined as the members of the OECD.

3. See, for instance, D. Dollar and A. Kray (2001), *Trade, Growth and Poverty*, World Bank Working Paper no. 2615, and J. A. Frenkel and D. Romer (1999), "Does Trade Cause Growth?" *American Economic Review* 89.

4. World Bank (2001), *Global Economic Prospects*, World Bank, Washington DC.

5. The counter to these figures is that this is a comparison of apples and oranges, i.e., that revenue (from trade) is offset by costs, while aid disbursements are in effect pure profit. More important perhaps is the question of allocation within countries and among them.

6. Oxfam (2002), *Rigged Rules and Double Standards: Trade Globalization and the Fight against Poverty*, Oxfam. Also available at http://www.maketradefair.com/stylesheet.asp?file=26032002105549&cat=2&subcat=6&select=13, pp. 47-48.

7. See, for instance, L. Hanmer, J. Healey, and F. Naschold (2000), *Will Growth Halve Poverty by 2015?* ODI Poverty Briefing, Overseas Development Institute and Oxfam (op. cit.).

8. Oxfam (op. cit.).

9. For the range of results, see World Bank (2002), *Global Economic Prospects*, World Bank, Washington DC (pp.166-173); K. Anderson (2001), "The Cost of Rich (and poor) Country Protection to Developing Countries," *Journal of African Economics*; P. Dee and K. Hanslow (2000), *Multilateral Liberalization of Services Trade*, Australian Productivity Commission Research Paper, Canberra; S. K. Dessus, K. Fukasaku, and R. Safadi (1999), *Multilateral Tariff Liberalization and Developing Countries*, OECD Development Center, Policy Brief No 18. See also the useful table (27) contained in SG/SD (2002) 2/ANN1 and reproduced as Table A5.1 to the present chapter.

10. UNCTAD (2001), *Statistical Profiles of the Least Developed Countries*, UNCTAD, New York.

11. R. E. Baldwin (2002), *Trade and Growth: Still Disagreement about the Relationships*, OECD Economics Department Working Papers, No. 264. See also F. Rodriguez and D. Rodrik (1999), *Trade Policy and Economic Growth: A Skeptic's Guide to the Cross-Country Evidence*, Center for Economic Policy Research, Discussion Paper Series, No 2143.

12. For a good outline of the kinds of policy measures and reforms that could be considered by developing countries, see in particular N. McCulloch, L. A. Winters, and X. Cirera (2001), *Trade Liberalization and Poverty: A Handbook*, UK Department for International Development (DFID) and the Center for Economic Policy Research.

13. For a good overview of the main issues, see H. Nordstrom, D. Ben-David, and L. A. Winters (2001), *Trade, Income Disparity and Poverty*, World Trade Organization, Geneva.

14. A. Winters (2000), "Trade and Poverty: Is there a Connection?" *Trade, Income Disparity and Poverty,* World Trade Organization, Geneva.

15. Critics have described the EU initiative as the "Everything but Farms" initiative. There is some justification for this criticism. The initiative focuses on the forty-nine least-developed countries, but it excludes sugar, rice and bananas, which are significant potential exports for many developing countries. ACP countries also have duty-free access to the EU for manufactured goods.

16. The Africa Growth and Opportunity Act that established unrestricted market access for selected African countries is time bound. Unrestricted access is offered for eight years for most goods, though for a significant minority, including many products of particular interest to African exporters, the most favorable provisions are available for only half that period.

17. UNCTAD (op. cit).
18. W. Chang and L. A. Winters (2000), *How Regional Blocs Affect Excluded Countries: The Price Effects of Mercosur*, World Bank (see: www.worldbank.org/html/dec/Publications/Workpapers/wps2000series/wps2157/wps2157.pdf).
19. Given that preferences do not affect prices in importing countries, consumption in those countries does not increase when preferences are changed.
20. See in particular K. Anderson et al. (2001), "The Cost of Rich (and Poor) Country Protection to Developing Countries," *Journal of African Economics*.
21. B. M. Hoekman and M. M. Koestecki (2001), *The Political Economy of the World Trading System: The WTO and Beyond*. Oxford University Press. See also the striking data contained in Table 7 of SG/SD (2003) 3/ANN1.
22. Idem.
23. B. M. Hoekman, F. Ng, and M. Olarreaga (2001), *Eliminating Excessive Tariffs on Exports of Least Developed Countries*, Policy Research Working Paper 2604, World Bank, Washington DC.
24. On the administration of TRQs, see WTO (2001), *Market Access: Unfinished Business*, WTO, Geneva; and OECD (2001), *The Uruguay Round Agreement on Agriculture: An Evaluation of its Implementation in OECD Countries*, OECD, Paris.
25. UNCTAD (2000), *The Post-Uruguay Round Tariff Environment for Developing Country Exports: Tariff Peaks and Tariff Escalation*, 28 January, TD/B/COM.1/14/Rev. 1.
26. For more information about this body, see the website at: http://www.acpsec.org/ which also offers access to the critically important Cotonu Agreement, providing guaranteed preferential market access across a range of sectors (http://www.acpsec.org/gb/cotonou/accord1.htm).
27. See, for instance, B. Borrell (1999), *Bananas: Straightening our Bent Ideas on Trade as Aid*, Center for International Economics, September, Canberra/Sydney.
28. For this reason, several developed countries (for example, New Zealand) have eliminated the GSP.
29. The Doha Declaration can be accessed at http://www.wto.org/english/thewto_e/minist_e/min01_e/mindecl_e.htm (paragraph 44 addresses the concept of Special and Differential Treatment).
30. M. H. Khan (2000), "Rural Poverty in Developing Countries," *Finance and Development*, December IMF, Washington DC.
31. See, for instance, IMF (2002), *World Economic Outlook Trade and Finance*, September, IMF, Washington DC.
32. Paragraph 13 of the Doha Declaration covers this point.
33. This assumes that agricultural production is replaced by more transfers into more productive sectors. ABARE (2001), *Export Subsidies in the Current WTO Agriculture Negotiations*, ABARE, Canberra.
34. The effect of eliminating subsidies would be to reduce agricultural production in export-subsidizing countries, because one of the incentives for overproduction has diminished, and production in more profitable sectors would rise. At the same time, agricultural production should also rise in those countries producing goods that had little support, particularly commodities that had been heavily supported by others.
35. R. Tyers and K. Anderson (1992), *Disarray in World Food Markets: A Quantitative Assessment,* Cambridge, Cambridge University Press.
36. It is also erroneous to argue that export subsidies reduce world hunger by cutting world prices. In fact, the use of export subsidies is not calibrated to meet developing country food demands. Rather, the mechanism is employed during periods of oversupply, i.e., support is timed to benefit producers in countries using agricultural

65. R. Chadha (1999), *GATS and Developing Countries: A Case Study of India*, New Delhi, National Center for Advanced Economic Research (mimeo).
66. OECD (2002).
67. World Bank (2001) *Global Economic Prospects*, World Bank, Washington DC.
68. Indeed, a recent report suggests that India can expect to garner annual revenues of more than $85 billion, and 2.2 million additional jobs by 2008 through the IT industry alone. Moreover, within the next decade IT services alone are expected to comprise up to 35 percent of India's total exports. World Bank (2001).
69. World Bank (1995) *Global Economic Prospects*, World Bank, Washington DC.
70. The movement of natural persons (Mode IV of GATS), which is of potentially enormous value to developing countries, is addressed elsewhere in this volume.
71. This example is drawn from the case study undertaken by the OECD (2002*) The International Fruit Container Organisation (IFCO) Returnable Packaging Initiative*, in Development Dimensions of Trade and Environment: Case Studies, OECD, Paris, COM/TD/ENV (2002) 87.
72. Arguably the most comprehensive attempt to assess the impact of standards on trade flows is the Cecchini study on the European Single Market. P. Cecchini (1988), *The European Challenge: The Benefits of a Single Market*, Gower. This study drew together the results of a survey of business and a number of case studies and offered powerful evidence on the impact technical standards were having on trade. Unfortunately, the study focuses on developed countries and offers few insights into the costs imposed on developing country exporters.
73. See, for instance, S. Henson, R. Loader, and A. Swinbank (2000), *The Impact of Sanitary and Phytosanitary Measures on Developing Country Exports of Agricultural and Food Products*, Paper Prepared for Agriculture and the New Trade Agenda from a Development Perspective: Interests and Options in the WTO 2000 Negotiations, World Bank, Geneva, November; S. M. Stephenson (1997), *Standards and Conformity Assessment as Non-tariff Barriers to Trade*, Policy Research Working Paper Number 1826, World Bank, 1997; and, in particular, K. E. Maskus, J. S. Wilson, and T. Otsuki (2000), *Quantifying the Impact of Technical Barriers to Trade, A Framework for Analysis*, World Bank, Washington DC.
74. See, for instance, T. Otsuki, J. S. Wilson, and M. Sewadeh (2001), *A Race to the Top? A Case Study of Food Safety Standards and African Exports*, World Bank, Washington DC, March; and the impressive range of case studies contained in OECD (2002) Development Dimensions of Trade and Environment: Case Studies, OECD, Paris, COM/TD/ENV (2002) 8. Most recently, F. Brouwer, ed. (2002), *Public Concerns, Environmental Standards and Agricultural Trade*, Agricultural Economics Research Institute, The Hague, Netherlands, considers issues such as pollution from agriculture, the quality of landscapes, animal welfare, food safety, and the kinds of standards, codes of good practice, and other policy measures many countries have developed to deal with such issues and, more significantly, relates them to agricultural trade and competition.
75. T. Otsuki, J. S. Wilson, and M. Sewadeh (2001), *Saving Two in a Billion: Quantifying the Trade Effect of European Food Safety Standards on African Exports*, World Bank, Washington DC.
76. J. S. Wilson and T. Otsuki (2002), *Food Safety and Trade: Winners and Losers in a Non-Harmonized World*, World Bank, Washington DC.
77. J. S. Wilson and T. Otsuki (2002), *To Spray or Not to Spray: Pesticides, Banana Exports and Food Safety*, World Bank, Washington DC.
78. On these points, see the useful overview of the issue by A. Markandya (1997), *"Eco-labeling: An Introduction and a Review,"* in S. Zarilli, V. Jha, and R. Vossenaar

(1997), *Eco-labeling and International Trade*, Macmillan, Basingstoke, pp. 147-8 of pp. 143-158; and K. P. Ewing and R. G. Tarasofsky (1997), *The Trade and Environment Agenda: Survey of Major Issues and Proposals, from Marrakesh to Singapore*, IUCN/ICEL, Environmental Policy and Law Paper, No 33.

79. Further detail on these three areas is contained in V. Vitalis (2002), *Private Voluntary Eco-labels: Trade Distortional, Discriminatory, and Environmentally Disappointing*, OECD, Paris.

80. Personal Communication, Abdulkhafiz Kayumov, director, UzbekOboshFruktoviProm, Tashkent, Uzbekistan, 10 October 2002.

81. On the Dutch Butterfly label, see in particular H. Verbruggen, S. Jongma, and F. van der Woerd (1997), *Eco-labeling and the Developing Countries: The Dutch Horticultural Sector*, in S. Zarrilli, V. Jha and R. Vossenaar (1997), *Eco-labeling and International Trade*, Macmillan, Basingstoke, pp. 147-8 of pp. 143-158.

82. Author's research based on a comparison of selected WTO tariff schedules (country offers) detailing commitments from 1994 onwards on four-digit and six-digit leather goods, textiles, and cut flowers (at the six-digit level) and the start dates of a range of new or modified eco-labels. For the negative impact on the Colombian cut flower industry, for instance, see in particular, the Colombian Government's submission to the WTO (Government of Colombia (1998), *Environmental Labels and Market Access: Case Study on the Colombian Flower-growing Industry*, WT/CTE/W/76 and G/TBT/W/60, 9 March.

83. For a good exposition of this argument, see D. Rodrik (1997), *Has Globalization Gone Too Far?* Washington DC, Institute for International Economics.

84. W. Martin and K. E. Maskus (2001), "Core Labor Standards and Competitiveness: Implications for Global Trade Policy," *Review of International Economics* 9, 2: 317-328.

85. Measure O sought to ensure that coffee sold in Berkeley City must be certified as either organic, meaning grown without chemicals; shade-grown, meaning grown under trees that protect the soil and provide bird habitat; or Fair Trade, meaning that growers received at least $1.26 a pound—$1.41 a pound for organic. If Measure O had come into law, it would have made it a crime, punishable by up to six months in jail, for anyone selling brewed coffee that wasn't certified as Fair Trade. The text of Measure O and the formal arguments for and against are available at: http://www.ci.berkeley.ca.us/elections/measures/2002/Ocoffee.htm See also http://www.arizonarepublic.com/news/articles/1103coffee03.html http://www.indybay.org/news/2002/07/136704.php http://www.baido.org/topics/environment/2002/tfusa_berkeley_coffee.php.

86. For further information about the Fair Trade label for chocolate, see http://www.divinechocolate.com/.

87. See *International Herald Tribune* (2002), "Coffee Controversy in California," 4 November and various websites including: http://www.alumni.berkeley.edu/Alumni/Cal_Monthly/February_2002/Coffee_break.asp which outlines the background to the initiative and http://www.enn.com/news/wire-stories/2002/07/07112002/reu_47813.asp which includes a Reuters report on the balloting initiative in Berkeley City.

88. DFID (1999), *Trade, Labour Standards and Development, Where Should They Meet?* DFID Background Paper.

89. See, for instance, McCulloch, Winters, and Cirera (ibid.), and K. Maskus (1997), *Should Core Labor Standards Be Imposed through International Trade Policy?* World Bank, Washington DC.

90. See, in particular, OECD (2001), *Non-Tariff Measures on Agricultural and Food Products: The Policy Concerns of Emerging and Transition Economies*, OECD, Paris.

91. An elaboration of this argument can be found in V. Vitalis (2002), *Private Voluntary Eco-labels: Trade Distorting, Discriminatory and Environmentally Disappointing*, OECD, Paris.

92. The OECD's annual Ministerial Communiqué in 2001, for instance, states that a priority is to achieve "improved economic, environmental and social policy coherence and integration." (The 2001 Ministerial Communiqué is available at http://www.oecd.org/oecd/pages/document/displaywithoutnav/0,3376,EN-document-notheme-1-no-no-5294-0, 00.html.) In 2002, OECD Ministers went a step further, re-emphasizing the need for policy coherence and noting that "successful poverty reduction requires mutually supportive policies across a wide range of economic, social, and environmental issues." (The 2002 Ministerial Communiqué is available at: http://www.oecd.org/oecd/pages/document/displaywithoutnav/0,3376,EN-document-notheme-1-no-no-29673-0,00.html.)

93. The key references on policy coherence in the Plan of Implementation are contained in the paragraphs on "Means of Implementation." The Plan of Implementation is available at http://www.johannesburgsummit.org/html/documents/summit_docs/2309_planfinal.htm.

94. Chapter III of the Implementation Plan is devoted to "Changing Unsustainable Patterns of Consumption and Production."

95. On this point, see OECD (2002), *Towards Sustainable Household Consumption? Trends and Policies in OECD Countries*, OECD, Paris.

96. For an early outline of this precise point, see the debate between N. Meyers and J. R. Vincent and T. Panayotou (1997), "Consumption: Challenge to Sustainable Development or Distraction?" *Science* 276 (5309): 53-57, 4 April.

97. See T. Rutherford (1992), *The Welfare Effects of Fossil Carbon Reductions: Results from a Recursively Dynamic Trade Model*, Economics Department, Working Paper No 112, OECD, Paris, and A. W. Wyckoff and J. M. Roop (1994), "The Embodiment of Carbon in Imports of Manufactured Products: Implications for International Agreements on Greenhouse Gas Emissions," *Energy Policy*, March 1994: 187-194.

98. See, for instance, Wyckoff and Roop (op. cit.). The countries examined were Canada, France, Germany, Japan, the UK, and the United States.

99. See, for instance, R. Sturgiss (1995), "Greenhouse Gas Emissions: The Impact of International Trade," *International Trade Papers 1995*, AGPS, Canberra.

100. R. Sturgiss (1996), "Integration, Trade Liberalization, and Climate Change" (unpublished paper) elaborates this argument in some detail (in relation to the FCCC) and offers important insights into the implications thereof.

6

The Development Impact of Rich Countries' Policies: The Case of Intellectual Property Rights

Charles Clift[1]

This chapter reviews first the nature of the intellectual property right (IPR), and then briefly summarizes the state of knowledge about the impact of IPR protection on developing countries, in each case drawing on the report of the Commission on Intellectual Property Rights (IPR Commission).[2] Section 3 of the chapter examines the process of policymaking on IPRs, and the interaction between developed and developing countries, and section 4 considers how research might influence policy, including the response to the IPR Commission's report. Section 5 seeks to identify priorities for future research and to suggest an institutional framework that would help to maximize the impact of that research. The appendix suggests how one might seek to measure the development friendliness of developed-country IPR policies.

What is the Nature of the Intellectual Property Right?

Some see IP rights principally as economic or commercial rights, and others see them as akin to political or human rights. The TRIPs agreement[3] treats them in the former sense, while recognizing the need to strike a balance between the rights of inventors and creators to protection, and the rights of users of technology (Article 7 of TRIPs). The Universal Declaration of Human Rights uses a broader definition recognizing "the right to the protection of the moral and material interests resulting from any scientific, literary or artistic production of which he is the author," balanced by "the right...to share in scientific advancement and its benefits."[4] The Commission on IPR saw the crucial issue as the reconciliation of the public interest in accessing new knowledge and the products of new knowledge, with the public interest in stimulating invention and creation that produces the new knowledge and products on which material and cultural progress may depend.

The difficulty is that the IP system, as now manifested in TRIPs, seeks to achieve this reconciliation by conferring a private right and private material benefits. Thus, the human right to the protection of "moral and material interests" of "authors" is inextricably bound up with the right to the private material benefits that result from such protection. And the private benefit to the creator or inventor is derived at the expense of the consumer. Particularly where the consumer is poor, this may conflict with basic human rights, for example, the right to life. And the IP system does not allow—except in rather narrow ways—discrimination between goods that are essential to life or education, and other goods such as films or fast food.

The Commission therefore considered that an IP right was best viewed as one of the means by which nations and societies can help to promote the fulfillment of human economic and social rights. It thought that there should be no circumstances in which the most fundamental human rights should be subordinated to the requirements of IP protection. IP rights are granted by states for limited times (at least in the case of patents and copyrights) whereas human rights are inalienable and universal. [5]

IP rights are nowadays generally treated as economic and commercial rights, as they are in TRIPs, and are more often held by companies than by individual inventors. But describing them as "rights" should not be allowed to conceal the very real dilemmas raised by their application in developing countries, where the extra costs they impose may be at the expense of the essential prerequisites of life for poor people.

IPRs should be considered as instruments of public policy that confer economic *privileges* on individuals or institutions solely for the purposes of contributing to the greater public good. The *privilege* is therefore a means to an end, not an end in itself.

Thus, for purposes of assessing the value of IP protection, IP protection may be compared to taxation. Hardly anybody claims that the more taxation the better. However, there is a tendency in some quarters to treat more IP protection as self-evidently a good thing. More taxation might be desirable if it delivers public services that society values more than the direct and indirect costs of taxation. But less taxation can also be beneficial, for instance if excessive taxation is harming economic growth. Moreover, economists and politicians spend much time considering whether the structure of the tax system is optimal. Are heavy social security taxes harming employment? Are particular tax breaks serving their intended purpose, or merely subsidizing their recipients to do what they are already doing? Is the effect of the tax system on the distribution of income desirable from a social point of view?

The Commission thought there were analogous questions for intellectual property protection. How much of it is a good thing? How should it be structured? How does the optimal structure vary with sectors and levels of development? Moreover, even if the level and structure of protection can be got right—in the sense of balancing the incentive to invention and creation against the costs to society, it is also necessary to worry about the distribution of gains from its imposition.

Evidence on the Impact of Intellectual Property Rights

Current Issues

During the last twenty years or so, the level, scope, territorial extent, and role of IP protection have expanded at an unprecedented pace. Genetic materials have become widely patented. IP rights have been modified or created to cover new technologies, particularly biotechnology and information technology. Technologies produced in the public sector are routinely patented. The TRIPs Agreement has extended minimum standards for IP protection globally. There are continuing discussions in the World Intellectual Property Organization (WIPO) aimed at further harmonization of the patent system, which may supersede TRIPs. Moreover, bilateral or regional trade and investment agreements between developed and developing countries often include mutual commitments to implement IP regimes that go beyond TRIPs minimum standards. Thus, there is sustained pressure on developing countries to increase the levels of IP protection in their own regimes, based on standards in developed countries.

The functioning of IPR systems raises genuine concerns even in developed countries. The submission of patent applications has increased tremendously in recent years—as has the perception that many patents of "low quality" and broad scope are being issued. Companies may incur considerable costs, in time and money, determining how or whether to conduct research without infringing upon other companies' patent rights, or in defending their own patent rights against other companies. This raises questions as to whether the substantial costs involved in patent litigation are a necessary price to pay for the incentives offered by the patent system, or whether ways can be found to reduce them. How does this proliferation of patents affect competition and research?

The concerns about the impact of IP in developed countries are important for developing countries as well. Developing countries can learn from the experience of developed countries in devising their own systems. In addition, the IP system in developed countries has had direct impacts on developing countries. Restrictions on access to materials and data on the Internet can affect everyone. IP rules and regulations may be hampering research on important diseases or new crops that affects developing countries but is actually carried out in developed countries. Developing countries may not be sharing appropriately in the benefits from commercialization of their knowledge or genetic resources when these are patented in developed countries.

Incentives work differently, depending on the supply response they evoke. They impose costs on consumers and other users of protected technologies. The balance of costs and benefits will vary according to how the rights are applied and according to the economic and social circumstances of the country where they are being applied. Standards of IP protection that may be suitable for developed countries may produce more costs than benefits when applied in developing countries, which rely in large part on knowledge generated elsewhere to satisfy their basic needs and foster development.

Although most developing countries do not have a strong technological base, they do have genetic resources and traditional knowledge that are of value to them and to the world at large. This gives rise to a further key question. Can the "modern" IP system help to protect these resources and knowledge and ensure that the benefits of their use are equitably shared? At the other end of the scale, the Internet offers enormous opportunities for access to scientific and research information needed by developing countries, whose access to traditional media may be limited by lack of resources. But forms of encryption and IP rules may paradoxically make this material less accessible than it is now in printed form.

Macroeconomic Issues

Patents and copyright inherently confer both costs and benefits on individuals and companies and on society at large. They provide an incentive for invention or creation that may benefit society, as well as the rights holder, but they also impose costs on the users of protected works.

Historically, now-developed countries used IP protection as a flexible instrument to help promote their industrialization. Discrimination against foreigners—by refusing them the right to IP protection or by charging higher fees—was common, as was the exclusion of entire sectors, such as food or pharmaceuticals, from patentability. In some developed countries, the patent system was fully implemented only well after the start of the twentieth century. The East Asian countries, the most successful recent examples of development, have developed their scientific and technical capabilities in the context of weak IP regimes. Now, under TRIPs and growing pressures for harmonization, most developing nations are restricted in how they can apply the IP system: they may not discriminate among fields of technology, or by nationality, and the use of various tools of IP policy that were used historically is circumscribed under TRIPs.

The contemporary evidence suggests that, because developing countries are large net importers of technology from the developed world, the globalization of IP protection will result in very substantial additional net transfers from developing to developed countries. Offsetting benefits to developing countries from IP protection would have to come from a dynamic stimulus to trade, the development of technology, investment, and growth.

In most developing countries these offsetting benefits are unlikely to outweigh the costs in the foreseeable future. Unlike in developed countries, where strong evidence suggests that certain types of companies, particularly the pharmaceutical industry, regard IPRs as essential in promoting innovation, in developing countries there is much less evidence that IPR systems of the kind practiced in the developed world are a key stimulus for innovation. For most developing countries with weak technological capacity, the evidence on trade, foreign investment, and growth suggests IP protection will have little impact. For more technologically advanced developing countries, the balance is finer; the benefits of IP protection may well outweigh the costs in the longer term, although there may be heavy transitional costs to other industries and consumers.

Perhaps the crucial issue in respect of IP is not whether it promotes trade or foreign investment, but how it helps or hinders developing countries to gain access to technologies that are required for their development. Countries such as Korea started at a low level of technological expertise forty years ago, comparable to many low-income countries today, but have now become innovators in their own right.[6] Technology transfer and the development of a sustainable indigenous technological capability are determined by many factors in addition to IPRs.

In today's liberalized and competitive environment, companies in developing countries can no longer compete on the basis of importing "mature" technologies from developed countries and producing them behind tariff barriers. And companies are more wary of transferring technology in ways that may increase the competition they face. The problem is less about obtaining mature technologies on fair and balanced terms, but more about accessing the sophisticated technologies that are required to compete in today's global economy.

TRIPs has strengthened the global protection offered to suppliers of technology, but without any counterbalancing strengthening of competition policies globally. Therefore, it may be unwise to focus on TRIPs as a principal means of facilitating technology transfer. A wider agenda needs to be pursued, as is currently being done in the WTO. Developed countries need to give serious consideration to their policies for encouraging technology transfer. In addition, they should promote more effective research and cooperation with and among developing countries to strengthen their scientific and technological capabilities.

Health

Without the incentive of patents it is doubtful that the private sector would have invested so much in the discovery or development of medicines. But the evidence suggests that the IP system plays hardly any role in stimulating research on diseases particularly prevalent in developing countries, except for those diseases (such as diabetes or heart disease) where there is also a substantial market in the developed world. Because the ultimate constraint on the volume of research is the lack of market demand for its products in developing countries, the globalization of IP protection will not by itself lead to greater investment by the private sector for the development of treatments for diseases that primarily affect developing countries.

The evidence also suggests that patent protection affects the prices charged for medicines. In developed countries, generic competition causes prices to fall quite sharply, particularly if the market is large enough to support a number of generic competitors. In developing countries, these competitive conditions are difficult to replicate. In the absence of patents in developing countries, more people would be able to afford treatments they need. When TRIPs comes fully into force after 2005, particularly when countries such as India must introduce patent protection on new medicines, the existing competition from generic suppliers will diminish.

The IP system is one factor among several that affects poor people's access to healthcare. Other important constraints on access to medicines in developing countries are the lack of resources, and the absence of a suitable health infrastructure (including hospitals, clinics, health workers, equipment, and an adequate supply of drugs) to administer medicines safely and efficaciously. Moreover, developing countries may adopt other policies, for example, taxes on medicines that adversely affect access.

As intellectual property rights are strengthened globally, the cost of medicines in developing countries is likely to rise, unless effective steps are taken to facilitate their availability at lower cost in these countries. The Commission identified a number of IP policies that both developed and developing countries can adopt to promote cheaper prices for medicines in developing countries without adversely affecting the incentives for research on relevant diseases. One of these is a mechanism called "compulsory licensing." This allows countries to license the manufacture of patented medicines to other manufacturers if there are good reasons to do so (for example, when the government considers the price of a medicine unjustifiably high). It can also be useful as a bargaining tool in price negotiations with producers of patented medicines. For instance, the United States envisaged this possibility when negotiating the price of Cipro following the anthrax attacks in 2002.

The importance of the IP system being used to improve access to medicines and public health was emphasized in a Declaration on TRIPs and Public Health at the WTO Ministerial meeting in Doha in 2001. A major issue at Doha was how countries without the capacity to manufacture medicines can procure them under the existing rules for compulsory licensing. The TRIPs Council in the WTO was asked to find a solution to this problem by the end of 2002. The IPR Commission's report discussed a number of ways to achieve this. A crucial issue is how to provide appropriate incentives for the potential suppliers of medicines and cheaper prices than the patentee is able to offer. The evidence of the negotiations in Geneva to date suggests that it will prove very difficult to negotiate a solution in the WTO at all, let alone one that will meet these criteria. If that proves to be the case, the threat of compulsory licensing will not be credible for most developing countries.

Apart from international measures to facilitate access to medicines, developing countries need to adopt IP rules in their legislation and practices that limit the extent of patenting and facilitate the introduction of generic competition. Doha allowed least developed countries (LDCs) to exempt pharmaceutical products from patent protection until at least 2016, but in practice most LDCs have already provided such protection and would need to amend their legislation accordingly.

Agriculture

The amount of public resources from developed countries going into funding research of relevance to poor farmers in developing countries is stagnant or declining. The dynamic element is private sector research, supported by IP protection and the demand from farmers in developed countries and the commercial sectors of a few developing countries. This combination of trends poses the danger that research priorities overall will be increasingly less relevant to the needs of poor farmers in developing countries. Moreover, the stagnation in public funding threatens, inter alia, the maintenance of national and international gene banks, which are the principal source of genetic material for future breeding efforts of relevance to poor farmers. While in recent years the IP rights of breeders have been increasingly strengthened, as required by TRIPs, little has been done in practice to recognize the services of farmers in the selection, development, and conservation of their traditional varieties that have provided the basis for modern breeding techniques. The recently agreed FAO Treaty on Plant Genetic Resources for Food and Agriculture seeks to protect the material in gene banks and in farmers' fields covered by the treaty from being directly patented, and also encourages countries to protect farmers' rights.

Under TRIPs, countries must apply some kind of IP protection to plant varieties, either patents or other kinds of protection (called *sui generis*). They must also allow microorganisms to be patentable. The evidence suggests that *sui generis* systems of plant variety protection (PVP) have not been particularly effective at stimulating research on crops in general or, particularly, on the kinds of crops grown by poor farmers. Systems of PVP designed for the needs of commercial agriculture in the developed countries (such as provided for in the UPOV[7] Convention) also pose a threat to the practices of many farmers in developing countries of reusing, exchanging, and informally selling seeds, and may not be appropriate in developing countries without significant commercial agriculture.

Patents are commonly used in developed countries both to protect plant varieties and to protect genetic material incorporated in plants. Because they offer a stronger form of protection than most PVP systems, they may offer a stronger incentive to research, particularly in developed countries, and the multinational agrochemical companies regard them as important. However, patents may also pose a threat to farmers' traditional practices of reuse and exchange. Moreover the proliferation of genetic patents owned by different companies has led to costly disputes, and difficulties in pursuing research without infringing other companies' patents. There is evidence that patents are one factor contributing to the rapid concentration in the agricultural biotechnology field, with adverse effects on the degree of competition. This is particularly important in developing countries where arrangements for enforcing competition are normally weak.

Traditional Knowledge

Motives for protecting and promoting traditional knowledge include the erosion of traditional lifestyles and cultures through external pressures, misappropriation, the preservation of biodiversity, and the promotion of its use for development purposes. Some wish to conserve traditional knowledge, and protect it against commercial exploitation, while others wish to ensure that it is exploited equitably for the benefit of its holders. Underlying the debate on the protection of traditional knowledge may be much larger issues such as the position of indigenous communities within the wider economy and society of the country in which they live, and their access to, or ownership of, land they have traditionally inhabited. Given the varied reasons for protecting traditional knowledge and the broad nature of the subject matter, there is no one way to protect or promote it. A multiplicity of complementary measures, many of which will be outside the field of intellectual property, will be necessary. For example, the types of measures required to prevent misappropriation of traditional knowledge may not be the same, indeed may not be compatible with, those needed to encourage its wider use. There is room for continued debate to clarify these complex issues.

Protection for traditional knowledge may be obtained both within the existing IP system and through the establishment of new or *sui generis* forms of protection. Recently, there have been a number of well-publicized cases of patents being granted for traditional knowledge that was already publicly known. To prevent the misappropriation of traditional knowledge through patenting, efforts are being made to catalogue traditional knowledge in digital databases that will be accessible to examiners in all patent offices. In other cases, patent laws and practices may allow patents on "inventions" that are little more than discoveries. Some countries do not recognize the use of knowledge in other countries, as opposed to their own, as a reason for not granting patents. Use elsewhere might demonstrate that the claimed invention is not novel, or is obvious, even though it has not been used domestically. Even if patents are granted for valid inventions derived from genetic resources or traditional knowledge, it may be that the communities that provided such resources or knowledge did not give their informed consent, and no arrangements for sharing any benefits from commercialization were agreed upon.

The Convention on Biological Diversity (CBD), which most countries have signed, seeks to encourage access to the world's genetic resources provided that access takes place with the informed consent of the holder of the resource and that any benefits deriving from the access are equitably shared. The extent to which the IP system should support the CBD has been the subject of much debate. At the heart of the debate has been the question of whether patent applicants should disclose in their applications the source of any genetic resource used in their invention.

A further debate in the WTO's TRIPs Council centers on whether the protection afforded under TRIPs to geographical indications (that is, indications that identify the origins of a product as a mark of quality and provenance) should be increased through either the establishment of an international register of protected indications or through the extension to other products of the additional protection that is currently available for wines and spirits. Lacking in this debate, however, is any real economic assessment of the impact of such proposals for developing countries.

Copyright

In a few cases, including the Indian software and film industry, developing countries have benefited from copyright protection. Other examples are hard to identify. Many developing countries have had copyright protection for a long time but it has not proved sufficient to stimulate the growth of copyright-protected industries. Because most developing countries, particularly smaller ones, are overwhelmingly importers of copyrighted materials, and the main beneficiaries are therefore foreign rights holders, the operation of the copyright system as a whole may impose more costs than benefits for them. International treaties such as the Berne Convention provide flexibilities in copyright, known as "fair use" or "fair dealing" provisions, to allow copying particularly for personal and education use. But these have not generally proved adequate to meet the needs of developing countries, particularly in the field of education.

Developing countries need to put in place effective systems for enforcing rights. However, in many cases (for example software) the absolute scale of estimated losses from illicit copying is higher in developed countries. And weak levels of enforcement have undoubtedly had a major impact in some areas on the diffusion of knowledge and knowledge-based products in the developing world. Indeed, many poor people in developing countries have only been able to access certain works through use of unauthorized copies available at a fraction of the price of the original. An inevitable impact of stronger protection and enforcement, as required by TRIPs, will therefore be to reduce access to knowledge-related products in developing countries, with potentially damaging consequences for poor people. For instance, the cost of software is a major problem for developing countries, and the reason for the high level of illicit copying. Copyright can also be a barrier to the further development of software specifically adapted to local needs and requirements.

Access to the Internet in developing countries is limited, although growing rapidly. The Internet provides an unrivalled means of low-cost access to knowledge and information required by developing countries. But the application of copyright rules to the Internet is problematic. And historic "fair use" rights may be restricted by forms of technological protection, such as encryption, which restricts access even more stringently than copyright. In the United States, recent legislation (the Digital Millennium Copyright Act) forbids the circumvention of such technological protection, even when the purpose of circumvention does not contravene copyright laws. The recently agreed EU Copyright Directive contains similar provisions. The EU has also introduced a special form of protection of databases (the "Database Directive"), which rewards investment in the creation of databases, and which may restrict access to data by scientists or others, including in developing countries. The 1996 WIPO Copyright Treaty contains elements that may restrict the access of developing countries to information.

The Policymaking Process in IPRs

World Intellectual Property Organization (WIPO) and World Trade Organization (WTO)

Traditionally, international IP policy discussions have taken place in WIPO or in its predecessor, BIRPI. BIRPI (the French acronym for the United International Bureau for the Protection of Intellectual Property) was established in 1893 to administer the two main international IP agreements—the 1884 Paris Convention (on industrial property) and the 1886 Berne Convention (on copyright). BIRPI transformed itself into WIPO in 1970, and became a specialized agency of the UN in 1974. But its function has remained to act as a forum for discussion and negotiation between members of the treaties and to promote standard setting internationally in IP. The provisions of these treaties allowed considerable flexibility in how countries managed their IP regimes and, of course, membership was voluntary.

For a period in the 1960s and 1970s, strong intellectual property protection fell into disfavor in developing countries, and in several of these countries in the wake of independence the strong IP protection inherited from the colonial powers was weakened. In the words of a former head of the USPTO:

> ...the political climate...in the 1970s was not hospitable to promote the global protection of intellectual property.... Inspired by the success of the OPEC oil cartel, a group of developing countries, the so-called "Group of 77," was formed within the United Nations with an agenda that was at odds with that of the industrialized countries. In fact, the Group of 77 argued for weakening rather than strengthening intellectual property rights. Under the economic policy of "import substitution," the Group of 77 favored substituting domestically produced goods and services for foreign imports, weak intellectual protection, and the compulsory licensing of patents and technology. In such a climate, the attempt to strengthen intellectual property rights under the Paris and Berne Conventions, which provided for "national treatment" but relatively low levels of minimum protection, proved impossible.

Thus, negotiations in WIPO on the strengthening of the Paris Convention went on for a decade but broke down in the face of developing country resistance. As a result:

> During the 1980s, the industrialized nations began to search for an alternative forum to negotiate increased standards of protection. The rise of knowledge-based industries, which was radically altering the nature of competition and the comparative advantage

of industrialized countries, gave new urgency to their demands. The cost of research and development was escalating, and the resulting new high-tech products and services became more vulnerable to unauthorized use and reproduction.[8]

Thus, under pressure from knowledge-intensive industries, the United States and then other developed countries forced the inclusion of IPRs in what became known as TRIPs in the Uruguay Round in the GATT. By choosing this forum, in preference to WIPO, the developed-country IP agenda could be advanced when the negotiations at WIPO had proved unfruitful. By combining a number of different trade-related agreements, which all GATT (then WTO) members had to subscribe to as a package, backed up by the enforcement procedure provided in the dispute settlement mechanism, the developed countries were able to exert powerful leverage on developing countries to accept TRIPs. While most developing countries were either unenthusiastic or uninformed about what TRIPs implied for them, they agreed to it on the basis that they would gain from the overall package, notably the promised liberalization of trade, in particular in agriculture and textiles. Moreover, while admitting the element of self-interest in their desire to establish minimum global intellectual property standards, industry groups and most developed country governments argued (and continue to do so) that it is in developing countries' interests to adopt IP protection.

In contrast to activist NGOs and many developing countries who believe it goes too far, most industry groups consider that TRIPs does not go far enough. The United States, but also other developed countries/groups, commonly seek to impose higher standards (so-called "TRIPs plus") in bilateral and regional trade agreements. In the United States it is explicit policy in trade agreements to ensure that the provisions provide for "a standard of protection similar to that found in United States law."[9] U.S. trade negotiators can thus use the "package approach" to incorporate stronger IP provisions in regional and bilateral agreements in exchange for other trade benefits that are valued more highly. This activity has the global effect of raising IP protection standards piecemeal, in large chunks. Apart from bilateral deals already signed (for example, by the United States with Jordan, Cambodia, and Vietnam), or in process, the single largest impact on developing countries will be through the establishment of the Free Trade Area of the Americas

(FTAA). The indications are that very few countries in Latin America or the Caribbean will be prepared to argue strenuously against higher IP standards, given that they perceive the other important trade and investment issues that are at stake to be of more immediate interest.

The advent of TRIPs has led to something of a revival of activity of WIPO's role. WIPO is now the forum where further upgrading of IP standards is considered. These include the WIPO Copyright and Performance and Phonograms Treaties of 1996, and the ongoing discussions on the WIPO Patent Agenda, whose ultimate goal is to harmonize patent laws and practices. WIPO's technical assistance activities have received a boost as developing countries seek advice on the implementation of their obligations under TRIPs. And WIPO has established a committee to look at the issues of the protection of traditional knowledge, genetic resources, and folklore.

Somewhat ironically it is in the WTO, as noted below, that developing countries have had the most impact in discussing the relationship between IP and development, particularly in the area of public health. WIPO, although it has much the same membership as WTO, is explicitly a body designed to promote IP protection worldwide and the harmonization of national legislation. WIPO's working assumption as an organization is that there is no conflict between strengthening IP protection and development—in fact, the organization dismisses or ignores the views of those who, like the Commission, believe that weaker IP protection may be appropriate in many developing countries. WIPO is 90 percent funded by fees from its patent activities (in effect by the private sector of the developed world—uniquely for a UN body). This association is reflected in the close involvement of developed-world IP industry umbrella groups in WIPO's work as observers. Moreover, WIPO delegates tend to be from the IP offices of countries represented, and in many cases WIPO meets the costs for developing country delegates traveling to Geneva. These delegates naturally tend to view stronger IP protection positively. The atmosphere is thus very different from that of WTO; the impact of IP rules and practices on development is much more rarely discussed than are the technical aspects of IP divorced from their economic and social context.

From the point of view of developing countries the danger of the patent harmonization process is as follows:

...a harmonized treaty would probably leave significantly less flexibility than does TRIPs. This is a problem if the harmonized structure ends up, as is likely, as a compromise between the U.S. and the European systems, for such a compromise is likely to include a low inventive step standard and a very broad subject matter standard, standards that are not in the interest of developing nations (nor, in the judgment of many, of the developed nations either). The question is what is the right strategy for the developing nations: to attempt to participate and seek a positive standard? To attempt to participate and seek special provisions for developing nations? To refrain from participation?[10]

WIPO remains a body based on voluntarism. As noted, countries may refrain from participating in treaties but, as with TRIPs, developed countries will always be able to "switch forums" to the WTO in a future trade round in order to bring about developing country compliance.

The Doha Declaration: A Case Study in Policymaking

In addition to industry, and the governments of developed and developing nations, activist NGOs have significantly affected the course of discussions since TRIPs entered into effect. This applies particularly to the impact of IPRs in the health sector, where public attention has been easy to attract because of the scale and gravity of the HIV/AIDS epidemic. A small number of NGOs (including Oxfam, Médecins Sans Frontières, Health Action International, and the Consumer Project on Technology) have had a major impact on the course of the international debate, which culminated in a Declaration on TRIPs and Public Health at the WTO ministerial meeting in Doha in 2001. This affirmed that "the TRIPs Agreement does not and should not prevent Members from taking measures to protect public health...and should be interpreted and implemented in a manner supportive of WTO Members' right to protect public health and, in particular, to promote access to medicines for all." This was widely perceived as a "victory" for developing countries over developed countries and their industry lobby groups. This alliance between developing countries and mainly international NGOS is thus significant as an indication of a strategy by which developing countries can increase their negotiating power vis à vis developed countries.

On the other hand, it has been claimed that Doha was really a "Pyrrhic victory" for NGOs and developing countries, and that it did not represent any fundamental change in the balance of power between the developed and developing world. There is support for this view in the outcome of the negotiations that were conducted subsequently in the WTO on the specific issue of compulsory licensing for countries without the capacity to manufacture (the so-called Para 6 question), to which the Doha Declaration had promised a solution by the end of 2002. These negotiations broke down at the end of 2002 when the United States—under pressure from the pharmaceutical industry—was unable to accept the consensus that all other WTO members, developed and developing, were prepared to sign up to. The specific issue was the desire of the pharmaceutical industry to limit the scope of compulsory licensing to infectious diseases principally affecting developing countries, and in particular to avoid the possibility of compulsory licensing on non-infectious diseases affecting both developed and developing countries (such as cancer, diabetes, asthma, and heart disease).

On this issue the implicit argument of the IPR Commission was that since IP protection in developing countries without manufacturing capacity contributes little or nothing to the incentives for R&D on either tropical or "western diseases," the research incentives of the pharmaceutical industry could not be undermined as a result of extending the ability to compulsorily license to these countries. Moreover, the Commission felt that in practice the utility of compulsory licensing was principally as a means of providing countries with a credible bargaining tool when negotiating prices with companies—particularly as competition from currently legal generic versions of patented drugs will decline after India complies with TRIPs in 2006. (Rather like the nuclear deterrent, it was the fact that it *could* be used, rather than its actual use, that would produce the desired competitive effect.) By contrast, the companies contend that once the tool is there it will be used frequently and indiscriminately, and that leakage from developing country markets will undermine their profits in developed countries, on which their funding of R&D depends. In particular, this is why they wanted to exclude the possibility of compulsory licensing on drugs for non-communicable diseases where current markets are overwhelmingly in developed countries.

The Doha Declaration illustrates a number of policymaking issues worth examination:

- The impact of the NGO/developing country alliance depended on the high public profile of the public health issue created over several years.

It did not extend to other aspects of IP rights as they affect developing countries in other areas important for development.

- The Declaration was a political statement of principles that TRIPs should be used in a manner supportive of public health. It was neither a legal document nor an operational one. Putting the Declaration into practical effect required further negotiations in the WTO, which have so far proved unsuccessful. In that sense it remains a "Pyrrhic victory."
- The role of NGOs remains contentious. It is said that they have power without responsibility for the consequences of their actions. In what way can they legitimately be said to represent the views of developing countries (which are obviously not homogeneous, for a host of economic and political reasons)? Or are they pressing on developing countries their own rather different agenda? For instance, opposition to the international pharmaceutical industry might be seen as a higher priority on the NGO agenda than on that of developing country governments. On the other hand, exactly the same criticism may be applied to official development agencies, both bilateral and multilateral, which have more power based on their financial clout, but no more responsibility for the consequences of the policies they have pressed on developing countries, many of which have been conspicuously unsuccessful.[11]
- Of course the subtext to this is the arm-twisting or horse-trading that occurs during these negotiations, either directly with delegates or back in their capitals. Governments, industries, and NGOs may all indulge in this lobbying activity, pulling developing countries this way and that. Again, for developing countries a preferred IP solution might be traded off against a more attractive promise in another area (or against the withdrawal of a threat). It is valuable for developing countries to have available a number of diverse sources of advice; there is less to be said for arm twisting backed by promised sanctions or rewards of different kinds.
- In the Para 6 case described above, getting an agreed solution by the end of 2002 also became a priority for WTO officials because of its symbolic importance to the future of the trade round launched in Doha. The fact that the United States rejected the solution agreed to by other nations is a further illustration of its aversion to multilateral deals that it perceives to threaten its vital economic interests.

Research and Its Impact

Such is the background against which the possible impact of research needs to be considered. In light of the above, how might research best contribute to the aims of the current initiative?

A central issue is how far research actually influences policy, fully recognizing that it would be naïve to see a direct influence. A recent report on the research-policy linkage usefully sets out the pitfalls:

...the report is critical of models which view the research/policy relationship as one of simple lineal progression. Interviewees described research knowledge as a source of power that can influence the policymaking process. But of course research knowledge is not the only source of power within politics, and its influence varies depending on who voices and holds it.... Research disseminated with the intention of influencing policy is a political intervention in a political context, and it is thus vulnerable to political exploitation and distortion. Interviewees referred to the exploitation of research to confer spurious objectivity upon predetermined policies, or to delay addressing politically sensitive issues. Interviewees also referred to the way in which dominant political ideologies act as constraints upon new research knowledge, determining which perspectives are deemed relevant and which are not at both national and international levels. Finally in this respect, attention was drawn to certain political contexts in which the prevalent attitude is one of indifference to development, and therefore to development research.

...Aside from the potential for exploitation and distortion which research knowledge encounters once it enters the political domain, interviewees gave testimony to the current weakness of capacity within developing country executives, legislatures and civil society organizations to carry out, engage with and use research. A lack of money, time or human resources, means that research is either not carried out, or is conducted by external consultants, often disconnected from the policy context. Governments may also be too overwhelmed by immediate crisis management and resource-scarcity to commission and consider any research other than that focused on short-term problems. Even where research is carried out and is of adequate quality and foresight, some developing country legislatures and bureaucracies lack personnel with the necessary educational background to engage with and use research."[12]

The response to the report of the IPR Commission is instructive on some of the points above. The Commission was careful to provide and to refer to a great deal of evidence in coming to its conclusions in the belief that policy should be evidence-based. Of course, evidence is seldom conclusive, particularly in the social sciences, so that the same evidence can be interpreted in strikingly different ways by people with contrasting views or interests. As one of the quite famous quotations in the report said:

...If we did not have a patent system, it would be irresponsible, on the basis of our present knowledge of its economic consequences, to recommend instituting one. But since we have had a patent system for a long time, it would be irresponsible, on the basis of our present knowledge, to recommend abolishing it.[13]

But the most notable feature of the responses to the report is how little they accept this evidence-based framework. Some parties and groups have simply endorsed the report because they agree with most of its conclusions, and its analysis of the problem and issues. It is not of interest to them to scrutinize the evidence to see if it justifies the conclusions.

More surprising is the extent to which critics of the report simply ignore or contradict the evidence, without presenting counter-evidence of their own. Rather they simply assert that the Commission is wrong—in a way that suggests that engaging with the evidence is not likely to be a fruitful way of advancing their point of view or group interest. For instance, the Pharmaceutical and Research Manufacturers of America (PhRMA) simply assert:

> The Commission began with a false premise—that intellectual property protection impedes economic development efforts and forces a transfer of wealth from poor nations to the rich. Clearly this is at odds with mainstream economic theory.... Countries at every stage of development benefit from protecting the intellectual capital of their people.... Respect for intellectual property rights helps developing countries build their economies and improve public health for their people.[14]

Put like that, there is not much room for dialogue. It does not matter that the Commission did not begin with that premise, and quoted a number of economists generally regarded as "mainstream": PhRMA's intention here is not to debate the evidence, but to discredit the report.

The International Federation of Pharmaceutical Manufacturers' Associations (IFPMA) paid a few slightly grudging compliments to the report but headlined its press release: "The CIPR Report: Possibly More Dangerous to Economic Development than the Alleged Costs of Patents and Copyrights." It then went on to say:

> The two major exceptions [to countries that have adopted TRIPs-level protection]— Argentina and India—had the only representatives from developing countries as members of the CIPR.... Developing countries have two models of IP protection to choose from: that of China, Brazil, Mexico where economic growth is strong, foreign investment is flowing in, there is no "brain drain" problem, and innovation is beginning to take place or that of Argentina and India, both beset by inadequate growth, a drain of skilled people to other countries, no opportunity for innovation and (as in the case of Argentina) financial chaos. I believe that the choice is clear.[15]

Again the somewhat bizarre use of "evidence" from which equally bizarre conclusions are drawn, demonstrates that IFPMA is not prepared to debate the Commission report on its own ground. There is an attempt to discredit, rather than to engage with, the report. Other critical commentaries have been more detailed, and less eccentric, but are still based principally on assertion, supported anecdotally by the evidence of experience or "common sense."

These examples of responses to the report indicate that evidence-based research is not for the most part an effective means of directly influencing the views or behavior of interest groups with a powerful stake in the IP system. Apart from the interests at stake, this kind of discourse deriving from the academic world is not something they are comfortable with. Moreover, there is an "all or nothing" syndrome. For them any suggestion for modifications of the IP system that shift the balance toward the users rather than producers of IP is tantamount to an attack on the foundations of the IP system and to be resisted in any way possible, irrespective of the fact that the Commission's agenda was entirely reformist rather than abolitionist.

To expect otherwise of these interest groups would perhaps be to exhibit naivety about the research-policy process. The most likely way in which change will occur, when there are powerful interest groups ranged against it, is through changing the dynamics and center of gravity of public debate and policy discussion in which research-based evidence does have an important role, particularly when linked to advocacy by several different constituencies. Key constituencies here include civil society groups, academia, think tanks, the press, politicians, civil servants, and, increasingly, pop stars. A coalition of these can be a counterweight to the power of particular interest groups. It can also change the terms and framework in which the debate is conducted. Perspectives or ideas that previously had been ruled out as irrelevant, dangerous, or "nutty" over a period of time become perceived as central. The way the international community overcame its deep-seated opposition to debt relief, and the catalytic role of Jubilee 2000, is a good example. On the other hand, there are many counter-examples. Years of research and campaigning about the iniquities of developed country agricultural policies—and their heavy costs both to consumers and taxpayers in developed countries and developing country agricultural sectors—have had minimal effect in bringing about reform.

Coalitions may also be more effective where they link presumed "losers" in developed or developing countries. For instance, the open-source software movement, essentially a developed-country movement, is potentially of great importance to developing countries as an alternative to ubiquitous proprietary software. Campaigns in the United States against the alleged extension of copyright terms beyond the "limited times" specified in the Constitution may also have important implications for developing country access to information. Similarly, moves to change the model of electronic publishing of scientific journals so that authors rather than consumers pay the costs of publication, also emanating from developed countries, may be of particular significance to scientists in developing countries.[16]

However, many developing countries have limited capacity to produce research, in particular research that responds to their own policy concerns rather the concerns of external funders. Similarly, their ability to absorb research, whatever its source, may be weak. The class of intermediary policy adviser who helps bridge the gap between the research world and the policymaker, such as exists in developed country governments, international organizations, or now NGOs, is relatively rare in developing countries. Any research program would need to consider how these capacity issues could be addressed.

Research Priorities

As we have noted, international rules on IP are developing rapidly. Very often the rules are changed in response to pressure from users of the IP system without any proper assessment of how they may impact on economic development or on the access of consumers and researchers to knowledge, products embodying knowledge, new technologies, and ideas. As the rules evolve, their actual and potential impact needs to be properly understood if policymaking is to be more firmly based on evidence, and less on preconceptions of the value or otherwise of these rules to developing countries.

This challenge has two principal aspects. First, there is a need for more evidence on the effect of introducing stronger IP protection in developing countries, particularly in those with low incomes that lack a viable technological base. Secondly, the range of emerging issues where the relationship between IP protection and development needs to be analyzed and understood is very broad.

The agenda over the coming five to ten years might include:

- The consequences of full implementation of TRIPs for the developing world, including the provisions relating to enforcement.
- The implications of the movement toward harmonization and integration of patent systems at the international level.
- Impacts of patents and other IPRs in new or rapidly advancing fields of technology, such as biotechnology and software.
- The impact of IP protection on access through the Internet to information crucial for development, including the impact of technological protection by publishers and other content providers, and of anti-circumvention legislation.

- The costs and benefits of geographical indications for developing countries.
- How best to build capacity for IP policymaking, administration, and enforcement in developing countries—and how donors can support this capacity building more effectively.

Currently, research on IP is sponsored and undertaken by a variety of public and private sector organizations: universities, NGOs, industry associations, IP institutes, and development agencies. WIPO commissions studies on particular topics, and occasional research papers, but, surprisingly, it does not support a more substantial and extensive research program directed at the emerging issues in its field. The WIPO Worldwide Academy currently focuses principally on training, but research is a part of its mandate. There would be value in WIPO building up the research work of the Academy as a means of better informing itself, and its members, about the impact of IP on developing countries at different stages of development. Currently, too little research work is focused on low-income developing countries, and even less is undertaken by developing country organizations themselves as part of national-level programs.

The system will only improve from a development perspective if we can develop a deeper understanding of the relationships between IP and development. It is important, therefore, for the community of research sponsors and practitioners around the world to meet this challenge. More research and collation of country case studies are certainly needed on subjects such as those listed above. But this is by no means a definitive list. Apart from questions of resources and research priorities, there would also be benefits from greater collaboration and coordination in this field between research sponsors and practitioners in developed and developing countries.

An international network and partnership initiative should be considered which would bring together development agencies, developing country governments, IP researchers, and NGOs. The aims would be to identify priorities and promote coordination of research programs; improve knowledge sharing among partners; and facilitate wider dissemination of findings through sponsorship of publications, conferences, and Internet-based resources. A steering committee could oversee the initiative's operations and working groups could be formed on particular subjects.

Appendix

Possible Indicators of Development Friendliness in IP Policy

No attempt is made here at quantification. The idea is to suggest the categories of policy and their composition that might be used to audit the extent to which developed country policies may have a development content.

Domestic IP Policies

Two main categories of domestic IP policy may affect the interests of developing countries:

- *Direct influence.* An example of this category includes the provision in U.S. patent law that excludes existing use overseas as a reason for refusing a patent application. Many of the examples of so-called "bio-piracy" arise through the legitimate patenting in the United States of plants or uses of plants that are commonly known about in the developing country concerned, but where such use has not been documented, or not been documented in a way that is accessible to U.S. patent examiners. Other developed countries do not have a similar provision and are therefore less likely to "wrongly" patent material from developing countries.
- *Indirect influence.* Domestic legislation, particularly in respect to electronic material, may have the effect of reducing access to "essential" information in third countries as well. For example, technological protection of scientific books and articles on the Internet may prevent the exercise of "fair use" rights, for example, to copy or even read extracts without authorization or payment.

International IP Policies

Again there are different categories that may be considered:

- *Policies on bilateral/multilateral agreements.* The Commission considered that IP obligations that went beyond TRIPs should not be imposed on developing countries, while recognizing that some countries might voluntarily consider some such policies beneficial to them. There is a gradation of the extent to which "TRIPs-plus" is routinely demanded in such agreements (with the U.S. at one extreme). There is also a gradation in the number of countries affected by such agreements. For example, EU numbers are probably greater than the U.S. because of the umbrella Cotonou agreement which covers all the EU's African, Caribbean and Pacific partners (the ACP countries), although the extent of TRIPs-plus impositions in that agreement is less than most U.S. agreements.

- *Policies in WTO/WIPO.* Negotiating positions in the WTO also exhibit variation. Typically, the United States is at one extreme and the EU often adopts a softer line, although this varies according to the particular IP policy issue being addressed.
- *Technical assistance policies.* Countries may be assessed as to how far their technical assistance policies recognize the need to tailor IP policies to countries' economic and social circumstances, as opposed to how far they reflect policies pursued in developed countries or, worse, are influenced by producer interests in developed countries. It needs to be noted that the major providers of technical assistance are WIPO and the European Patent Office.

Notes

1. The author is a member of the UK Department for International Development and was formerly head of the secretariat of the Commission on Intellectual Property Rights. The views expressed here do not necessarily represent those of the Commission on Intellectual Property Rights or of the UK Department for International Development.
2. The Commission's report, "Integrating Intellectual Property Rights and Development Policy," and associated background documents can be downloaded from its website www.iprcommission.org. Hard copies can be obtained by e-mailing ipr@dfid.gov.uk.
3. WTO Agreement on Trade-related Aspects of Intellectual Property Rights.
4. United Nations (1948), *"Universal Declaration of Human Rights,"* UN, Geneva, Article 27. Source: http://www.un.org/Overview/rights.html.
5. UN Sub-Commission on the Promotion and Protection of Human Rights (2001), *"Intellectual Property Rights and Human Rights,"* UN, Geneva, p.6, paragraph14, Document No. E/CN.4/Sub.2/2001/12. Source: http://www.unhchr.ch/Huridocda/ Huridoca.nsf/(Symbol)/E.CN.4.Sub.2.2001.12.En?Opendocument.
6. See, for instance, Linsu Kim, "Technology Transfer and Intellectual Property Rights: Lessons from Korea's Experience." UNCTAD/ICTSD, October 2002. Source: http:/ /www.ictsd.org/iprsonline/unctadictsd/docs/Kim2002.pdf.
7. The French acronym for the International Union for the Protection of New Varieties of Plants.
8. Both quotations from Bruce Lehman, "WIPO at the Center: A Brief Description of the Global Intellectual Property System." Speech in Miami, Florida, August 2000. Source: http://www.iipi.org/newsroom/speeches/Miami%200800.pdf.
9. The Trade Act of 2002.
10. J. Barton, "Integrating IPRs in Development Strategies," Background Paper for Bellagio Meeting, 30 October–2 November 2002.
11. See, for instance, William Easterley, *The Elusive Quest for Growth: Economists' Adventures and Misadventures in the Tropics*, Cambridge, MIT Press, 2001.
12. "id21: Tracking Routes towards Impact: Summary," 2002 Source: http:// www.id21.org/id21-info/impact/summary.pdf.
13. From Fritz Machlup on the U.S. patent system, *IPR Commission Report*, September 2002, 16.
14. PhRMA Press Release, 13 September 2002. Source: http://www.iprcommission.org/ graphic/Views_articles/Pharmaceutical_Research_and_Manufacturers _of_America.htm.

15. IFPMA Press Release, 13 September 2002. Source: http://www.iprcommission.org/ graphic/Views_articles/International_Federation_of_Pharmaceutical_ Manufacturers_Associations.htm
16. See "Free Journals to Boost Access to Medical Science," SciDevNet, 20 December 2002. Source: http://www.scidev.net/frame3.asp?id=2012200209543647&authors= Katie%20Mantell&posted=19%20Dec%202002&c=1&r=1&t=NB.

7

Migration as a Factor in Development and Poverty Reduction: The Impact of Rich Countries' Immigration Policies on the Prospects of the Poor

Kathleen Newland[1]

> *International migration is the missing link*
> *between globalization and development.[2]*

Migration remains very much the exception rather than the rule of human behavior. About 175 million people today are estimated to be living in a country other than the one in which they were born. Another way of saying this is that approximately 97 percent of humanity has stayed home. Why then does international migration suddenly loom so large on the international policy agenda? Much of the answer lies in the domestic politics of migrant-receiving countries, where immigration has become a wedge issue exploited by right-wing parties, and part lies in the abrupt demographic transition that the major countries of destination are going through (Box 7.1). Another element is concern about the consequences of human-capital flight, or "brain drain." More positive reasons for the interest in migration include growing optimism about the developmental potential of financial flows associated with remittances and investment from emigrant populations. These and other factors add up to a greatly heightened consciousness about the importance of migration as a force of globalization and economic change.

Box 7.1
The Demographic Decline of the West

According to the UN Population Division, Europe's population declined from 728 million in 2000 to 726 million in 2003, and is projected to continue to decline to 632 million in 2050.[a] At the same time, the populations of developed countries will be aging rapidly—in Europe's case, the median age is projected to increase from 37.7 in 2000 to 47.7 in 2050.

According to the European Union's statistical office, in 2001 there were more deaths than births in 43 percent of the 211 regions that make up the European Union. The population in one out of every four regions declined even when immigration was taken into account. The *International Herald Tribune* points out that "Towns and villages in southwest France, southern Italy, northern Spain, and here in Eastern Germany, among other places, are shrinking or in some cases disappearing. Maintaining roads, telephone networks, and other basic services is becoming expensive in areas that are not economically self-sustaining."[b]

This combination of a declining and aging population means that labor markets will be caught between a dwindling supply of workers and a surging demand for services like health care and domestic work. Many observers conclude that the result of these trends will be a dramatic increase in the demand for immigrant labor.

Immigration alone, however—particularly as it is currently practiced—is not a realistic "solution" to population aging. Immigrants also age, and tend to adopt the fertility habits of their host country. According to UN projections, Germany, for example, would need an average immigrant inflow of 3.4 million people a year every year through 2050 in order to maintain its current ratio of working age to retirement age people.[c] As a result, there is likely to be renewed interest in temporary labor mobility, which could give developed countries access to a huge supply of labor without bringing in many new permanent residents. The clear need for increased migration gives some urgency to consideration of how to accommodate the increased flows in policy terms, and how migration flows might be managed to bring greater advantage to the migrants' countries of origin.

[a] United Nations Population Division, *World Population Prospects 2002 Revision*, New York: United Nations, February 2003.
[b] *International Herald Tribune*, 12 December 2002.
[c] United Nations Population Division, *Replacement Migration: Is it a Solution to Declining and Aging Populations?* New York: United Nations, 2000.

This chapter focuses on the impact of the migration policies of rich countries on the development prospects of poor countries. The state of knowledge about the causal effects assumed here is imperfect to say the least. Basic data about, for example, remittance flows (which are reported by the receiving countries) are not disaggregated by source country, making it very difficult to say with precision that the immigration policy of a particular country has had a specific effect on the flow of resources to the home country of the migrants. And because so much of the remittance flow moves through informal channels, recorded remittances are believed to be a fraction of the actual funds sent home by migrants.

The rich industrial countries are experiencing the consequences of a dramatic decline in fertility, which, along with increasing life expectancy, results in a rapidly aging society whose population will in time shrink if current trends in fertility, mortality, and net migration continue. Many observers conclude that the fertility/mortality trends will dramatically increase the demand for immigrant labor. The desire and the apparent opportunity to turn increased migration flows to the greater advantage of the migrants' countries of origin prompts renewed attention to the potential of migration policy as an instrument of development.

Theoretical Explanations[3]

Each of the most common theoretical explanations of international migration captures only part of the complex reality of the phenomenon and therefore offers only limited guidance for policy thinking and research. Neoclassical economic theory sees migration as the process that, in the absence of obstructions, equalizes the return to one of the major factors of production—labor. It looks at migration as a reaction to disequilibria between wages (and working conditions) in countries of origin and destination; individuals move in order to maximize their earnings after weighing the potential gains against the costs and risks of migration. Basic supply and demand factors, described in migration terms as "push" and "pull" factors, are the engine of migration, and changing patterns are brought about by convergence (or divergence) in labor markets.

A new economics of labor migration portrays a more complex landscape of decision-making in which the household rather than the individual is the basic unit of decision-making. The migration of one or more members is part of a household strategy to minimize risk, increase the security of the family under difficult conditions at home by diversifying its participation in different labor markets, and overcome the local constraints on household income, production, and/or capital accumulation. The broad economic motives of migration are not played out only through the labor market; in fact, labor migration is not the most common form of migration to rich countries from poor countries: family reunification is.

Segmented labor market theory focuses on forces operating at higher levels of aggregation: immigration is driven by the hierarchical structure of modern industrial economies. The duality between permanent well-paid jobs and unstable, temporary, low-status, poorly paid jobs creates the permanent demand of the modern economy for immigrants. Every hierarchy must have a bottom rung, and it becomes more and more difficult to attract native-born workers to take these jobs as expectations rise and the social safety net is strengthened. Employers remain reluctant to raise wages for lower productivity jobs, which either cease to exist or are exported, mechanized, or filled by new immigrant labor. Even if the lowest segment of jobs disappears, the next lowest will take its place as the least desired and the hardest to fill with native-born workers.

In emerging theories of globalization, and in older structural explanations such as world systems theory, migration is seen as a natural consequence of economic integration, for better or for worse. The structural change inherent in market-driven economic development is inherently destabilizing of established employment patterns. With structural reform in agriculture and other traditional modes of production, labor is released in amounts that cannot be absorbed locally. Domestic urbanization is the most common result, but trade and political links may encourage international migration as well.

Social capital theory emphasizes the role of transnational networks in facilitating international migration. These networks provide a powerful explanation of why migration is so unevenly spread. Average per capita incomes are low throughout China, but contemporary Chinese emigration originates overwhelmingly from a single province, Fujian, which has a long history of out-migration. Similarly, 60 percent of Indian immigrants in the United States come from the state of Gujarat. Familial, community, or ethnic ties between migrants abroad and intending migrants at home, particularly as they become institutionalized, lower the costs and raise the returns of relocation. Each of these theoretical approaches contributes insight into the complex phenomenon that is migration.

Types and Patterns of Migration

Immigrants to rich countries from among the poor flow through three major streams: the family stream, the employment stream, and the humanitarian stream.

In the advanced industrial countries, family reunification accounts for the great bulk of immigration: about 60 percent in the European Union and 75-80 percent in the United States. Governments set the rules for family migration, but it is not easy for them to control the numbers. The right to integrity and unity of the family is widely recognized as a fundamental human right. Very few countries place legal restrictions on the right of citizens to sponsor a spouse or minor children for immigration. Some add parents under certain conditions. Legal permanent residents who are not citizens also normally have some rights to family reunification.

The second largest immigration stream to the United States is employment related. But compared to family-based immigration it is small, at an annual rate of only about 107,000, or 13 percent of all migrants, for permanent residence. (There is also a sizable temporary labor category, many of whom eventually gain permanent status.) The employment category is the most controllable, and most welcome in public policy terms. In Europe, however, it is only in third place among sources of immigrants, at about 7 percent.

The third steam of immigration—the humanitarian—is the one part of the immigration stream over which governments have deliberately relinquished a considerable degree of control. As of January 2003, 145 governments have signed the UN Convention Relating to the Status of Refugees, which obligates them not to return a refugee against her will to a place where her life or liberty would be in danger. Another clause of that treaty says that a refugee should not be penalized for entering a country illegally in order to seek asylum.

The asylum channel is one of the very few ways in which a person without previous ties in a country can legally remain there, and it has become a major channel of migration. Roughly one-third of all entries to European countries now are asylum seekers. Many of them are suspected of coming for economic motives rather than to escape persecution, although the greatest number come from some of the most violent and oppressive countries on earth—Afghanistan, Iraq, Iran, Somalia, and Sudan all being high on the list of source countries. The United States, with its more expansive family and employment entry, receives only 8 percent of its total legal immigration through humanitarian programs.

Although migration is a long-term constant in human history (and, indeed, pre-history), it has historically moved in fits and starts. In the past, the great waves of international migration have been interrupted by catastrophes; two world wars and a global depression put a stop to the last great wave. Without these catastrophic interruptions, migration acquires a tremendous momentum, in large part because of the phenomenon of *chain migration*, which is driven by family reunification and community networks. One member of a family establishes himself—or, increasingly, herself—in a new country, and in time is able to bring the spouse or children or parents she left behind. Then the spouse brings his parents, and they bring their other adult children, who bring their spouses, siblings, in-laws, and so forth. The communities of origin often develop a culture and a political economy of migration, so that it becomes an expected part of life's pattern and develops a powerful momentum if it is not interrupted by some external factor.

No war or depression on a scale large enough to disrupt migration patterns has occurred since migration recovered from the aftereffects of World War II. The earth-shaking events of the last twenty years have been such as to promote migration—the collapse of the Iron Curtain; the removal of internal borders in Europe as part of the process of European integration; and the technological revolution that has put long-distance travel and communication within reach of people of modest means. The protracted civil wars of the late twentieth century, rather than disrupting migration patterns, have created new ones as refugees have sought safety in other countries. The worldwide total of refugees peaked in early 1990s and has remained high, as the resolution of many long-standing conflicts proves elusive.

Costs and Benefits of Migration from the Perspective of Poor Countries of Origin

The balance of costs and benefits accruing to the source countries from migration is controversial. The argument usually comes down to one of remittances vs. brain drain, and the evidence on both sides is weak. Developing tools to identify with greater precision the effects of both factors on development, growth, and poverty reduction is necessary in order to reach any confident conclusions about the impact of migration policy on development. There are, however, many other factors that impose costs and confer benefits, and it is important that they, too, be taken into account even though the state of knowledge about them is similarly patchy.

There is little doubt that voluntary migration from a poor to a rich country almost always benefits the individual migrant, who may easily find himself or herself earning in an hour what he or she earned in a day in the country of origin. The question is whether the benefits to individuals (and, commonly, their relatives left behind) aggregate to a general benefit to the home country. The evidence is contradictory and fragmentary. Much of the research that supports beliefs about the overall costs and benefits of migration is "micro" (the impact of remittances on inequality in five villages in Punjab), and cannot conclusively demonstrate the validity of "macro" conclusions.

Remittances

The most often cited support for the positive side of the argument is the observation that remittances from international migrants play an extraordinary role in the economic accounts of many developing countries, one far more important than official development assistance. Worldwide, remittances are estimated to exceed $100 billion a year, and approximately 60 percent of remittances are thought to go to developing countries.[4] Official development assistance (ODA) from the DAC countries was $54 billion in 2000. In Nicaragua and Haiti, remittances account for 25 percent and 17 percent, respectively, of GDP. Even in a larger and stronger economy such as that of Mexico, remittances equal 10 percent of the value of exports and about 80 percent of the value of foreign direct investment, and are nearly as large as the earnings from the second largest source of income, tourism.[5] They are the most important source of income for the Dominican Republic, El Salvador, and Honduras. They account for 20 percent of the GDP of Jordan, and for 10 percent of urban household spending in Morocco. The estimates are notoriously imprecise, however, because remittances often move through private, unrecorded channels. Moreover, as ODA has been declining, remittances seem to have been rising strongly, even in the face of weak economic performance in the host countries. Flows from the United States to Mexico and Central America grew from less than $1 billion in 1980 to more than $14 billion in 2002.[6] In 2002, according to the Bank of Guatemala, wire transfers to Guatemala more than doubled, to $1.4 billion from $560 million the previous year.[7]

Despite these numbers, many experts believe that labor migration does not significantly improve the development prospects of the country of origin. Source countries have had great difficulty in converting remittance income into sustainable productive capacity. In addition, most states are able to exercise little control over the composition of their labor exports, which tends to be determined by foreign labor markets and may bear no relation to "surplus" labor at home. A few countries have focused quite deliberately on "producing" skilled labor for foreign markets—Philippine nurses and Indian computer programmers come to mind—but most are passive in the face of international supply and demand.

In addition, it is argued that remittance income is rarely used for productive purposes. Remittances go in small amounts to poor people (the average size of a transfer from the United States to Latin America is about $200),[8] and are used mostly to support direct consumption as well as some housing, health care, and education. A very small proportion of remitted funds seem to go into income-earning, job-creating investment. Moreover, remittances may increase inequality, encourage consumption of imports, and create dependency. They are often delivered with stunning inefficiency; as much as 20 percent of their value is said to disappear commonly through high transfer fees and poor exchange rate offerings.

The benefits of remittance income to source *countries* do not necessarily explain the full impact of remittances on poverty. Remittances may not constitute a rising tide that lifts all boats, but they do have a very important effect on the standard of living of the households that receive them, constituting a significant portion of household income. A review of the literature on remittances by Deborah Waller Meyers reports a fairly strong consensus on their use, across countries. "For the most part, remittances are used for daily expenses such as food, clothing, and health care.... Funds are also spent on building or improving houses, buying land or cattle, and buying consumer goods such as washing machines and televisions."[9] Families also spend remittance income on education. Meyers concludes that remittances are spent in the same ways that income from other sources is spent by people in similar situations.

Remittances are an important social safety net for poor families, possibly reducing additional out-migration in particularly difficult times. Studies in the Dominican Republic showed that residents at all economic and social levels received remittances, but that the poor relied on them most heavily, as one would expect. In a 1991 study, 33.8 percent of Dominicans received remittances, which provided on average 60 percent of family income.[10] Governments in Central America recognize the safety net aspects of migrant remittances. In the aftermath of the devastating Hurricane Mitch in 1999, the government of El Salvador asked the United States government not for additional humanitarian aid, but for extended permission for Salvadoran immigrants to stay legally in the United States so that they could send money to storm-affected relatives back home.

The relatively small portion of remittances that are used for investment (apart from human capital investment through education and health spending) reflects not only the immediate consumption needs of poor families, but also the discouraging investment climate for the poor. Until problems such as poor infrastructure, corruption, lack of access to credit, distance from markets, lack of training in entrepreneurial skills, disincentives to savings, and so forth are tackled, it is unrealistic to expect remittances to solve the problem of low investment in poor communities. In the meantime, remittances lift many recipients out of poverty, if only for as long as the transfers continue.

Brain Drain

If remittances are the major benefits of migration from the point of view of the source countries, the loss of human resources—particularly highly skilled people—is the most serious cost. The market for advanced skills has become truly a global market, and the most dynamic industrial economies are admitting—sometimes even recruiting—significant proportions of the highly trained professionals from poor countries.[11] *The Economist,* in a September 2002 article about emigration, assembled the following random snapshots of the brain drain:

- About 30 percent of all highly educated Ghanaians and Sierra Leoneans live abroad.
- 12 percent of Mexico's people with higher education are in the United States, as are 30 percent of its Ph.Ds.
- 75 percent of Jamaicans with higher education are in the United States.
- Albania lost one-third of its qualified people in the decade after the fall of communism.
- Half of all foreign students who get Ph.Ds in the United States are still there five years later.

Ironically, emigrants from countries in which a very small proportion of people gain tertiary education are not only better educated than their compatriots, but also tend to be much more highly skilled than the people of their destination countries. A study of new legal immigrants to the United States found that 21 percent have at least seventeen years of education—a level reached by only 8 percent of U.S. native born.[12]

The loss of skilled people imposes several different kinds of costs on their countries of origin. The most obvious is perhaps the cost of the education itself, which in almost all cases has been heavily subsidized by the state. The emigration of the educated thus represents a transfer from the poor country to the rich. There are also fiscal costs associated with the brain drain, in that the country of origin loses the tax revenue that these potential high-earners would have paid into the national exchequer. A study by Mihir A. Desai, Devesh Kapur, and John McHale examined the direct fiscal losses associated with the emigration to the United States from India of a key element of the tax base. Estimating what highly skilled professionals would have earned and paid in taxes if they had stayed in India, it concluded that the net fiscal losses ranged (depending on the methodology employed) from 0.24 percent to 0.5 percent of India's GNP. Indian expatriates are high earners even compared to their U.S. contemporaries. Although they comprise only 0.1 percent of India's population, their aggregate income abroad is equivalent to 10 percent of India's national income. The study also demonstrated that it is "the best and the brightest" who tend to emigrate: the proportion resident abroad was higher among graduates of the most prestigious Indian institutions, among those graduating higher in their academic classes, and among those in the most sought-after fields of specialization.[13]

The net developmental losses from the brain drain are more difficult to estimate. Losses of highly skilled professionals may in the extreme case—in which dire economic mismanagement, conflict, poor working conditions, and low levels of reward conspire with opportunities abroad—be the final blow that cripples institutions and sectors of an economy. A Communication from the European Commission on Migration and Development reports that "three-quarters of doctors with Zambian nationality left the country, in just a few years. Nigeria saw 21,000 medical doctors emigrating to industrialized countries."[14]

The developmental impact of the brain drain is most severe in source countries with weak human resource bases, where educational systems are not capable of replacing those who emigrate. A "musical chairs" game of replacement migration from other countries is captured by Jonathan Crush's description of the impact of emigration on South Africa's health sector. He quotes the South African High Commissioner to Canada: "The cycle, as I understand it, is that your (Canadian) city doctors go to the States for richer pickings. And then your rural doctors come here (to urban centers) and our doctors go to your rural areas. And we get Cuban doctors."[15] In Crush's account, the mystery is not South African doctors' emigration (spurred by recruiting from Canada among other places), but why South Africa has not in turn engaged in replacement recruiting. South Africa is exposed to the stings of globalization but political obstacles to immigration in this otherwise open economy impede it from enjoying the potential benefits.

Sub-Saharan African countries such as Zambia, Liberia, or Zimbabwe represent an extreme. For countries in crisis, the brain drain is only one manifestation of a more general problem of an economy in free-fall. Many other countries that are seeing high levels of skilled immigration are beginning to think in terms of labor—and even skills—export as a comparative advantage, and to think of ways to maximize its benefits (Box 7.2).

In the right circumstances, the employment abroad of skilled people may bring benefits to their countries of origin. Once they have migrated, highly skilled people do not necessarily abandon their home countries. Given the right opportunities, they will invest in their home countries or outsource production to it. They will also contribute expertise—Silicon Valley-based Taiwanese migrants

Box 7.2
The Philippines: Labor Export as Official Policy

In the Philippines, labor export has been an explicit part of the government's economic plan. The government's policy goals have been consistent: migration should be temporary and it should be done through official channels.

All employment abroad must be approved by the Philippines Overseas Employment Administration (POEA), which also contracts directly with foreign companies and government to provide temporary labor of all types. Through POEA, workers can receive health and insurance benefits for themselves and their families, pre-departure briefings and counseling, an ATM card that can be used to send remittances, and the right to make claims against their employer through an adjudication process. In addition, POEA makes some effort to verify the work conditions of official workers: it recently suspended labor migration to Hong Kong in response to the persistent abuse of Philippine domestic workers. The government also tries to thicken the social and political links tying Filipinos to their homeland by allowing migrants to vote from abroad and sponsoring Philippine cultural events in host countries.

It is difficult to judge the impact of this activist policy in making emigration from the Philippines more temporary, legal, humane, and productive. The government estimates that 2.9 million temporary workers were abroad via official channels in 2000. However, an estimated 1.8 million Filipinos were abroad having moved irregularly, and 2.5 million Filipino citizens were permanent residents of another country.[a]

Labor migration has become an important industry, with official remittances amounting to about 8.9 percent of GDP.[b] Other industries, such as education and tourism, derive a large part of their revenues from serving would-be and current migrants. But the return of temporary workers has been disappointing as a development tool. Although studies show that migrants often return with useful new skills, they generally stay unemployed until their next deployment abroad.

[a] Philippines Overseas Employment Administration, web page http://www.poea.gov.ph, 2 April 2003.
[b] International Monetary Fund, *Balance of Payments Yearbook 2002,* Washington DC: IMF, 2003; World Bank, *World Development Indicators 2002,* Washington, DC, 2003.

earned the name "astronauts" in the 1980s because they "lived in the air" commuting between California and Taiwan (Box 7.3). Associations of migrant professionals, such as the South African Network of Skills Abroad, contribute expertise and help keep researchers in the source country abreast of international advances. And highly skilled migrants sometimes return permanently, particularly if change in their home country (democratization or growth of the economy, for example) presents them with real opportunities to use their skills. "Brain circulation" is the other side of the coin to "brain drain."

Box 7.3
Taiwan: Brain Drain or Brain Gain?

Developing countries lament the emigration of highly skilled people because it robs the domestic economy of the rewards to publicly subsidized investment in education. The case of Taiwan, however, shows that high skill emigration can play a more benign, and even positive, role in development.

In terms of the number of emigrants, Taiwan has suffered from "brain drain" as badly as any developing country. Over 90,000 Taiwanese left for study abroad in the second half of the last century, and in some years returns were fewer than 10 percent of departures.[a] But these emigrants did not carry large amounts of publicly subsidized education with them; Taiwan had invested mostly in primary, secondary, and vocational education and began heavily subsidizing higher education only recently, as the domestic economy began to demand those skills. This forced Taiwanese students who wished to continue in university to migrate, but their education abroad was financed privately— and often subsidized by the governments of their host countries.

Once gone, these emigrants were not forgotten. As Taiwan's high-tech sector grew and demanded more skills, emigrants abroad contributed their considerable expertise, experience, and business connections. They began to return, sometimes with the help of a government database that tracked skilled migrants and matched them with job opportunities in Taiwan. Many returned to start businesses, particularly in places like the Hsinchu Industrial Park, where the government built Western-style housing and sponsored international conferences in order to build a critical mass of well-educated returnees. The lesson: good public policy can be a catalyst for "brain circulation" when combined with a healthy economy that can make real use of the skills that highly educated migrants have to offer.

[a] Luo, Yu-Ling and Wei-Jen Wang. "High-skill migration and Chinese Taipei's industrial development." In OECD, *International Mobility of the Highly Skilled*. Paris: OECD, 2002.

Beyond Remittances vs. Brain Drain

Trying to net out the benefits of remittances and the costs of the brain drain is seen by a growing body of analysts as too limited a framework for assessing the impact of migration on development. Other kinds of financial flows may have more concentrated developmental impacts than remittances, which, as we have seen, are used primarily for current consumption. Foreign direct investment from emigrants back to their countries of origin has tremendous potential, and is already important for some countries. Chinese emigrant communities, for example, numbering about 55 million worldwide, invest about $60 billion in China. By contrast, India's 20 million expatriates invest only about $1 billion in India.[16] *Tourism* from immigrant communities to the "old country" is a major earner for countries from Ireland to Vietnam. *Philanthropy* by "home town associations" (Mexico), returnee associations (Jamaica), charitable foundations (Egypt), or by individual expatriates provides significant resources for community development at the local level. *Fundraising* for political candidates or causes targets diaspora communities. Nostalgia for the foods and products of the country of origin creates *markets* for those products in the immigration country, fostering local production and international trade. All of these interactions are fostered by the growth of transnational networks that sustain deep and thick relations among migrants, their countries of origin, and the countries in which they have settled. In an age of swift and cheap transport and communication, emigration no longer represents the break with the home country that it once did. And in this context, social and economic capital can no longer be neatly segregated analytically. Many students of migration agree that these transnational networks are today the most important developmental resource associated with international migration.[17]

Transnational networks are not a new phenomenon, but they are relatively new as objects of interest to development analysts and policymakers. Jagdish Bhagwati suggests, "A realistic response requires abandoning the 'brain drain' approach of trying to keep the highly skilled at home. More likely to succeed is a diaspora model, which integrates past and present citizens into a web of rights and obligations in the extended community defined with the home country as the center."[18] Increasingly, the governments of countries of origin are seeking to cultivate ties with the diaspora, seeing them as a source of investment, overseas market openings, foreign exchange, expertise, and political support (in domestic campaigns as well as vis-à-vis the governments of their new countries of residence). The Government of India, for example, collaborated with the Federation of Indian Chambers of Commerce in January 2003 in sponsoring a conference of "non-resident Indians" and "people of Indian descent," which was attended by nearly 2,000 people.[19] It is preparing to offer dual citizenship to overseas Indians in Australia, Canada, New Zealand, and Singapore, the United Kingdom, and the United States, and to relax constraints on overseas investment by Indian nationals. Other governments are following similar courses of action, seeking to encourage close transnational ties within the diaspora.

How Development Friendly Are the Migration Policies of Rich Countries?

It is possible to answer this question with conviction but not with a very solid basis of incontrovertible evidence, mainly because so much is unknown about the complex relationship between migration and development. Are policies that permit large-scale immigration inflows development friendly? The answer is yes if one is convinced (as this author is) that migration is fundamentally a positive force in development; and no if one is preoccupied with the brain drain and skeptical of the influence of the diaspora. There are questions about the fundamental relationship between migration and development, and questions about which elements of that relationship are susceptible to policy intervention.

A certain number of policy arenas can be identified without much risk as being important to the migration-development relationship, although clear causal connections are hard to identify.

The *transactions costs* that migrants incur in transferring resources back to their home countries are high. Government actions that encourage competition in financial services to migrants and require transparency on fees, exchange rates, and such will increase the value of remittances that actually reach the intended beneficiaries. In 1996, two companies had 97 percent of the U.S. market in remittance transfers. A successful lawsuit against them on grounds of price gouging has resulted in greater oversight and greater involvement by the companies in the communities they serve. Moreover, competition is driving down prices. In January 2003, the retailing giant Walmart announced that it would offer money transfer services at lower rates than those currently prevailing. Improved services need to be offered on the receiving end of these transactions as well. Minimizing paperwork and identification requirements can encourage migrants to use banks and credit unions, which may be unfamiliar and intimidating. The current U.S. policy of allowing banks to accept consulate-issued identification cards when opening an account, for example, has helped banks market their services to undocumented immigrants, making the U.S. money-transfer market more competitive and fueling a price decline. New requirements placed on money-transfer services to combat money laundering and financing for terrorist organizations may move in the opposite direction, however, and raise transactions costs.

Transferability of pensions benefits source countries by encouraging return migration and infusing substantial funds into countries of origin as retirees repatriate their savings. Returning migrants bring their expertise and experience as well as their money.

The *recruitment policies* of rich countries such as Australia and Canada have been criticized as exacerbating the brain drain from poorer countries. The South African minister of health has stated "Countries that systematically under-produce skilled workers because it is cheaper to poach them from poorer countries are guilty of exploitation."[20] Yet recruitment for skilled workers is a central part of the immigration policies of such countries as Australia and Canada. The negative development impact of such recruitment in poor countries might be mitigated by support for education and training in the countries of origin, particularly in fields where needed skills are in short supply.

The *legal status of migrant workers* has a major impact on their ties with their home countries in a number of ways. Unauthorized migrants earn less for comparable work than those who work legally, and therefore are able to remit more to relatives at home. For migrants who use smugglers because they lack authorization to enter, the often-substantial fees reduce the benefits of moving. Unauthorized migrants are less able to seek recourse when their rights are violated, including labor rights. In 2002, the U.S. Supreme Court ruled in the case of *Hoffman Plastic Compounds, Inc.* that unauthorized workers cannot be awarded back-pay remedies, even if they are discharged in violation of the National Labor Relations Act— thus reversing a well-established trend that unauthorized workers are entitled to the same labor protections as authorized workers are. Policies that open paths to legal status for migrants are likely to increase their earnings by putting them in a stronger position to assert their labor rights and thus to send more money home to families and communities.

Studies have demonstrated that the lack of legal status combined with harsh border enforcement makes migrants less likely to return home periodically for family visits, which may lessen their ties with family left behind, discourage the flow of remittances, and convert temporary or circular migrants to permanency, given the risks and expense of repeated border crossings. As Doug Massey points out, "Immigration policies should...recognize that most international migrants are not initially motivated to settle permanently in developed nations, and that hardening the border through repressive police actions only undermines the inclination to return, ultimately reducing the flow of people and migradollars back to sending regions to choke off their development. A smarter strategy would be to cultivate the natural inclination of migrants to remain abroad temporarily by facilitating return migration and the repatriation of funds."[21]

Temporary labor mobility programs—when well designed and executed—are seen as being in the best interest of both sending and receiving countries. Temporary migration often better reflects the desires of migrants themselves and benefits countries of origin by promoting the continued flow of remittances and the return of migrants, along with any skills and capital they may have acquired while working abroad. For receiving countries, such programs represent a way to obtain needed labor without some of the social impacts of permanent migration. However, past temporary labor programs have all too often resulted in long-term illegal immigration and/or the exploitation and abuse of migrants.

Admissions of foreign students for tertiary education provide developing countries with an important educational resource, sometimes subsidized by governments or private institutions in the host country. On the other hand, foreign students often stay permanently (or semi-permanently) in the receiving country, so educational admissions also play a role in the "brain drain" controversy.

Family unity policies also have an impact on the development potential of migration, again through the mechanism of remittances. Harsh policies that make it difficult for families to reunite may encourage migrants to send money to relatives left at home, but that is hardly a recommendation for them. Governments have been known to resist more generous policies for that reason, however. The Government of Mozambique discouraged South Africa from taking the long overdue step of allowing Mozambican miners in South Africa to bring their families with them, on the grounds that remittance flows would shrink. In the diaspora model of transnational ties, reunited families are less likely to be seen as a threat to financial flows. More generally, *immigrant integration* policies may follow the same pattern of being good for immigrants but bad for remittances, unless strong transnational ties are established and maintained.

Western European countries have in recent years moved to *coordinate migration control and development policies* more closely. Seeking to address the root causes of migration from the major sources of unauthorized migration, the European Union set up a "High Level Working Group" in 1998 to prepare action plans on border control, coordination of aid, and reallocation of aid flows to six major source-countries and regions.[22] Underlying the assignment was the concept of "co-development" put forward originally by France, which recognized that the source and destination countries of migration occupy a single transnational space. There remains considerable suspicion among some of the partners that the goal is much more strongly to control migration than to contribute to development.

This is merely a selection of some of the most salient migration policies that have an impact on development. Many others could be explored. The relationship between migration and development is complex and uncertain; that between migration and poverty reduction even more so. A recent authoritative study on the migration development nexus, carried out by the Center for Development Research in Copenhagen for the Danish Ministry of Foreign Affairs, came to the following unequivocal conclusion: "There is no direct link between poverty, economic development, population growth, social and political change on the one hand and international migration on the other. Poverty reduction is not in itself a migration-reducing strategy."[23]

Priorities for Research

Migration research has produced various and sometimes contradictory conclusions on who wins and who loses from international migration. In the winners' column are:

- Migrants themselves, who usually succeed in bettering their earnings in the country of destination, although often at considerable personal cost.
- Employers, who are more easily able to hire the staff they need at the wage they are willing to pay, both of which contribute to their competitiveness.
- Consumers, for whom the costs of goods and services are kept down.
- Native-born employees in enterprises that would shut down or relocate if immigrant labor were not available.
- Taxpayers, whose funding obligations in pay-as-you-go pension schemes are supported by the social security payments of immigrants.
- Non-bank financial services sector, whose firms profit from transferring migrant remittances.
- Relatives left behind who receive remittances from migrants.

Some of the same categories appear as losers in different kinds or levels of analysis. They include:

- Unskilled and low-wage laborers in receiving countries (including immigrants), whose wages may be slightly suppressed by continuing inflows of new immigrants.
- Highly skilled professionals in receiving countries, whose pricing power for their services may be undercut by the admission of skilled immigrants.
- Taxpayers in receiving countries, especially at the local level, who bear the costs of public services (of which schooling is much the most important) to immigrants and their families.
- Residents of source countries who have to pay more for professional services or endure lower availability or quality of such services.

These lists are by no means exhaustive, but a comparison of the two reveals that considerable uncertainty persists about the impact of migration, reflecting the parlous state of knowledge about what makes migration beneficial, under what circumstances, and for whom.

Some very basic research is needed to answer some of the big questions about migration, such as who migrates, where, and why. A feminization of migration has occurred over the past two decades. What does that trend imply for development? Voluntary migrants do not come from the ranks of the poorest of the poor; what are the enabling conditions for migration? This chapter has dealt only with voluntary migration. Does forced migration produce a different kind or level of development dividend to the country of origin? Is temporary migration truly an alternative to permanent migration? Or does it simply strengthen the ties and the knowledge that encourage migration?

In order to grasp the development impact of the migration policies of rich countries, better data should be a priority. Remittance data need to be disaggregated by country of origin (of the remittances) so that correlations between policy and financial flows can be made. It is also important to keep in mind that while remittances are a major factor in development prospects, the development impact of migration goes far beyond remittances. Migrants remit more than money. With migration come transfers, exchanges, and sharing of social and political capital.

Almost every topic mentioned in this chapter has research topics embedded within it, because so few are thoroughly understood. A comprehensive research agenda on migration and development would attempt to better understand the behavior of migrants, assess the impact of public policies, and compile a store of lessons and best practices. Research areas and policies that merit particular attention include:

Remittances: Remittances are one of the topics where knowledge gaps plague policymaking on migration and development. Data on even those remittances that flow through official channels are not disaggregated by source country, are not comparable across countries, and may include other forms of money transfers. No large-scale, reliable estimates of informal remittance flows have been made. Questions also remain about the ways remittance income affects household spending and community economies, and the evolution of remittance behavior over time and with changes in the legal status of the migrant.

Meanwhile, development professionals should examine innovative ways of better leveraging remittances for development. For example, remittances are increasingly seen as a way of introducing the poor to the formal financial system in both the sending and receiving country. Banco Soladario, in Ecuador, now offers a complete migration package providing a loan to finance migration (repaid through remittances or by the migrant's family), a cheap remittance-sending service, and the opportunity for the migrant to control how remittances are used (by directing them to a mortgage payment or savings account, for example).[24] Remittance-backed bonds are a new option for banks and micro-finance institutions in developing countries.

As the private sector experiments with new projects and services, public policymakers in both sending and receiving countries need more information about the influence of government banking regulations on competition (and thus on the cost of sending remittances). For example, financial controls implemented after September 11th 2001 were associated with an almost ten-fold increase in officially recorded remittances to Pakistan from the United States as the informal, but highly efficient, Hundi (halawa) system was shut down.[25] Conversely, the United States' decision to continue to allow banks to accept foreign identification documents when opening bank accounts helped promote competition that has led to recent price declines in remittance transfers. However, most of the obstacles to lower prices lie in the poor banking infrastructure in developing countries; the effect of public policy on competition there should be a research priority.

The brain drain: The migration of highly skilled people deserves continued examination primarily because it represents a growing proportion of legal immigration into developed countries. Past discussions of the brain drain have often been poorly informed about the *opportunity costs* of emigration by highly skilled people. In countries with grave economic and/or political problems, highly educated people may not be able to use their skills, and thus may not be very productive. In this case, the loss to the sending country inflicted by migration may be outweighed by any remittances sent back. In more stable environments, however, the opportunity cost of the migration of human capital is greater. The *fiscal costs and benefits* to developing countries and *multiplier effects* of high-skill migration and their interaction with a number of areas of public policy are also significant. In countries that supply highly skilled labor on a large scale, such as India and the Philippines, the education of future migrants is a major industry—but could represent a real fiscal waste if subsidized by the state.

Beyond a strictly economic view, little is known about the effect of the loss of educated, innovative people on institutions and the political culture of the sending country. Both dimensions of human capital loss merit further exploration.

Diasporas and development: The role of a country's diaspora in development is more important and less understood than that of the brain drain. Critical evaluations of the role of diasporas and returned migrants in the development of the Indian software industry, the Taiwanese high-tech sector, or Chinese manufacturing should focus on discovering what enabling policies promote diaspora investment and outsourcing of production to migrants' countries of origin. Anecdotal evidence suggests that migrant investors are better equipped to navigate the cultural and bureaucratic obstacles of investment in their home country. They may also be willing to take greater risks or accept lower returns if they feel their home communities will benefit.

Small scale, low-tech efforts to tap these resources should receive the same attention as the celebrated successes in Taiwan or India. A government program in Mexico matched Mexican investors living in the United States with small-scale textile enterprises in Mexico. Despite flaws in the initial business plans and the unexpected withdrawal of government support, the migrant investors continued to play an active role in the ventures, contributing not just capital but expertise.[25] Research on efforts like this one should critically evaluate the role of the state in such projects.

Philanthropy, both individual and collective, by migrants in their communities of origin represents a tiny but growing fraction of the money that moves between destination and host countries. The state of Zacatecas, Mexico, tried to encourage such contributions and channel them to municipal governments through a program that matched donations from emigrants with money from the government. Migrant donations over seven years totaled $4.5 million, exceeding the capacity of the government to match them.[26] The effect of government incentives and government involvement in this case and others is not clear. Governments in both source and destination countries may have a role to play in encouraging and assisting philanthropy, but it is far from certain what that role should be.

On the negative side, diasporas also finance civil conflicts and terrorism—examples of groups funded by emigrants include the Irish Republican Army and the Tamil Tigers. More broadly, research is needed to identify financial controls that effectively block financial support of terrorism and civil conflict or money laundering but do not interfere with the legitimate flow of remittances.

One of the most complicated questions within the sphere of migration and development is the effect of efforts by source countries to maintain their emigrants' political and social ties. Allowing (and enabling) the members of diasporas to vote is not new, but has received increased attention from developing countries. Some view it as a way to further encourage the diaspora to remit, invest, or return. But there are other expectations: "Our overseas countrymen cannot be bought, intimidated, or hoodwinked," said the president of the Philippine Senate after passing a 2003 law allowing Filipinos to vote from abroad.[27] The downsides of dual citizenship and overseas voting are difficult to see, but for countries with large diasporas of permanent emigrants, they may force a reevaluation of the nature of citizenship.

Return migration: Despite documented cases in which migrants have returned to start factories, high tech firms, or other new initiatives with skills, connections, and capital acquired abroad, return migration is often a disappointing tool for development. In many cases, migrants return only to retire, start a low value-added business such as a taxi service, or remain unemployed until their next stint working abroad. Migrants who return early or without the resources for de facto retirement may be viewed as failures and thus effect little change in their home communities. In addition, skills learned in the host country may not be applicable upon return. More research is needed about what types of migration lead to the acquisition of useful skills, what incentives can encourage migrants to return, and what support can help migrants be more productive upon return.

The effects of new ideas and social attitudes carried by returning migrants should be examined. Those who have lived in democratic market economies may bring new standards of intolerance toward corruption, for example, and new expectations about the rule of law, political participation, and gender equality. But the effects of the migration experience are unpredictable: some migrants are radicalized by their time abroad, as the involvement of a few migrants in anti-Western terrorism has shown at the extreme.

Policies by developing countries such as multi-annual seasonal visas and transferable pensions are thought to be among the most powerful tools to promote return, but have not been implemented widely, even on an experimental basis.

Temporary labor mobility: Trade economists estimate that the efficiency gains to liberalizing the movement of labor even slightly far exceed the returns to any additional liberalization of trade.[28] Most of the wealth generated by such a liberalization would accrue to the migrants themselves—and thus benefit their countries of origin. However, liberalizing labor mobility under multilateral agreements, such as the WTO's GATS Mode 4, is still politically and socially contentious. Workable temporary labor migration programs will be a likely prerequisite for treating labor mobility as an economic issue. New visa structures, effective social protection systems, and return incentives should be goals of future research and policy experimentation.

Migrant behavior: Effective migration policy must be based on realistic views of how migrants behave. Little is known about the decision to migrate (or not migrate) and the choice of destination. Further, because the very poorest are not usually voluntary migrants, greater knowledge about the enabling conditions for migration is needed to better understand the effect of development upon migration. The effect of border controls on the decision to migrate and the decision to return (or not return) are of high interest to both sending and receiving countries.

Understanding the credit relationships within families that send migrants could help banks and other financial institutions develop more attractive products. More evidence is needed on the relationship between remittance behavior and both legal status and citizenship in both the sending and receiving country. Finally, the decision to return and behavior after return are of critical importance both to development policy and to the success of temporary labor programs.

As if this list of policy and research needs were not long enough, the task ahead includes the need to ensure that policies are built on an understanding of local needs and local behaviors. Advances in the understanding of migration and development will require partnerships involving researchers from countries of origin and destination. The cooperation of governments will be essential in dealing with the data requirements. A major goal of any research agenda should be to establish common parameters for data collection. Finally, and most difficult of all, policymakers in both developing and developed countries need to be willing to experiment with policy, assess its impact, and adapt to new circumstances and information.

Conclusion

Is the pendulum swinging, after decades of benign neglect, toward more institutionalization and regulation of migration and migration-related financial flows? In the case of migration, such a trend could be beneficial, since the "open market" for migrants is largely one of undocumented flows, which leave migrants open to exploitation and abuse against which they have little recourse. If greater efforts to manage migration are primarily restrictionist in nature, however, ignoring labor market needs and family ties, they will impose high costs (not least through the growth of organized crime) and are likely nonetheless to be ineffective. Regulation of remittances and migrant investment has less obvious upside potential. Regulatory schemes have often amounted to a tax on earnings, a tax on competitiveness, or a distortion of returns on investment. Apart from regulations aimed at illicit end-uses, such as money laundering or support for terrorism, positive incentives have the best chance of influencing the channels or uses of financial flows associated with migration.

There are not many fora in which cooperative migration policies can be agreed at a global level. International migration policy is marginalized to a remarkable degree within global (as opposed to regional) inter-governmental organizations. The sole exception concerns refugee flows, which are dealt with by the office of the UN High Commissioner for Refugees (UNHCR). This fact reflects the extent to which migration continues to be seen as an issue that lies firmly within the prerogatives of the sovereign state, as well as the reluctance of states to be bound by international agreements pertaining to migration. Three international treaties deal specifically with the human and labor rights of migrants, but have been ratified by few states and consequently have little impact. United Nations programs and agencies deal with migration sporadically, when it intersects with their major preoccupations, but not consistently. Given the untapped potential of migration as a factor in development, and the essential and growing role it is likely to play in the advanced industrial societies in the next twenty years, the relative silence of international organizations is an anomaly.

It is ever more apparent that no state finds it easy to control migration single-handedly. At the regional level, discussion and even cooperation on migration is increasingly common. It seems likely that the pressures on global organizations to take up migration issues will grow along with the attention to this prominent aspect of globalization.

Notes

1. The author is co-director, Migration Policy Institute, Washington DC. The author would like to thank Kevin O'Neill of the Migration Policy Institute for his assistance with this chapter.
2. Rubens Ricupero, secretary-general of the UNCTAD, quoted in Carlo Dade, "Transnational Communities and Grassroots Development: From Remittances to Community Co-Development," unpublished concept paper, Inter-American Foundation, 4 October 2002.
3. The author is indebted to Douglas S. Massey for his elegant précis of these theoretical explanations in a number of chapters and papers, on which this section draws for a much simpler overview. See, for example, Douglas S. Massey, Joaquin Arango, Graeme Hugo, Ali Kouaouci, Adela Pellegrino, and J. Edward Taylor, "Theories of International Migration: A Review and Appraisal," *Population and Development Review* 3 (September 1993): 433-466.
4. Countries such as Greece, Italy, Portugal, and Spain (all, until fairly recently, countries of emigration), receive substantial remittances as well.
5. Manuel Orozco, "Globalization and Migration: The Impact of Family Remittances in Latin America," in *Approaches to Increasing the Productive Value of Remittances, IAF and Other Case Studies in Financial Innovations and International Cooperative Community Ventures,* papers presented at a conference held at the World Bank, 19 March 2001. Washington DC: Inter-American Foundation, 2001.
6. Ibid., p. 24; Roberto Suro, summary of the study "Billions in Motion: Latino Immigrants, Remittances and Banking," *Migration Information Source* (www.migrationinformation.org), February 2003 edition.
7. Jacob H. Fries, "Business of human smuggling slowed only briefly after 9/11," *Denver Post,* 5 January 2003.
8. Roberto Suro, summary of the study "Billions in Motion: Latino Immigrants, Remittances and Banking," *Migration Information Source* (www.migrationinformation.org), February 2003 edition.
9. Deborah Waller Meyers, "Migrant Remittances to Latin America: Reviewing the Literature," paper commissioned by the Inter-American Dialogue and the Tomas Rivera Policy Institute. Washington DC, 1998.
10. Ibid.
11. Emigration of the highly skilled is not a problem peculiar to poor countries. Australia, Canada, and the United Kingdom among others lose highly trained people to the United States.
12. *The Economist,* "Outward Bound" 28 September 2002.
13. Mihir A. Desai, Devesh Kapur, and John McHale, "The Fiscal Impact of the Brain Drain: Indian Emigration to the US." Unpublished paper prepared for the Third Annual NBER-NCAER conference, 17-18 December 2001.
14. Commission of the European Communities, "Communication from the Commission to the Council and the European Parliament: I. Migration and Development." Brussels, 3.12.2002 COM (2002) 703 final, p. 24.
15. Jonathan Crush, "The Global Raiders: Nationalism, Globalization and the South African Brain Drain," *Journal of International Affairs* 56, 1 (Fall 2002).
16. Amy Waldman, "India Harvests Fruits of Diaspora," *New York Times,* 12 January 2003.
17. Alejandro Portes, "Introduction: The Debates and Significance of Immigrant Transnationalism," in *Global Networks* 1, 3 (2001): 181-194.
18. Jagdish Bhagwati, "Borders Beyond Control," *Foreign Affairs* (Jan/Feb. 2003).

19. Waldman, op. cit.
20. Quoted in Crush, op. cit.
21. Masy et al., op cit., p. 157.
22. Afghanistan and neighboring regions, Morocco, Somalia, Sri Lanka, Iraq, and Albania and surrounding regions.
23. Ninna Nyberg Sorensen, Nicholas Van Hear, and Poul Engberg-Pedersen, "The Migration-Development Nexus: Evidence and Policy Options," CDR Working Paper 02.6. Copenhagen: Center for Development Research, March 2002, p. 1.
24. Santiago Ribadeneira, Presentation at Multilateral Investment Fund Conference on Remittances as a Development Tool in Ecuador, Quito, Ecuador, 12 May 2003.
25. Dilip Ratha, Workers' Remittances: An Important and Stable Source of External Development Finance," in *Global Development Finance 2003*, Washington, DC: World Bank, 2003, p. 171.
26. World Bank, "Migrants' Capital for Small-Scale Infrastructure and Small Enterprise Development in Mexico," World Bank: Washington, DC, 4 January 2002.
27. Jim Gomez, "Arroyo Signs Law Allowing Millions of Filipinos to Vote Overseas," Associated Press, 13 February 2003.
28. L. Alan Winters, Terrie Walmsley, Zhen Kun Wang, and Roman Grynberg. "Negotiating the Liberalization of the Temporary Movement of Natural Persons," Discussion Paper 87, University of Sussex: Brighton, October 2002.

8

Impacts of the Policies of Rich Countries on the Prospects for Growth and Poverty Reduction in Poor Countries: Focus on the Environment[1]

Frances Seymour[2]

Introduction

The purpose of this chapter is to inform a discussion about research priorities regarding the impacts of the policies of rich countries on the prospects for growth and poverty reduction in poor countries, with particular reference to the environment. The potential scope of such a discussion is enormous. Industrialized countries dominate global environmental management directly through the heavy ecological footprint of their production and consumption patterns, and indirectly through their influence over global regimes governing trade, investment, and the global commons.

Rich country policies that impact the prospects for growth and poverty reduction in poor countries through environmental means include the following:

- *domestic environmental* policies of rich countries that, for example, influence the trade and investment opportunities of poor countries;
- *international environmental* policies of rich countries that, for example, impose standards on or provide technical assistance to poor countries;
- *domestic non-environmental* policies of rich countries that impact the environment in poor countries, for example through degradation of the global commons; and

215

- *international non-environmental* policies of rich countries that impact the environment in poor countries, for example through shaping the rules of international trade and investment regimes.

Impacts on developing countries are thus driven by both the domestic and international policies of industrialized countries, and by both the presence and the absence of policies designed to promote environmental sustainability within and beyond national borders. The significance of these impacts was recognized in 1994 by economist Herman Daly upon his resignation from the World Bank, when he observed that "[t]he major weakness in the World Bank's ability to foster environmentally sustainable development is that it only has leverage over the South, not the North" (Daly, 1994).

Impacts on the growth and poverty reduction prospects of developing countries can take several forms:

- *economic* impacts on poor countries, for example through creation or restriction of trade and investment opportunities;
- *environmental* impacts on poor countries, for example through pollution and natural resource depletion, which in turn have implications for growth and poverty reduction; and
- *political* impacts on poor countries, for example through corruption related to providing access to natural resources to foreign governments.

Underlying Assumptions

Two assumptions underpin the analysis in this chapter. The first concerns the relationship between environmental sustainability and growth and poverty reduction objectives. Although there are certainly very real trade-offs in the short run and across geographic units, this analysis assumes that overall environmental sustainability is necessary for sustainable growth and poverty reduction in the long run and at significant geographic scale. In particular, it is not in the interest of developing countries to base growth and poverty reduction on economic development strategies that are environmentally unsustainable.

This assumption is supported by analysis suggesting that a "grow now, clean up later" strategy results in significant economic and human costs that could be avoided by earlier investment in environmental protection (Panayotou, 1997). For example, the World Bank's environment strategy makes the case that environmental protection can promote poverty reduction through protecting livelihoods based on natural resources, mitigating health risks caused by polluted air and water, and reducing vulnerability to "natural" disasters caused by environmental mismanagement (World Bank, 2001a).

The second assumption is that in those instances in which there are trade-offs between environmental sustainability objectives and actions to promote growth and poverty reduction, decisions, to the extent possible, should be taken through democratic processes that are representative of and accessible to relevant stakeholders at the appropriate level. Principle 10 of the Rio Declaration (United Nations, 1992), which was recently reaffirmed at the World Summit on Sustainable Development (United Nations, 2002a), articulates this standard of environmental governance. While many could consider democratic decision-making to be a value in its own right, evidence is accumulating that more participatory decision-making results in both better and more robust decisions (Petkova et al., 2002).

Although it is not possible to consult all relevant stakeholders in decisions that have impacts that span generations, there is nevertheless significant room for improving the access afforded to the present generation in decision-making that affects the environment. For example, the report of the World Commission on Dams (2000) suggests a "rights and risks" approach to development decision-making, in which all those who hold rights or face risks from a proposed intervention should be consulted. However, the fact that the Commission's report was controversial underlines a message to be developed later in this chapter: that exploration of alternative conceptions of equity—in terms of both procedure and outcome— is a high priority for further research and advocacy.

These two assumptions should be borne in mind in considering whether a given impact of rich country policies on poor countries is positive or negative with respect to prospects for growth and poverty reduction: Does it promote long-term environmental sustainability, both locally and globally? To the extent that it does not, have affected stakeholders participated in an informed decision to choose the trade-off?

Scope of the Chapter

Because of the broad range of policies that affect the environment, the topics treated in this chapter are of necessity selective and illustrative. We begin with a focus on the disproportionate use by industrialized countries of the world's natural resources, and the impacts of production and consumption by the North on the development prospects of poor countries. Section 2 highlights climate change as an example of a global commons issue, and because it is the environmental challenge with the most significant prospective negative impacts on developing countries and on the poor within those countries. Section 3 focuses on the marine fisheries issue as an example of how Northern commercial interests, supported by national government policies, exploit the natural resources of developing countries. Sections 4 and 5 briefly assess what is known about how domestic environmental regulations and standards in industrialized countries impact the development prospects of developing countries through international investment and trade. They include brief discussions of the alleged displacement of environmentally damaging industry from North to South, and "green protectionism." Section 6 addresses how rich countries affect the development of poor countries through their dominant influence in global environmental governance regimes. Each of these sections provides a brief summary of the issue and the discourse surrounding it, a description of possible impacts on developing countries, an assessment of the winners and losers from possible policy changes by industrialized countries, and suggested priorities for further research, monitoring, and advocacy.

Section 7 highlights additional issues at the interface between environment and other policy arenas: aid, trade, investment, migration, and intellectual property rights. The final section of the chapter summarizes the themes that emerge from the previous sections, and concludes with a suggested approach for further research. The appendix offers an assessment of various efforts to measure impacts of rich countries on poor countries in the context of environmental sustainability.

The focus of the chapter is on the impacts of policies (or their absence) in rich countries on poor countries, even though for many of the topics covered, there are significant North-North, and South-South, and South-North interactions.[3] It does not address the many environmentally unsustainable policies of industrialized countries that have environmental impacts largely within the countries' own borders.[4] Neither does it attempt to cover policies of industrialized countries specifically designed to promote environmental sustainability in developing countries, for example, through bilateral and multilateral development assistance programs.

Another limitation of the chapter is that it tends to generalize policies of the North and impacts on the South. While the grouping "rich" or "industrialized" countries includes a diversity of national policy regimes, and the grouping "poor" or "developing" countries includes a variety of associated impacts, the scope of this chapter allows only minimal attention to exceptions to broad generalizations.

Degradation of the Global Commons: The Example of Climate Change

One important pathway through which the policies of rich countries affect the development prospects of poor countries is degradation of the global commons. Many would argue that industrialized countries use more than their fair share of the global commons, either by exploiting renewable and non-renewable resources (for example, mining the oceans for marine life and minerals) or by using up the capacity of the commons to absorb waste (for example, carbon released into the atmosphere). Indeed, some advocacy groups suggest that industrialized countries and multinational corporations owe the rest of the world an "ecological debt" based on their appropriation of global resources (International Climate Justice Network, 2002). Others invoke the concept of "ecological space" needed by developing countries for growth as the basis for calling on industrialized countries to reduce their burden on the global environment (Gomez-Echeverri, 2000). Whatever one's views on what would constitute fair regimes for sharing the global commons, most would agree that current regimes are biased against developing countries.

A complete treatment of global commons issues would include attention to degradation of the atmosphere (climate change, ozone depletion), loss of biological diversity, exploitation and pollution of the oceans, disruption of global nutrient cycles (for example, nitrogen), and the global transport and accumulation of toxic chemicals. Among these, climate change is likely to have the most significant impacts on developing countries, and is in large part driven by the past and present policies of industrialized countries. The discussion below thus focuses on those impacts, and the likely winners and losers from policy changes, as an illustrative example of how the policies of rich countries affect poor countries through degradation of the global commons.

The scientific consensus around the causes and likely impacts of climate change is well documented by working groups organized under the Inter-governmental Panel on Climate Change (IPCC) (Houghton et al., 2001, McCarthy et al., 2001, Metz et al., 2001). Climate change is predicted to have catastrophic impacts on developing countries through a variety of mechanisms. These include changes in weather patterns (affecting agricultural production), increased frequency of severe weather events (affecting coastal communities and ecosystems), spread of vector-borne disease, and sea-level rise (affecting the very existence of small island states).

That greenhouse gas emissions from industrialized countries are the primary cause of climate change is non-controversial. According to the World Resources Institute, industrialized countries—home to only 20 percent of the world's population—are responsible for 63 percent of the carbon dioxide that has accumulated in the atmosphere from fossil fuel burning and land use changes from 1900 to 2000 (Baumert and Kete, 2002). It is important to emphasize the role of *cumulative* emissions as the driver of carbon dioxide concentrations in the atmosphere, and thus climate change, as the current debate often focuses on *current* emissions across countries. Figure 8.1 illustrates the contributions of various world regions to the level of carbon dioxide currently in the atmosphere.

A recent report highlights the astonishing disparities in absolute and per capita emissions between the United States, the largest emitter of greenhouse gases, and the developing world (National Environmental Trust, 2002). The United States, a nation of 288 million people, is responsible for more emissions than the combined emissions of 151 developing countries, which are home to more than 2.6 billion people. In 1999, the per capita emissions of Texas were 47 times higher than those of 119 countries whose combined emissions were lower than those of Texas (National Environmental Trust, 2002). Continued excessive emissions in industrialized countries result in large part from explicit and implicit subsidies to technologies and development patterns that drive fossil fuel use and hinder transitions to less emissions-intensive development paths.

Figure 8.1
Contributors to Climate Change

Percent of total accumulated atmospheric CO2 from industrial
sources and land use changes, 1990-2000

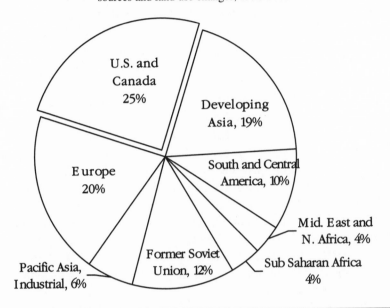

Notes: Data include net CO_2 emissions from fossil fuel combustion (1900-2000), cement manufacturing (1900-1979), and changes in land use (1900-1990), such as harvesting of forest products, clearing for agriculture, and vegetation re-growth. *Source*: World Resources Institute, compiled from data in Marland et al. (2000), EIA (2002b), and Houghton et al. (2000).

Impacts on Developing Countries

Climate change will have disproportionately negative impacts on poor countries and poor communities within those countries. Developing countries will fare worse than industrialized countries for two reasons. First, developing economies are more vulnerable to climate change. Characteristics of geography—such as low-lying small island states, heavily populated deltas, and drought-prone arid regions—all render developing countries at risk from the sea-level rise, increased frequency and intensity of extreme weather events, and disruptions in precipitation patterns associated with climate change.

Second, developing economies have limited capacity to adapt to climate change (McCarthy et al., 2001). Compared to industrialized countries, they have less economic wealth, technology, information and skills, infrastructure, institutions, and equity, all of which seem to determine the adaptive capacity of societies. According to Munasinghe (2000), "it is generally believed that developing countries and disadvantaged groups within all countries are more vulnerable to the impacts of climate change as a result of limited resources and low adaptive capacity."

Of course, vulnerability to climate change varies across developing countries and regions, depending on geographic and socioeconomic attributes. Food security in parts of Africa, for example, is vulnerable to changes in precipitation patterns, given the dependence of supplies on arid and semi-arid agriculture, while in some Asian countries large numbers of people are at risk from flooding in lowland urban areas. The most extreme cases of vulnerability are small island developing states (SIDs), whose very existence is threatened by sea level rise and other impacts of climate change. Table 8.1summarizes the likely impacts of climate change for the developing world, with particular reference to prospects for growth and poverty reduction.

Estimates of the relative magnitude of potential economic losses associated with a doubling of carbon dioxide in the atmosphere range from 1.3 to 1.6 percent of GDP for OECD countries, and from 1.6 to 2.7 percent of GDP for developing countries overall (Pearce, 2000). Current carbon dioxide concentration is already 35 percent above pre-industrial levels, and stabilizing concentrations at double those levels is widely considered to be an extremely optimistic target (Baumert, 2002a). Figure 8.2 illustrates the upward trajectory of the concentration of carbon dioxide in the atmosphere over the last century.

One study analyzing the effects of a 2.5 degree C global warming estimated that impacts would range from a net benefit of 0.7 percent in output for Russia (due largely to improved agricultural conditions) to a net damage of almost 5 percent of output for India (due largely to its dependence on monsoons) (Nordhaus, 1998). Another estimate places the potential cost to countries in Africa and South and Southeast Asia as high as 8.7 and 8.6 percent of GDP, respectively (Pearce, 2000). Such numbers are at best or-

Table 8.1

Likely Impacts of Climate Change on Developing Regions

Region	Likely Impacts
Africa	• diminished food security due to decreased grain yields and water availability • extended ranges of infectious disease vectors • exacerbated desertification • increased incidence of droughts and floods • coastal settlements adversely affected by sea-level rise
Asia	• diminished food security due to decrease in agricultural productivity and aquaculture • increased exposure to vector-borne infectious disease • decreased water availability in arid and semi-arid regions • increased incidence of floods, droughts, forest fires, and tropical cyclones • decreased tourism attraction
Latin America	• decreased crop yields and threats to subsistence farming in some regions • extended ranges of infectious disease vectors • decreased water supply and quality • increased intensity of tropical cyclones; more frequent floods and droughts • coastal settlements adversely affected by sea-level rise
Small Island States	• erosion, loss of land and property, displacement of populations, salt-water intrusion due to sea-level rise • decreased water availability • increased vulnerability of agriculture • bleaching of reefs and threats to livelihoods based on reef fisheries • severe disruption of tourism

Source: Adapted from Table SPM-2 in McCarthy et al., 2001.

der-of-magnitude estimates, but they are likely to understate the disproportionate impacts on poor countries, given the greater ability of OECD countries to adapt (Pearce, 2000).

Other country-specific estimates of the economic losses likely from climate change and adaptation costs provide a sense of the magnitude of the problem. For example, Hurricane Mitch—an example of extreme weather events to which Central America is vulnerable and which are potentially exacerbated by climate

Figure 8.2
Atmospheric Carbon Dioxide (CO$_2$) Concentrations, 1750 to Present

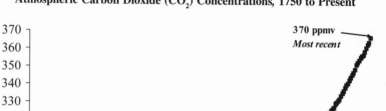

Source: C. D. Keeling and T. P. Whorf, Atmospheric CO$_2$ Concentrations (ppmv) derived from in situ air samples collected at Mauna Loa Observatory, Hawaii, Scripps Institute of Oceanography, August 1998. A. Neftel et al., Historical CO$_2$ Record from the Siple Station Ice Core, Physics Institute, University of Bern, Switzerland, September 1994. See http://cdiac.esd.ornl.gov/trends/co2/contents.htm.

change—resulted in estimated losses to Honduras and Nicaragua amounting to 70 and 45 percent of GNP, respectively (McCarthy et al., 2001). Islands in the Indian and Pacific Oceans are estimated to face the highest costs of protecting vulnerable populations from sea level rise (Pearce, 2000). One study estimated that the cost of protecting the coast of the Marshall Islands from the erosion, flooding, and groundwater loss caused by a one-meter rise in sea level by 2100 would be four to six times the country's current GDP (Slade and Werksman, 2000).

While useful for illustrative purposes, such estimates fall short of the comprehensive and comparable cost estimates of climate impacts or adaptation needed to inform policymaking. For example, even for sectors such as water, agriculture, and natural resources, for which it should be possible to attach financial values, "there are few if any published data on the economic impacts of climate change on these sectors in Africa" according to the IPCC (McCarthy et al., 2001). Further, "[t]here are…few comprehensive estimates of the costs of adaptation" (McCarthy et al., 2001).

Given the lack of estimates of the costs of impacts and adaptation, it is not surprising that information on the distributional implications of climate change—beyond the broad patterns outlined above—is also inadequate. According to the IPCC, "[r]esearch into the distribution of impacts of climate change is in its infancy, in large measure because this research poses several methodological challenges." These challenges include how to synthesize different kinds of costs, fill knowledge gaps (particularly regarding developing countries), include adaptation responses, and establish links to other socioeconomic trends (McCarthy et al., 2001). In addition, "few studies have explicitly examined the distribution of impacts on the poor relative to other segments of society" (McCarthy et al., 2001).

Winners and Losers from Policy Change

Scenarios indicate that greenhouse gas emissions can be significantly reduced through a portfolio of changes, including transitions to more efficient technologies for energy use, transitions to more efficient and/or low- or no-carbon energy supply, and increased carbon sequestration in terrestrial ecosystems (Metz et al., 2001). Countries can choose from among numerous policies to effect these changes, including "emissions, carbon, or energy taxes, tradable permits, subsidies, deposit-refund systems, voluntary agreements, non-tradable permits, technology and performance standards, product bans, and direct government spending, including R&D investment" (Metz et al., 2001).

Conceptually, "mitigation capacity" is analogous to "adaptation capacity" (Metz et al., 2001), suggesting that rich countries are better positioned to reduce their (already greater) emissions than poor countries. But there is significant diversity within and between rich countries in taking action: while the European Union Council of Environment Ministers recently reached agreement on the world's first regional emissions trading scheme (European Union, 2002), the United States Government continues to oppose domestic action. Policies within rich countries may also pull in opposite directions. For example, while Germany has encouraged development of one of the strongest wind energy industries through production and investment incentives (Roodman, 1998), it is also among the countries that has dramatically slashed public and private spending on energy research and development in recent years (Dooley and Runci, 1999).

Overall, the magnitude and distribution of the costs and benefits of changing rich country policies that drive climate change are contested in the political arena, and further analysis is clearly needed. Provisionally, however, likely winners and losers can be identified within and between countries and country groupings, sectors, firms, and income groups.

Climate change will have costs for developing countries, but so may policies to constrain emissions in rich countries. For example, a carbon tax could result in reduced revenues for oil-exporting countries such as Mexico, Nigeria, and Venezuela. At the same time, other developing countries could enjoy lower oil prices, but might also be adversely affected by price increases of carbon-intensive imports (Metz et al., 2001).[5]

Some of the industrialized countries would have more difficulty than others in shifting to a lower-emissions trajectory. Countries such as Australia, Canada, and the United States, which have significant carbon-intensive natural resources, relatively low energy efficiency, and extensive transport networks to serve widely dispersed populations, face different challenges than countries with fewer such resources, higher energy efficiency, and more compact transport systems, such as Japan.

However, the economic impact of a transition to more climate-friendly policies on industrialized economies depends on a range of variables. Repetto and Austin (1997) showed that the predictions of models designed to estimate the costs of climate protection to the U.S. economy depend critically on assumptions related to substitution among energy sources, potential efficiency improvements, technological innovation, availability and cost of non-fossil energy resources, emissions trading, and carbon tax regimes. Their simulations indicate that "doomsday" predictions of heavy economic losses are implausible, and that carbon dioxide emissions can be reduced with minimal economic impacts. Further, they estimate that if the benefits of averted damages from climate change and air pollution are included in the analysis, the overall economic impact could even be positive (Repetto and Austin, 1997).

The distributional impact across sectors in rich countries will also be uneven. Carbon-intensive sectors—such as coal and oil—will suffer, while renewable energy industries will likely benefit (Metz et al., 2001). Mitigation would strengthen an existing trend away from heavy manufacturing in favor of services and information-based industries (Metz et al., 2001).

The insurance industry is potentially a big loser from the failure to mitigate climate change, if extreme weather events increase claims for life and property losses. Already, insurance losses from such events have mounted in recent years, with losses from natural disasters having increased fifteen-fold over the last four decades (*E/Environment Magazine*, 2002). There also is concern that the global insurance industry's financial reserves are insufficient to cover claims from a confluence of several such events in a single year (Meyer, 1997). Developing country consumers, who currently enjoy almost no protection from economic losses due to extreme events (Chartered Insurance Institute, 2001) will also likely be losers, as the insurance industry becomes more cautious about extending coverage to high-risk areas.

The economic impact of climate-friendly policies in many sectors also depends on which policies are chosen. For example, analysis by Faeth and Greenhalgh (2000) indicates not only that "implementation of policies that address climate change will not be an economic disaster for U.S. agriculture," but that there is significant scope for "win-win" policies that would meet climate and other objectives simultaneously. For example, a nutrient trading regime under the Clean Water Act and/or expansion of the Conservation Reserve Program would make it financially attractive for farmers to take land out of traditional production, causing energy and fertilizer emissions to go down while increasing soil carbon sequestration (Faeth and Greenhalgh, 2000).[6]

At the firm level, there are also winners and losers. Austin and Sauer (2002) have demonstrated that even within an industry—oil and gas— that is likely to be a "loser" under any climate protection regime, individual companies are differently positioned. According to scenario analysis, those companies with more assets in oil rather than gas and those positioned more "upstream" in the value chain are more likely to be adversely affected (Austin and Sauer, 2002). Thus, under the scenario deemed most probable, BP's shareholder value would increase slightly, while Repsol YPF, Enterprise Oil, and Occidental Petroleum could lose about 4 percent of their shareholder value (Austin and Sauer, 2002).

Across income groups within rich countries, there is reason for concern about the distributional impacts of climate-friendly policies. For example, "the distributional effects of a carbon tax appear to be regressive unless the tax revenues are used either directly or indirectly in favor of the low-income groups" (Metz et al., 2001).

Priorities for Further Research, Monitoring, and Advocacy

This brief analysis suggests several priorities for further research on the impacts of rich country policies on poor countries via degradation of the global commons. While the following recommendations focus on climate change, by analogy they could be extended to other global commons issues.

First, there is a need for better estimates of the economic costs of climate change impacts for developing countries, and estimates of the costs of adaptation to that change. As described above, currently available estimates are inadequate even for relatively straightforward financial impacts on key productive sectors, and even more inadequate for impacts that are more difficult to value financially, such as impacts on human health and well-being and catastrophic risks. In addition, according to the IPCC, "[a]ny comprehensive assessment of adaptation costs (including benefits) would consider not only economic criteria but also social welfare and equity"(McCarthy et al., 2001). Such research should to the extent possible be conducted in developing countries and led by researchers from developing countries.

Second, there is a need to combine analyses of mitigation costs in rich countries with estimates of impact/adaptation costs in poor countries to reframe the issue as a cost/benefit analysis. Such an approach would contrast with the IPCC's current separation of the analyses of the cost effectiveness of various mitigation options from analyses of impact/adaptation costs. IPCC's Working Group III has itself suggested strengthening the links between policymaking related to mitigation and policymaking related to adaptation (Metz et al., 2001). Juxtaposition of the costs of various mitigation options in rich countries with the costs to be incurred by poor countries under various climate change scenarios could illuminate a social justice dimension to the climate issue in at least some national and international policy arenas. Such analysis could empower negotiators from developing countries to demand more action from rich countries, and could also supply powerful moral arguments to advocates for policy change within rich countries.

Third, more research is needed on "win-win" mitigation opportunities in specific industrialized countries to build political constituencies for policy change. In addition, comparative research across rich countries could highlight effective policy models as well as successful political strategies that might have relevance in other countries.

Finally, increased collaboration between OECD and developing countries in energy sector research and development would both build capacity in developing countries and ensure that future technology options address the particular needs of poor countries.

Extraterritorial Exploitation of Natural Resources: The Example of Marine Fisheries

Another important environmental pathway through which the policies of rich countries affect the prospects of poor countries is the exploitation of natural resources in developing countries. If markets fully internalized the environmental externalities of natural resources development, and if developed countries negotiated on an equal footing with industrialized countries for access to natural resources, such exploitation might not pose a problem. However, many would argue that raw materials are seldom priced at their "ecological value," and that current patterns of international trade include a "hidden subsidy from South to North in the form of externalized environmental degradation (Gupta, 1997). For example, in the context of the Convention to Combat Desertification, the Center for Science and Environment has argued that "[t]he South has been forced to sell its goods in the global market at very low prices, taking on the burden of the North's consumption at the cost of its land degradation" (Agarwal, Narain, and Sharma, 1999).

A complete treatment of issues related to the extraterritorial exploitation of natural resources could thus potentially include all agriculture and extractive industry in the South destined for export to the North, including tree crops, timber, fisheries, oil, gas, and mining. In this chapter, however, attention is limited to natural resources exploitation in developing countries in which Northern corporations and/or governments are directly involved in resource extraction.[7]

Marine fisheries provide an illustrative example of how the policies of rich countries affect poor countries through the exploitation of natural resources beyond their borders. Current production patterns are driven in part by industrialized country subsidies to overcapitalized fishing fleets and strong-arm tactics used by rich countries to gain access to the waters of poor countries. Marine fisheries are interesting because (1) the resource is very important to both local livelihoods and potential export revenues of many developing countries; (2) very little is known about the status and trends of the resource; and (3) the appropriate venue and approach to handling the issue at the international level is currently controversial.

Marine fisheries are in trouble worldwide. According to the Food and Agricultural Organization of the United Nations (FAO), three-quarters of the world's fisheries are already fully exploited, overexploited, or depleted (FAO, 2000). While FAO statistics are probably inaccurate—based as they are on national reporting not subject to independent verification—they nevertheless provide some sense of relevant data. World marine capture fisheries production dropped to 78 million tonnes in 1998 from an average of about 85 million tonnes a year in the mid-1980s (FAO, 2000). Top producing countries were China, Japan, the United States, the Russian Federation, Peru, Indonesia, Chile, and India, accounting collectively for about half of total production in 1998 (FAO, 2000). World fisheries landings have been declining slowly since the late 1980s, by about 0.7 million tonnes per year (Pauly et al., 2002).

Overfishing is caused by a complex set of factors, including poor management, and most fisheries are effectively "open access" regimes. However, poor management is exacerbated by subsidies to the fishing industry provided in various forms by governments around the world. Together, these factors are estimated to have resulted in a global overcapacity in major food fisheries of 30 percent (Milazzo, 1998).

In a paper commissioned by the World Bank, Milazzo (1998) provided a conservative estimate of $15 to $20 billion dollars per year in subsidies to marine fisheries, representing one-quarter to one-third of total revenues in the sector. A subsequent analysis by WWF came up with a similar figure (Schorr, 2001). About three-quarters of these subsidies are estimated to be provided by rich countries to their domestic fishing fleets (Milazzo, 1998).

Impacts on Developing Countries

Overfishing is a global problem with significant North-North, South-South, and even South-North dimensions. However, for the purposes of this chapter, the key issue is that fishing fleets from industrialized countries are decimating the marine fisheries in tropical coastal zones, threatening current and future productivity that could and should provide growth and poverty reduction benefits to developing countries.

Distant-water fishing fleets of rich countries accelerated their penetration of the fisheries of developing countries in the 1980s. In 1982, the United Nations Convention on Law of the Sea (UNCLOS) established the jurisdiction of coastal states over marine life in exclusive economic zones (EEZs) extending up to 200 nautical miles from shore (Runge et al., 1997). As coastal states expanded their own fishing fleets, distant-water fleets were displaced, and "tended to seek new grounds in unmanaged international waters or off the coasts of developing countries" (Milazzo, 1998).

While UNCLOS provides that coastal countries should make the unused surplus of EEZ resources available to the fleets of other countries, "eagerness for foreign exchange, political pressure and illegal fishing" has led to a harvesting intensity rivaling that of human exploitation of terrestrial ecosystem productivity (Pauly et al., 2002). In effect, the excess capacity of rich country fishing fleets has been transferred to the waters off developing countries, thereby undermining both the economic and environmental interests of the latter (Milazzo, 1998), as well as further complicating governance of the resource.

Of particular concern are the methods used by rich countries to gain access by their distant water fleets to the EEZs of developing countries. Rich country governments make direct payments to developing country governments, and offer access-for-trade and access-for-aid deals. Milazzo estimates that the European Union spent $350 million in 1996 on such payments to developing countries, including states in West Africa, East Africa, and the Indian Ocean (Milazzo, 1998). For the same period, Milazzo estimates that Japan made $100 million in payments for access, mostly to developing countries in the Western Pacific and elsewhere, as well as another $100 million in foreign assistance to the fisheries sector linked to continued access (Milazzo, 1998). By comparison, the United States made $14 million in payments to Pacific Island states for access to tuna fisheries (Milazzo, 1998).

These payments are problematic from the perspective of poor countries for several reasons. First, they facilitate the entry of distant-water fleets into EEZ fisheries that may already be fished to capacity, compromising the sustainability of the resource. This is significant for those countries highly dependent on seafood exports (Schorr, 1998). Case studies undertaken in Argentina and Senegal revealed how increased fishing effort with the entry of foreign fleets resulted in depleted stocks and diminished catch (UNEP, 2002).

Second, more technically advanced distant-water fleets compete for the same fisheries resources as local fishermen, with the potential of undermining local food security. Milazzo (1998) recounts how the fishing industries in Mauritania and Senegal objected on these grounds to EU access arrangements negotiated with the EU.

Third, the distant-water fleets capture export opportunities that would otherwise support the development of domestic fisheries. For example, the World Bank estimates that Pacific Island fleets landed only about 11 percent of the value of tuna captured in the region in 1998, with the rest caught by the distant-water fleets of Japan, Korea, Taiwan, and the United States (World Bank, 2000). Fourth, the negotiated payments are too low to compensate developing country governments for the economic value of the resource. For example, in 1996 Papua New Guinea decided to end its long-standing policy of granting tuna licenses to foreign vessels, having determined that revenues represented only a tiny fraction of the boats' export earnings (Milazzo, 1998).

Finally, the non-transparency of these payments provides ample opportunity for corruption. Unfortunately, there are few if any examples of fisheries rents being reinvested in the sustainability of the resource (Riggs, 2002).

Winners and Losers from Policy Change

To address the problem of overfishing globally and the inequitable position of poor countries in the exploitation of marine fisheries, several policy changes are needed. Clearly, these include implementation of improved fisheries management regimes by all coastal states. However, rich countries in particular should take the lead in reducing harmful subsidies to their fishing fleets, both those fishing in domestic waters (due to the "spillover" effect of overcapacity to developing countries) and distant-water fleets.

In the short run, the losers from such policy change would be the fishing industries of industrialized countries. For example, Europe's fishing industry is estimated to employ 15 million people, either directly or indirectly (Schiermeier, 2000), and in 1996 the agreements for access to foreign fisheries directly and indirectly generated 45,000 jobs (Milazzo, 1998). According to World Wildlife Fund (1999), EU subsidies tend to favor large companies rather than poor coastal fishing communities. The EU's Commissioner for Agriculture and Fisheries has proposed redirecting the $450 million subsidy earmarked for renewal and modernization of vessels over 2003-2006 to pensions and retraining for fishermen, to reduce fishing. However, he is expected to face opposition from Spain, Portugal, and France, which have large fishing industries (Schiermeier, 2000).

However, existing subsidy payments have not prevented the economic decline of fishing industries in rich countries. In Japan, for example, despite generous subsidies to coastal fishermen, the sector has not achieved economic viability. Instead, subsidies have at best slowed down a steady downward trend in profitability, while at the same time exacerbating the overfishing that is a cause of declining revenues (Milazzo, 1998), along with other factors, such as coastal habitat destruction. In the long run, the fishing industry "has everything to lose if fish stocks continue to decline" (Schiermeier, 2000).

A new avenue for addressing the issue of fisheries subsidies multilaterally opened up in 2001, when it was specifically mentioned in the Doha WTO Ministerial Declaration (WTO, 2001). Advocacy groups such as WWF have put forward proposals to close gaps in current WTO rules that fail to address the special needs of fisheries. These include, for example, the need to expand the definition of subsidy (to include access payments), the need to address damage not only to exporters who lose market share, but also to fishermen who lose access to fish, and the need to strengthen reporting requirements (WWF, 2002a).

Over the last year, members of the WTO Negotiating Group on Rules have disagreed as to whether the issue should be treated as a separate agenda item or lumped under a discussion of general subsidies issues. The winners and losers among countries from reform of the subsidy regime can perhaps be inferred from how countries have lined up on this issue. A group informally known as "Friends of Fish"—including Argentina, Chile, Ecuador, Iceland, New Zealand, Peru, Philippines, and the United States—have advocated separate negotiations, with support from Norway, Barbados, Mexico, Malaysia, and Thailand. They argue that "[a] distinctive feature of fisheries sector subsidies is the effect that over-capacity and over-fishing by subsidized producers can have in limiting other producers' access to the shared resource" (WTO, 2002a). Japan and South Korea have adamantly opposed such negotiations, with the EU and Canada occupying intermediate positions (ICTSD, 2002a-2002e).

Some have raised concerns that developing countries could be losers from new trade disciplines related to fisheries subsidies. Grynberg (2002) points out that some countries are highly dependent on access fees—which represent up to 40 percent of GDP for Kiribati and Tuvalu—and may need to provide subsidies to support development of local industry and provide support to artisanal fisheries. Others assert that the interests of developing countries would be protected by allowing exemptions to prohibitions against subsidies for those countries with underdeveloped fisheries sectors (Porter, 2002).

Priorities for Further Research, Monitoring, and Advocacy

This brief analysis suggests several priorities for further research on the impacts of rich countries' exploitation of natural resources in poor countries. While the following are focused on marine fisheries, by analogy they could be extended to the exploitation of other natural resources such as forests and minerals.

Further research on the marine fisheries issue needs to begin with better data on the fisheries themselves as well as on the magnitude of subsidies and their impacts on developing countries.[8] Better surveillance of global fisheries activity and independent verification of national statistics is necessary to increase confidence in data on the status and trends in the resource itself.

Data on fisheries subsidies is also problematic. According to Schorr (1998), data on fisheries subsidies remain "obscured by endemic lack of transparency in subsidy regimes as well as by the definitional uncertainties and logistical complexity of the issue."

Reporting requirements are widely disregarded. Schorr (1998) estimates that in 1996, governments reported only about 7-8 percent of fisheries subsidies that should have been reported to the WTO. While Milazzo's (1998) estimates have been attacked by environmentalists as too low and by Japan as too high (WTO, 2002) they remain the only numbers available to inform the debate. Milazzo (1998) states that "[t]ransparency is generally insufficient; information on major players like China and most of the developing countries is woefully inadequate."

Porter proposes several procedural options to the international community to agree on relevant criteria and methodologies for measuring subsidies (Porter, 2002). Milazzo (1998) suggests that "some categories of assistance, like "upstream" subsidies and user fees, are inherently difficult to analyze." Schorr (1998) adds that "[t]he problems arising out of implicit subsidies provided by coastal states to foreign distant water fleets are especially difficult analytically." These data and methodological problems can only be addressed through a collaborative North-South research agenda closely linked to relevant policy arenas. Better data on fisheries resources and subsidies can then support better analysis of the links between rich country subsidies and overfishing in poor countries. Analysis of the costs and benefits to developing countries of subsidy regimes is also needed to support bilateral and multilateral negotiations for more equitable regimes for sharing the resource.

Impacts via Domestic Environmental Regulation

Domestic environmental standards in industrialized countries can have consequences, both intended and unintended, for developing countries. This section discusses what is known about the consequences of regulation of industry that is alleged to drive "dirty" economic activity to developing countries.

The so-called "pollution havens" hypothesis—also referred to as "industrial flight"—suggests that when industrialized countries impose regulations on domestic production to protect the environment, industry will move to developing country jurisdictions where environmental regulation is not as strong. Such regulation could include production and remediation standards imposed on extractive industry, and emissions standards imposed on manufacturing industry. It is argued that firms will relocate to escape environmental standards and enforcement, resulting in a "race to the bottom" among jurisdictions.[9] A related concept is the "industrial specialization" hypothesis, which suggests that weak environmental standards and enforcement will lead to specialization in pollution-intensive industries by domestic firms (Wilson et al., 2002).

Despite numerous studies over the last decade, evidence to support the pollution havens hypothesis remains thin (Repetto, 1995, Zarsky, 1999, Wilson et al., 2002). Repetto found that "the many economists who have investigated the impact of environmental standards on trade and investment and those who have reviewed the research literature consistently found that regulatory differences among jurisdictions have no significant impact on the direction or magnitude of trade and investment flows, even in industries whose compliance costs are relatively high." A review of statistical studies found that "differences in environmental standards and/or abatement costs have not made a significant difference to firm location decisions" (Zarsky, 1999). Overall, the literature suggests that the costs of compliance with environmental standards are not high enough to affect competitiveness, and that access to markets and natural resources are more important drivers of firm location decisions.

Nevertheless, anecdotal evidence from case studies suggests that environmental standards may drive investment decisions in some sectors and circumstances (Zarsky, 1999). For example, many foreign mining companies left the Philippines following a strengthening of social and environmental impact assessment procedures in the wake of a major disaster in 1996 (La Viña, 2002). In addition, some sectors remain poorly studied. For example, there has been little empirical analysis of the impact of environmental standards and enforcement on the agriculture sector (Grote, 2002). Further, while the desire to attract investment might not result in a "race to the bottom" on environmental standards, it might leave weak or poorly enforced standards in developing countries "stuck in the mud" if officials hesitate to strengthen them (Zarsky, 1997).

Finally, if reductions in environmental impacts in rich countries are merely displaced to developing countries, it is possible that "leakage" could undermine global environmental regimes. For example, there is concern that if industrialized countries take policy actions to meet targets for reducing greenhouse gas emissions, and those policies push up production costs for carbon-intensive products, then the production of those products will simply move to developing countries not yet subject to such targets. For all of these reasons, the topic merits continued attention.

Impacts on Developing Countries

The impact of displacement of pollution-intensive industry from rich to poor countries could have both positive and negative implications for development and poverty reduction. On the one hand, industry relocation could be seen as positive in terms of increased investment, employment, and export revenue, at least in the short run. If environmental regulation reduces the competitiveness of industries in the North, then it must enhance that of industries in the South.

On the other hand, pollution-intensive industrial relocation and specialization in the South would likely have negative short-term impacts on the local environment and on health, especially in light of the less well-developed physical and regulatory infrastructure for dealing with environmental impacts. And in the long run, the sustainability of the economy could be compromised. Collectively, all developing countries could be put at risk if "leakage" were to undermine international climate protection efforts.

There appears to be little empirical work on the distribution of the positive and negative impacts of the relocation of dirty industry from North to South. If location decisions are driven by access to markets and natural resources, it is likely that manufacturing would relocate to the "emerging market" countries that take the lion's share of North-South foreign direct investment, while extractive industry would relocate to poorer but resource-rich countries. Within countries, benefits would more likely be enjoyed by governments in the form of increased tax revenues, with local communities benefiting from employment opportunities as well as suffering from environmental impacts. Zarsky (1999) suggests that while "pollution havens" cannot be proven, a pattern of agglomeration of pollution is discernible, one based not on differences in national environmental standards, but on differences in income and/or education of local communities..."there are clearly 'pollution zones' of poorer people, both within and across countries...."

Winners and Losers from Policy Change

Downward harmonization of environmental standards and enforcement in rich countries would not be a viable or desirable policy option. On the other hand, rapid upward harmonization by developing countries to industrialized country environmental standards and enforcement would impose significant costs on poor countries. Recent econometric analysis by Wilson et al. (2002) of trade in five pollution-intensive products among twenty-four countries suggests that upward harmonization would depress exports from non-OECD countries more than OECD countries.

To address the potential negative impacts for developing countries of relocating pollution-intensive industry, rich countries could support stronger environmental regulation and enforcement, and in particular better information disclosure and citizen participation in environmental management (Petkova et al., 2002). Such a strategy would build on the observation that incremental improvements in corporate environmental performance currently underway around the world are "primarily in response to effective national regulation and/or local community pressure" (Zarsky, 1999).

To address the "leakage" aspect of relocation of pollution-intensive industry and its potential to undermine global environmental management regimes, rich countries could support efforts to account for the natural resources and/or pollution "embedded" in traded products. In a climate protection regime, for example, greenhouse gas emission reduction targets would capture consumption of carbon-intensive products as well as direct production.

Priorities for Further Research, Monitoring, and Advocacy

Despite the many studies already in the literature, there is scope for additional statistical and case studies—particularly in specific sectors—to illuminate various aspects of the pollution-intensive industry flight/specialization issue. First, more analysis is needed of the impact of pollution-intensive foreign direct investment on broad-based "sustainable development" rather than on the narrow environmental performance of firms (Zarsky, 1999). In addition, research is needed on the distributional impacts of such investment within countries, particularly the net impact on the poor.

Second, more research is needed on how improved environmental procedural rights (access to information, public participation in decision-making, access to justice) affect the environmental performance of firms, as well as on the distribution of costs and benefits of pollution-intensive industry. Anecdotal evidence—reactions to the report of the World Commission on Dams, mining industry flight from the Philippines—indicates that corporations are more concerned about procedural rights such as prior informed consent than they are about compliance with environmental standards per se. Research synthesizing experience across a large number of investments could illuminate the degree to which additional costs incurred in the short term, to comply with more onerous procedural requirements, are outweighed by the benefits of less conflict in the long run.

Impacts via Environmentally Related Product Standards

When markets in industrialized countries discriminate among traded products in the interest of environmental protection, there is potential for harm to producers in developing countries. Such discrimination may be reflected in regulations, for example in standards regarding the amount of pesticide residue allowed in foods. Recently, there has been an explosion of voluntary standards, such as labeling schemes to identify "sustainably" produced commodities. Discrimination may be designed to protect domestic environmental quality or health, for example through standards on the lead content of gasoline. Discrimination may also be designed to promote environmental sustainability in other countries or at the global level, as in tropical timber certification schemes or bans on trade in endangered species.

The complex and contentious international debate on trade and environment is far beyond the scope of this chapter. But, in short, there are profound disagreements on several issues. First is the legitimacy of discriminating among products on environmental grounds, particularly with respect to how the product is produced. By far the most controversial cases have involved the validity of trade restrictions as a way of influencing foreign "process and production methods" (PPMs).

Second, there is disagreement regarding the appropriate forum for adjudicating trade and environment disputes (for example, the overlapping jurisdictions of multilateral trade agreements and multilateral environmental agreements). Environmental advocates are generally against the use of trade forums to deal with environmental issues, due to their lack of appropriate mandate and expertise, and tendency to favor trade rather than environment interests when the two conflict. Environmentalists' concerns have been exacerbated by specific GATT and WTO decisions.[10]

Finally, there is disagreement regarding the degree to which voluntary schemes should be brought under multilateral disciplines. On the one hand, developing countries are deeply suspicious that rich countries will use multilateral trade forums to legitimize "green protectionism" to satisfy domestic constituencies. On the other hand, they would prefer to see "proliferating eco-labeling schemes, particularly those formulated and administered by private bodies...brought under multilateral disciplines on the basis of equivalencies and mutual recognition" in which each country could set its own standards (Raghavan, 1996).

Impacts on Developing Countries

The impact of environmental discrimination among products on developing countries is potentially significant. Developing country voices at the United Nations have declared that "standards that developed countries applied to exports from the developing world were a major trade barrier" and decried the "new protectionism" implicit in attempts to impose new environmental and labor standards (United Nations, 2002). Product discrimination can result in a loss of market access, with attendant losses in export revenues and employment. A survey of nine trade-environment disputes in multilateral forums in the early 1990s estimated an average of $50 million a year in trade losses resulting from measures intended to protect a particular species, and $250 million per year resulting from more general measures (Lee, 2001). The Mexican National Chamber of Fishing and Aquaculture recently filed a claim against the U.S. canned tuna industry for $1 billion in damages resulting from the 1990s embargo on tuna caught by methods that harmed dolphins. The suit alleges hundreds of millions of dollars in lost export revenues and job losses from processing plant closures (Atuna, 2002).

Developing countries may also suffer loss of competitiveness from either regulatory or voluntary standards in industrialized countries. Eco-labeling schemes have had adverse trade impacts in several countries and sectors (Grote, 2002). Developing countries are disadvantaged in their efforts to comply with standards due to their relative lack of technology and capacity, as well as the high cost of independent verification (UNCTAD, 2002). Such barriers are likely to prove more significant for the poorest countries than for emerging market countries, and for small and medium enterprises (SMEs) and artisanal producers within countries (UNCTAD, 2002). Further, smaller producers may be particularly disadvantaged by verification costs. For example, while some of the most "sustainably" produced timber may come from smallholder or community-based producers, the costs of obtaining independent certification for their products could be prohibitive, especially in remote areas.

In the medium to long term, however, product standards could drive improved environmental management in developing countries, and create new markets for developing country producers of more sustainable alternatives (for example, certified wood products). It is possible that such benefits could differentially benefit the poor. A recent review of 240 cases from sixty countries published by the International Finance Corporation (2002) found that export-oriented companies can gain access to markets and sometimes price premiums. The report further documents the "business case" for sustainability in emerging markets by demonstrating that small and medium enterprises (SMEs) benefit most from the cost savings that result from more attention to sustainability, and also higher revenues and improved market access especially for environmental products and services.

Developing countries may also derive long-term benefits at the economy-wide level. According to UNCTAD (2002), "...in certain cases the national economy of developing countries may derive longer-term advantages from trade-induced shifts to more stringent standards in terms of greater resource efficiency, higher occupational safety, improved health conditions and less environmental pollution." For example, eco-labeling schemes have reduced the fertilizer and pesticide intensity of flower production in several developing countries (Grote, 2002). Since the poor suffer more from pollution and resource degradation, improvements in environmental quality that result from more environmentally friendly production processes could differentially benefit lower-income groups.

Winners and Losers from Policy Change

As with policy options to deal with industrial flight, neither upward nor downward harmonization of environmental standards to a single global standard is viable or desirable. Constituencies in rich countries for sustainable trade are vocal, while markets for "sustainably" produced products are growing. But rapid upward harmonization would impose unacceptable costs on producers in poor countries.

Instead, promising options appear to be steps that minimize the negative impacts of rich country environmental standards and maximize the benefits. As an example of the former, product and process standards should be developed with the participation of developing country producers, and designed so as to recognize differences in socioeconomic conditions as well as such factors as climate, population density, and availability of natural resources (Grote, 2002). As examples of the latter, developing country producers should be given adequate time and resources to adjust to new standards to enable them to take advantage of new export opportunities (UNCTAD, 2002).

Priorities for Further Research, Monitoring, and Advocacy

Several kinds of research are needed to support the strategy mentioned above. First, more independent empirical work is needed on the sectoral impacts of specific regulatory and voluntary product standards. In particular, it would be useful to know the distribution of costs and benefits across individual countries and types of producers (for example, large firms, small firms, smallholders). In addition, it would be useful to know how these costs and benefits and their distribution change over time, as producers adjust. Such research should be conducted to the extent possible in developing countries, and led by developing country researchers. Such research could inform the design of international policies regarding the volume, timing, and distribution of assistance provided for adjustment.

Second, more research is needed on alternative production methods suitable for local conditions in developing countries (UNCTAD,

2002). Ideally, research efforts could be undertaken collaboratively between North and South, linking knowledge of the particular environmental interests of rich countries with the interests and particular conditions of poor countries. If appropriately linked to advocates in both North and South, such research could inform developing country participation in international standard-setting exercises, both in official forums and in voluntary certification regimes.

Impacts via Dominance of Global Environmental Governance Regimes

Previous sections of this chapter have highlighted how certain policies of industrialized countries governing natural resources and environmental management systematically disadvantage the interests of poor countries. One reason for the persistence of such policies is that industrialized countries dominate global environmental governance regimes. Such regimes could be used to achieve meaningful multilateral agreements and support national-level implementation of natural resources and environment policies in a way that is equitable for developing countries.

Northern bias in global environmental governance affects the interests of developing countries in a number of ways. Agarwal, Narain, and Sharma (1999) and Agarwal et al. (2001) provide a wealth of information and analysis related to global environmental governance regimes from a developing country perspective. Only a few aspects can be highlighted here.

First, industrialized countries are selective in their engagement in global environmental forums. For example, industrialized countries—and in particular the United States—exercised strong leadership to achieve international agreement on the Montreal Protocol on Substances that Deplete the Ozone Layer in 1987 (Benedick, 1991). Among other consequences, disappearance of the ozone layer would have increased the risk of skin cancer for populations with fair complexions in temperate latitudes, perhaps explaining the industrialized country political behavior in this case (Agarwal, Narain, and Sharma, 1999). By contrast, industrialized countries have been relatively uninterested in the Convention to Combat Desertification—dubbed a "second class convention"—which is of most interest to African countries (Agarwal, Narain, and Sharma, 1999).

Only in 2002 was agreement reached on using the Global Environment Facility as a funding mechanism, eight years after the Convention was adopted in 1994.

Further, industrialized countries influence which international forum deals with a particular issue. Developing country observers perceive that the industrialized countries have intentionally shifted the leadership role away from United Nations forums to the Bretton Woods Institutions, which appear to them more biased toward Northern interests (Gupta, 1997) and corporate interests (Agarwal et al., 2001). A related point is that industrialized countries are better positioned to make links across issues and policy arenas (Dubash, 2002). For example, rich countries are able to condition debt relief on specific environmental commitments.

Second, industrialized countries are selective in their engagement on issues within global forums. For example, within the context of the UN Framework Convention on Climate Change, industrialized countries have neglected issues of equity, adaptation, and stabilization of atmospheric greenhouse gas concentrations—issues that are of interest to developing countries—relative to the attention they have focused on the so-called "flexibility mechanisms," which are designed to reduce the burden of mitigation efforts on rich countries (Sokona et al., 2002).

Attention to environmental issues in multilateral trade and investment forums has also been selective. Developing country observers are suspicious that rich countries will selectively use the newly invigorated WTO Committee on Trade and Environment to satisfy the interests of domestic constituencies with a "mini-package of 'environmental decisions'," but then be unresponsive to the issues of interest to developing countries (Raghavan, 1996).

Third, developing countries are "handicapped" in their negotiating power by a variety of constraints (Gupta, 1997). They are often represented in international environmental negotiations by smaller delegations with less experience and knowledge than those from industrialized countries. In addition, the mandates of developing country negotiators from their governments may be "hollow," as developing countries do not see international environmental issues as first-order interests (Gupta, 1997). As a result, their engagement is more reactive than proactive. According to one observer, "a true irony of the climate change negotiations is that those countries that are most vulnerable to the impacts of climate change are also those with the weakest, least consistent negotiating teams" (Gomez-Echeverri, 2002). Another aspect of this weakness is the difficulty faced by developing country negotiators in forming coalitions among themselves (Gupta, 1997).

Karlsson (2002) elaborates on what she calls the "North-South knowledge divide" and the ways that it undermines equitable international environmental negotiations. She observes, for example, that the scientific advisory bodies to environmental conventions are dominated by scientists from developed countries. She and others suggest that the dominance of the North in producing the science that informs international policymaking biases both priorities and analysis toward the interests of the industrialized countries (Karlsson, 2002; Agarwal, Narain, and Sharma, 1999). For example, despite the future importance of developing country energy trajectories for climate change, more than 95 percent of the world's public sector research and development in the energy sector is performed in only nine OECD countries (Dooley and Runci, 1999).

Fourth, the structures and norms of international institutions and agreements exacerbate developing country capacity constraints. Most obvious is voting weighted by share in international financial institutions, which increasingly have become the de facto centers of significant international environmental policymaking. In addition, "framework" agreements, and agreements not grounded in clear principles and definitions, require continuous negotiations over long periods of time that are more difficult for financially strapped developing countries to sustain consistently (Baumert, 2002a; Agarwal, Narain, and Sharma, 1999). Norms that allow industrialized country groupings to meet informally prior to negotiations exclude developing countries from meaningful participation in agenda-setting (Kwa, 2002). Finally, international environmental standard-setting regimes tend to be driven by standards developed in industrialized countries, which are not necessarily appropriate for developing country contexts.

Impacts on Developing Countries

The Northern bias of international environmental governance regimes leads to several impacts on developing countries, and the poor within those countries. Perhaps most important, there is limited progress on issues of particular interest to developing countries, and therefore limited international funding for those priorities and necessary policy changes in industrialized countries. Examples include limited funding for implementation of the Convention on Desertification, and slow progress in the UNFCCC toward restraining emissions from industrialized countries.

Second, because international environmental negotiations are not well articulated with domestic policy arenas in developing countries, there is poor "ownership" of the outcomes of those negotiations on the part of developing country governments and other stakeholders. The resulting limited implementation of commitments undermines the effectiveness of the agreements overall (Gupta, 1997).

Third, international standards driven by the experience and/or preferences of industrialized countries could inappropriately constrain the choices of developing countries through restrictions on aid and trade. For example, some developing country voices have accused Northern NGOs of "carbon hypocrisy" for calling on international financial institutions to end lending for fossil fuel-based energy development (Agarwal et al., 2001). Developing country representatives on the World Bank's board have long complained about the costs imposed by compliance with the Bank's environmental safeguards.

Fourth, the structures and norms of international governance regimes—both those explicitly environmental, and those that impact the environment through such mechanisms as trade—do not currently provide adequate opportunities for disadvantaged communities to represent their interests. La Viña (2002b-g) has produced a series of papers detailing those interests, and suggesting strategies to advance them.

Winners and Losers from Policy Change

Leveling the playing field in international environmental negotiations through increased investment in capacity building and redesign of structures could lead to more robust agreements with more likelihood of implementation. At the same time, such changes would likely be resisted by countries and constituencies accustomed to dominating global environmental governance regimes, and could lead to their opting out. The United States Government's decision to withdraw from the Kyoto Protocol in 2001 provides an unfortunate example of a decision to opt out rather than to be a "loser" in a regime more balanced toward the interests of developing countries. Environmental advocates would also consider themselves losers if attention to developing country concerns about poverty and equity were understood to be at the expense of attention to global environmental challenges (as opposed to integrated in a sustainable development agenda).

A promising parallel approach to improving international environmental governance is experimentation with alternative multi-stakeholder forums as vehicles to synthesize knowledge, develop consensus on contentious issues, and legitimize new norms of behavior. The World Commission on Dams illuminates both the advantages and disadvantages of such an approach. While the Commission produced an aspirational report that has strongly influenced the international debate on large dams, its legitimacy was implicitly or explicitly rejected by powerful stakeholders including the World Bank and the Governments of India and China (Dubash et al., 2001). While winners included constituencies such as indigenous peoples not usually granted a seat at the table in such deliberations, those used to wielding more power clearly saw themselves as losers in a more inclusive approach. Indeed, the effective withdrawal of support from the World Commission on Dams by the governments of India and China could be interpreted as decisions to opt out rather than be "losers" in a forum more inclusive of civil society interests.

To deal with the dominant influence of industrialized countries on international environmental standards, investment in capacity building and increasing the participation of developing countries in standard-setting processes is clearly appropriate. In addition, however, increased emphasis should be placed on harmonizing procedural standards rather than substantive standards, as the former are likely to prove more acceptable to advocates of environment and development alike. In the case of environmental standards for bilateral export and investment promotion agencies, for example, emphasis could be given to requiring increased information disclosure and opportunities for public comment and appeal related to the environmental assessment of proposed projects, rather than prohibiting or requiring particular technologies.

Priorities for Further Research, Monitoring, and Advocacy

The project of democratizing global environmental governance suggests a wealth of research topics. First, echoing the needs identified in previous sections, there is a need for more research on the interests of developing countries that are at stake in international negotiations. Because of the suspicion accorded to the analysis generated by research done in the North by industrialized country researchers (Gupta, 1997), it is important that such research be conducted by developing country researchers. Karlsson (2002) further suggests that Northern researchers conduct more research in the South, and that research efforts be broadened to include nontraditional researchers, disciplines, and types of knowledge.

Second, more research is needed on alternative conceptions of equity of both process and outcome in the context of international environmental governance. In the climate arena, for example, a key deadlock in negotiations has been disagreement over the appropriate timing and contributions by industrialized and developing countries toward reducing emissions growth (Gupta, 1997). Such research should be linked to ongoing consensus-building dialogues linking advocates from both developed and developing countries.

Finally, research could illuminate how the processes and structures of global agreements affect the ability of developing countries to represent their interests effectively, and suggest reforms that could improve both the effectiveness and the perceived equity of governance regimes. Comparative research could be conducted among official regimes, both within the realm of environmental agreements and between that realm and agreements covering trade, human rights, other policy arenas. In addition, further work on the role of "global public policy networks" and other multi-stakeholder forums, and the degree to which they complement official forums in providing political space for the articulation of the interests of poor countries and marginalized communities, would be a fruitful area for collaborative research.

Links between Environmental and Other Policy Arenas

This section highlights the links between the environment and other policy arenas not otherwise covered in this chapter. The context remains the impacts of policies of rich countries on the prospects for growth and poverty reduction in poor countries. Links between the environment and trade, intellectual property rights, investment, aid, and migration are treated in turn.

Links between Environment and Trade

As suggested above, trade-and-environment debates are among the most complex and contentious in today's international policy arenas. In addition to the trade and environment issues discussed in prior sections, many others could be the subject of further research on how rich country policies affect poor countries.

One currently controversial issue is the degree to which European standards related to genetically modified organisms (GMOs) will constrain agricultural development, particularly in Africa. The refusal of certain African countries to accept food aid from the United States for fear of contaminating seed stock with GMOs has raised concern about immediate costs. Further research on the potential long-term costs—and particularly on the distribution of winners and losers—of refusing new technologies, as well as on the risks of those technologies, would inform a highly polarized debate.

Another issue mentioned but not elaborated above is the assertion that commodities exported by developing countries are underpriced because they do not reflect the environmental externalities caused by their production. More research on the magnitude of this gap for particular commodities in particular countries, and the distribution of associated costs and benefits, would illuminate the scale of the problem and its impact on equity within and between countries. Research on the policy changes necessary to internalize those externalities in developing countries—and on the political economy of effecting changes in multiple national jurisdictions through environmental policy, versus addressing the problem multilaterally in trade forums—would also be highly relevant to current debates.

Links between Environment and Intellectual Property Rights

The most important issue at the intersection between the environment and intellectual property rights relates to biodiversity. The issue is access to and benefit-sharing of genetic resources. According to La Vina (2002b), there are two aspects to the debate.

First, there is the question of how to share genetic resources between developing countries (which harbor much of the genetic material) and industrialized countries (which have the science and technology to use it). Second, there is the question of how corporations and research institutes—mostly in the North—negotiate with local communities in developing countries for access to genetic material, and how the traditional knowledge regarding that material is reflected in intellectual property rights.

Research to quantify the actual benefits at stake could help ensure that negotiations among countries, and between companies and communities, are equitable. Further research is needed on mechanisms to underpin an equitable global regime on genetic resources. For example, case study research could illuminate prospective global norms on such practices as prior informed consent of local communities, and benefit-sharing mechanisms that provide both short-term and long-term benefits (La Vina, 2002b).

Links between Environment and Investment

One of the most important drivers of North-South private investment flows is the bilateral export credit and investment promotion agencies—usually known as ECAs—that most OECD countries use to support investment abroad. The environmental implications of ECA-supported investments are significant both globally and locally for the recipient countries. For example, Maurer and Bhandari (2000) found that ECAs provided disproportionate support to emissions-intensive industries in developing countries, at the same time that their governments were calling on developing countries to pull their weight in international climate protection efforts.

Environmental impacts of ECA finance at the national level have included severe ecological and social disruption from large dams, and forest destruction resulting from ECA finance of overcapacity in the wood-processing industry. ECA finance of environmentally and socially harmful projects often runs against the articulated goals of development aid involving the same donor and recipient countries; further, ECAs do not meet the same standards of transparency and public consultation that rich countries have insisted be adopted by multilateral development banks (Seymour, 2002). Such policy perversity is ripe for further research.

Because a significant portion of the foreign debt of developing countries is to ECAs, a related issue is the relationship between debt and the environment. Anecdotal evidence suggests that the pressure to service a debt burden leads to unsustainable natural resource exploitation to generate revenues, while at the same time constraining budgetary resources for environmental protection. Further research on the relationship between debt, environmental sustainability, and associated impacts on poverty and equity would make an important contribution to debates on the debt issue.

Another area that is ripe for further research is how international capital markets can be harnessed to promote environmental sustainability. Stronger disclosure standards for corporations listing on stock exchanges could force companies to disclose environment-related risks so that investors could discriminate among shares on environmental grounds. As suggested earlier, recent research by the World Resources Institute suggests that different multinational companies are positioned quite differently to benefit or be harmed by such disclosure (Austin and Sauer, 2002). Further research could illuminate how companies based in developing countries could be affected. For example, assuming improved disclosure, should favorable tax treatment of "green" investment funds—such as has been implemented in the Netherlands—be treated as a green product standard?

Links between Environment and Aid

Both bilateral and multilateral aid agencies have invested a portion of their resources in recent years in the environment sector, and particularly in helping developing countries build the institutional infrastructure for environmental regulation. While there have been some reviews of the efficacy of such support, continued analysis of "what works" is probably needed.

More important, however, is the problem of mainstreaming environmental sustainability into development aid, that is, integrating environmental considerations into sectoral and macroeconomic engagement beyond the environment sector per se. Despite a commitment to such mainstreaming since the early 1990s, for example, the World Bank has failed to make significant progress on the mainstreaming agenda, and there is even some evidence of backsliding (World Bank, 2001b). Further research exposing the failure to mainstream environmental sustainability considerations into development aid, and its consequences for growth and poverty reduction in developing countries, could help call political attention to the problem in rich countries. Such research could also demonstrate to poor countries how mainstreaming is in their own national self-interest, rather than a cost imposed by rich countries, as is often claimed.

Development aid also has a key role to play in addressing the causes and consequences of global environmental challenges. According to the IPCC, for example, "activities required for enhancement of adaptive capacity are essentially equivalent to those promoting sustainable development" (McCarthy et al., 2001). A recent set of guidelines issued by the OECD's Development Assistance Committee (DAC) provides a number of recommendations for how donor agencies can better exploit synergies among such environment and development objectives (OECD, 2002). Further research to identify the most significant "win-win" opportunities could help inform investment priorities for development aid.

Links between Environment and Migration

Links between demographic change and the environment are controversial, and discourse on the subject is constrained by sensitivity about calls for population control to serve the objective of environmental protection. With respect to the immigration policies of rich countries, a key issue is how to respond to the problem of "environmental refugees," which is expected to worsen in coming years. For example, the IPCC warns that "further increases in the frequency and intensity of severe weather systems as a consequence of climate change can trigger mass migration," as could sea level rise (McCarthy et al., 2001). The Pacific island nation of Tuvalu, which has experienced a decade of cyclones and flooding, has recently struck an agreement with New Zealand to accept a number of its citizens every year "effectively as environmental refugees" (Center for Science and Environment, 2002).

Perhaps less dramatic triggers of migration, but nevertheless significant, could be climate impacts on human health (such as the spread of disease vectors) and decreases in food security. Research on how to prepare for and respond to such migration would be an important complement to research on climate change mitigation strategies by rich countries and climate change adaptation strategies by poor countries.

Summary and Conclusions

The examples presented in this chapter illustrate a number of pathways through which the policies of rich countries that govern natural resources and the environment can affect poor countries. They further suggest the potential significance of these impacts for the prospects of developing countries for growth and poverty reduction. Climate change threatens the most severe and widespread impacts, but extraterritorial resource exploitation, and environmental regulations in industrialized countries, can also have significant implications for particular countries and sectors in the developing world. Further, rich country dominance of global environmental governance regimes impedes progress in making those regimes more development-friendly.

The distribution of "winners" and "losers" from current policy regimes and prospective reforms varies significantly depending on the issue. Among industrialized countries, for example, the United States stands out as the country most needing to change its policies related to climate change, while the European Union and Japan stand out as countries most needing to change their policies related to fisheries in the waters of developing countries. Among developing countries, geographic characteristics strongly determine vulnerability to climate change, while economic characteristics determine vulnerability to environmentally driven restrictions on trade.

Overall, it appears that both within and between countries, the poor tend to suffer more from perverse rich country policies. For example, the poorest countries are least well positioned to adapt to climate change, and artisanal producers are least well positioned to take advantage of market opportunities created by eco-labeling schemes. Further, it appears that the costs of changing policies for industrialized countries tend to be front-loaded in the short term, with the benefits enjoyed in the long run. For example, in the marine fisheries sector, withdrawal of subsidies could result in unemployment in the short term, but healthier fish stocks in the long run.

In addition, the analysis suggests that the persistence of rich country policies that undermine the interests of poor countries is at least partly due to the systematic bias of global environmental governance regimes toward the interests of rich countries. Further, across all of the topics treated, there is a paucity of policy-relevant data and analysis specific to developing country interests.

Previous sections of this chapter have suggested priorities for research related to the specific topics covered. However, the analysis suggests several cross-cutting priorities for research as well.

First, there is a need for improved methodologies to estimate and additional empirical studies to measure the actual economic impacts of various rich country policies on developing countries. Such research should to the extent possible be done in developing countries and led by developing country researchers. In particular, more work is needed to illuminate the distributional consequences both within and between countries of current and prospective policies. Such data and analysis would not only serve as a platform to address individual issues; it would also underpin some priority-setting among issues based on their relative significance.

Second, there is a need for further research on policy options that minimize the negative impacts of rich country policies and maximize the positive opportunities for poor countries. In the realm of extraterritorial exploitation of natural resources, for example, more work is needed on how payments from rich countries to poor countries for access to resources can be made more transparent and can be invested in ensuring sustainability. Such research should be conducted in the context of North-South collaborations and, to the extent possible, should identify and disseminate best practices where they are shown to be effective.

Third, in rich countries, there is a need for more research that exposes the perversities of current policies, with respect to their impacts on poor countries and to the distribution of costs and benefits within rich countries. Such research should be designed to speak to latent constituencies for reform within rich countries, including regions, industries, and income groups that are disadvantaged by current policies.

Fourth, and perhaps most importantly, more research is needed on how global environmental governance regimes can be reformed to democratize decision-making across North and South, and on how equity can best be pursued both in terms of both process and outcome. Such research could include, for example, questions regarding the appropriate choice of forum for various issues, the structure of regimes and institutions, the capacity of developing countries, and the generation and use of knowledge. Such research should be undertaken collaboratively between developed and developing country researchers, and be linked to advocates active in global environmental governance arenas.

Finally, there is a need for more research at the level of specific sectors and commodities to provide policy-relevant indicators for reform. Highly aggregated data, and analytical generalizations across sectors, are seldom useful to inform specific policy reforms. For example, better information on the level of effective fossil fuel subsidies across countries would support better indicators of progress on action to prevent climate change.

Appendix

Measurement Tools

This appendix provides a brief review of various tools that have been developed to capture the trans-boundary dynamics of environmental sustainability, that is, the impact of economic activity in one country on the environment in other countries and/or on the global environment. Many indicators of environmental sustainability have been advanced in recent years (Hales and Prescott-Allen, 2002), but none is adequate to the challenge of providing simple, comprehensive, and policy-relevant information on the impacts of industrialized country policies on the growth and poverty reduction prospects of developing countries. Three alternative approaches are assessed below: ecological footprint methodologies, material flows analyses, and indices of environmental sustainability.

Ecological Footprint Methodologies

The concept of an "ecological footprint" was developed in the mid-1990s (Wackernagel and Rees, 1996), and has been promoted by Redefining Progress and WWF-International (Redefining Progress, 2002; WWF 2002b). The methodology attempts to measure a population's consumption of renewable resources, and to compare that consumption level with nature's biological productive capacity, both expressed in terms of land area. The ecological footprint of a country is the total land area required to produce the resources that it consumes. The total footprint is built up from calculations of the land (or sea) area needed to produce crops, provide grazing land for livestock, produce timber products, produce fish and seafood, provide land for infrastructure, and sequester the carbon dioxide emissions resulting from fossil fuel energy use. The total or per capita land requirements to support a country's economy are then compared to the "biocapacity" of that country or available on a global per capita basis (respectively) to arrive at an "ecological deficit," the degree to which a country is "overshooting" its endowment of renewable natural resources or its share of global resources.

Popular efforts conceptually similar to the ecological footprint include calculations of "food miles" and "ghost acres." Food miles are defined as "the distance food travels from where it is grown or raised to where it is ultimately purchased by the consumer or other end-user" (Pirog et al., 2001). These data are then used to correct for the environmental externalities of fossil fuel used in transport. The potential significance of such externalities is suggested by the recent increase in agricultural imports to the United States—26 percent from 1995 to 1999 (Pirog et al., 2001). Ghost acres are the land areas in developing countries used to grow commodities for export to rich countries. For example, 44 million ghost acres in Thailand are used to supply manioc for European cattle (Lobstein, 1999). Food miles and ghost acres calculations are apparently designed to inform consumers of the environmental impacts— including impacts in other countries—of their purchases, as well as to promote more local food production.

An advantage of the ecological footprint is that it reduces a variety of forms of consumption to one number, and graphically portrays different levels of consumption across countries. Importantly, it also attempts to incorporate the trans-boundary impacts of consumption, by adding imports and subtracting exports, and in particular, by including the carbon embodied in imported products. It thus enables the identification of "ecological debtors" and "ecological creditors" among countries (Sturm et al., 2000). This highlighting of gross imbalances could raise public awareness and be a useful trigger for further attention and investigation by policymakers. The ecological footprint has also recently been used in conjunction with the World Economic Forum's global competitiveness rankings to demonstrate that eco-efficiency offers a competitive edge (Sturm et al., 2000).

However, the ecological footprint approach has been criticized on a number of grounds. First, there is concern that the weaknesses in the underlying data—particularly those used to estimate indirect consumption—render the calculations prone to error (Carpentier et al., 2002). Second, the methodology rests on the defensibility of aggregating very different kinds of numbers. While it may be relatively straightforward to estimate the land area needed for crop, livestock, and timber production, the conversion of fish and seafood consumption and energy consumption into land area is more problematic (personal communication, Matthews, 2002). Also, the use of global average land productivity penalizes countries such as the United States, where productivity is high (personal communication, Matthews, 2002). In addition, the methodology treats "sinks"—the capacity to absorb pollution and waste—only for carbon dioxide emissions, thereby failing to capture important elements of pollution and ecosystem disruption (personal communication, Matthews, 2002). Finally, several critics have pointed out that the methodology is a static "snapshot" rather than a model with predictive power (McDowell, 2002). An advisory group convened by the Commission for Environmental Cooperation of NAFTA concluded that "while provocative and occasionally useful as a way of exploring certain limited kinds of environmental impacts...the ecological footprint...has too many flaws to serve as a guide for national or international policies addressing the environment" (Carpentier et al., 2002).

Material Flows Analyses

"Material flows" is an accounting methodology developed by a consortium of research institutes in the United States, Europe, and Japan (Adriaanse et al., 1997, Matthews et al., 2000). The purpose of material flows analysis is to offer a set of physical accounts parallel to economic accounts to track the movement of "stuff" through the economy. Using metric tonnes as a common unit, the methodology estimates the total weight of materials displaced or extracted from the natural environment to support economic activity. One objective of material flows analysis is to capture the "hidden flows" of materials—such as soil erosion—that are not captured by economic accounts. Another is to account for the physical disruption that takes place in other countries to generate economic goods that are imported. Material flows analysis proposes as a summary measure the "Total Material Requirement," which accounts for both hidden and extraterritorial flows.

A related measure and concept are the "Material Input per Unit of Service" and the "ecological rucksack" developed by the Wuppertal Institute (Schmidt-Bleek, 2001). As implied by its name, the MIPS estimates the material intensity—including materials, energy, and transport—of a particular product throughout its life. The ecological rucksack refers to the weight of the metaphorical baggage of materials used to produce a finished good.

The advantage of material flows analysis is that it draws attention to the physical reality underpinning economic activity. In addition, it allows tracking of where displaced materials end up—for example, dispersed into air, water, or land—and accounting for material flows by sector. It also allows for the tracking of the "dematerialization" of economies over time—for example, progress toward "Factor10" objectives, which seek to reduce dramatically the natural resource inputs necessary to achieve the current standards of living in industrialized countries—while elucidating how gains in production efficiency can be more than overcome by increases in scale in the generation of wastes.

However, the methodology also has several disadvantages. First, it is highly data-intensive, and data to support "hidden flows" are scarce. Second, the methodology does not attempt to assign a value to different materials in terms of their environmental or health impacts; thus a ton of toxic waste is equivalent to a ton of eroded soil (Carpentier et al., 2002). Third, the methodology does not treat water. Nevertheless, based on analyses of regional dynamics in the agriculture and forestry sectors, the CEC advisory group concluded that material flows analysis can "reveal patterns of material use not always apparent from monetary data, thereby demonstrating the promise of the methodology" (Carpentier et al., 2002).

Environmental Sustainability Indices

The Environmental Sustainability Index (ESI) is produced by the Center for International Earth Science Information Network at Columbia University and the Yale Center for Environmental Law and

Policy in collaboration with the World Economic Forum. The ESI purports to measure the "overall progress toward environmental sustainability" of individual countries in a way that enables quantitative cross-national comparisons (Yale Center for International Law and Policy, 2002). The 2002 index is built up from 68 data sets and 20 indicators that are clustered into five "core components": environmental systems, reducing stresses, reducing human vulnerability, social and institutional capacity, and global stewardship. All variables of the index are weighted equally.

The index attempts to measure the prospects for long-term sustainability by combining measures of current environmental and social conditions (such as air and water quality and health indicators) with drivers of environmental change (such as total fertility rate) and measures of institutional arrangements to address sustainability (such as control of corruption). The ESI core component of "global stewardship" includes six indicators related to consumption of global resources (marine fish catch and consumption of CFCs and seafood) and trans-boundary environmental impacts (sulfur dioxide exports and carbon dioxide emissions per capita and per dollar of GDP). The 2002 index ranks 142 countries. Finland, Norway, Sweden, Canada, and Switzerland come out on top, while Haiti, Iraq, North Korea, Kuwait, and the United Arab Emirates come out at the bottom (Yale Center for International Law and Policy, 2002).

The "Dashboard of Sustainability" under development by the Consultative Group on Sustainable Development Indicators appears to be following a similar approach (International Institute for Sustainable Development, 2002). Clusters of indicators are being developed for environment (such as air and water quality), economy (such as employment), and society (such as poverty). Like the ESI, all indicators are weighted equally. The society cluster includes indicators of international cooperation, and so has at least some relevance for trans-boundary impacts.

The 2001 ESI was criticized by *The Ecologist* and Friends of the Earth (2001) for being biased in favor of rich countries. The alleged bias results from the inclusion of too many indicators of socioeconomic conditions (such as under-5 mortality rate), and the inclusion of indicators of "capacity" (such as private sector participation in the World Business Council for Sustainable Development) not strongly correlated to environmental outcomes. In particular, the ESI was criticized for weighting all variables equally, with the result that key variables such as carbon dioxide emissions and global impacts more generally were underweighted. *The Ecologist* produced an alternative index correcting for these flaws, and the country rankings were dramatically altered. For example, the United States moved from 11th place in the ESI ranking to 112th place in *The Ecologist*'s alternative.

A strength of the ESI is its transparency, which allows the sort of recalculation by others described above. Individual indicators most related to the impacts of rich country policies on poor countries— such as those included in the "global stewardship" component— could be pulled out and weighted to illuminate this aspect of sustainability more effectively.

Considered separately, the global stewardship component does provide a somewhat different rank ordering among rich countries than the ESI overall, particularly in terms of the worst performers. Of the ten high-income OECD countries that score the highest in the ESI over all, seven are also in the top ten from that group that score the highest in the global stewardship component. At the bottom end, however, only Japan is in the bottom five high-income OECD countries in the ESI overall and in the global stewardship component.

However, the global stewardship component is itself implicitly weighted toward issues of greater interest to the North than to the South: six variables relate to international cooperation and funding related to ozone depletion, acid rain, endangered species, and the Global Environment Facility, while only five related to climate change and marine resources. In addition, while the latter do capture the North's disproportionate consumption of global resources, they do not capture the policies that drive that consumption.

Priorities for Further Research

None of the approaches reviewed above scores high across the board on the criteria for sustainability indicators proposed by IISD (2002): policy relevance, simplicity, validity, time series data, availability of affordable data, ability to aggregate information, sensitivity, and reliability. For the purposes of assessing the impact of rich country policies on poor countries, issues of policy relevance, data availability, and ability to aggregate information appear to be particularly constraining.

None of the approaches described above attempts to capture key features of rich country *policies*, as opposed to consumption patterns, that directly impinge on developing countries. Accordingly, a first priority is to develop new indicators that could capture progress in changing the policies that drive resource use. For example, in addition to measuring carbon intensity and carbon emissions per capita, it would be useful to compare the degree to which rich countries tax (or subsidize) fossil fuel consumption in their domestic economies, and the degree to which policies encourage investment in less carbon-intensive alternatives. And while not without severe methodological difficulties, some attention should also be given to developing indicators to capture subsidies to extraterritorial extractive industries, such as distant-water fishing fleets. The activities of bilateral export and investment promotion agencies would likely be an important component of such indicators. Overall, the development of such indicators would require further work on distinguishing "good" subsidies from "bad" subsidies from an environmental perspective on a sector-by-sector basis.

A second priority is to improve the database for monitoring environmental sustainability. All of the measurement approaches reviewed above are constrained by inadequate data. Particular attention should be given to information that is poorly represented in more traditional economic data sets and official statistics, including the "hidden flows" of natural resources that do not enter the market, and capturing the informal (often illegal) exploitation of natural resources such as forests and fisheries. Better methodologies for estimating the environmental impacts "embedded" in resources flows, such as carbon and water, would also be useful.

A third priority is to address the "apples and oranges" problem that compromises the utility of aggregating various indicators, either by focusing on sectoral indicators or by improving methodologies for aggregation. Most effort to date has gone into approaches that focus on arriving at a national-level aggregate measure or index that allows overall comparisons across countries. While such efforts are quite useful for drawing attention to the significant differences in overall consumption patterns, particularly between North and South as well as among industrialized countries, their direct utility for policymaking is limited. Focused analysis of the direction, magnitude, and environmental impacts of specific commodity flows could be more usefully tied to specific policy options. Initial effort by the Sustainability Institute to model commodity flows and their environmental impacts was a step in this direction (Johnston et al., 2000).

At the same time, the message conveyed by aggregate indicators would be more credible with improved methodologies for aggregation. For example, better justification for conversion factors of various resource uses into hectares would improve ecological footprint methodologies, while attention to discrimination among different kinds of materials of equal weight would improve the policy relevance of material flows analysis.

Finally, all the approaches would benefit from adherence to the highest standards of transparency, making underlying data, assumptions, and calculations available to the public. Assumptions, implications, and sensitivity analyses of alternative weightings of variables is an important component of such transparency.

Notes

1. This chapter was written by Frances Seymour based on research conducted by Suzanne Ehlers. Invaluable contributions were also provided by Kevin Baumert of World Resources Institute on the climate section, by Peter Riggs of Rockefeller Brothers Fund on the fisheries section, and by Emily Matthews of World Resources Institute on the measurement section. Navroz Dubash and Antonio La Viña of World Resources Institute and Robert Picciotto of the Global Policy Project provided helpful comments on an earlier draft. Linda Shaffer-Bollert of World Resources Institute provided research and editorial assistance.
2. Frances Seymour is director of the Institutions and Governance Program of the World Resources Institute. The World Resources Institute is an environmental think tank based in Washington, DC, that goes beyond research to create practical ways to protect the earth and improve people's lives. WRI's mission is to move human society to live in ways that protect earth's environment for current and future generations.
3. For example, environmental policy regimes in European countries constrain exports from the United States (for example, genetically modified organisms); predatory timber companies and fishing fleets from developing countries exploit the forest and marine resources of other developing countries; and the emissions of ozone-depleting substances by developing countries lead indirectly to impacts in industrialized countries.
4. However, it is useful to note that reform of those policies can have important positive externalities for developing countries. To cite one example, subsidies to the sugar industry in the United States have driven degradation of the Everglades through water pollution and conversion of wetlands to cane production. Removal of those subsidies would not only promote conservation of a globally important nature reserve, but would also create significant export opportunities for developing countries.
5. The issue of "carbon leakage" is treated in a subsequent section of this chapter.
6. Shifting of agriculture sector subsidies from production to conservation would of course also have more direct and immediate positive impacts on developing countries as well as on the environment.

7. While beyond the scope of this chapter, it is important to acknowledge that rich countries' dependence on natural resources affects the political economy of the developing countries that produce them. Natural resource extraction is often associated with extreme corruption and violence, as developing country elites vie to control sources of wealth and power, and developed country elites look the other way when strategic "partners" violate international norms of transparency and human rights. A report by Oxfam America found that oil and mineral dependent states suffered from unusually high rates of corruption, authoritarian government, government ineffectiveness, military spending, and civil war (Ross, 2001). Further, the study found that higher levels of mineral dependence are strongly correlated with higher poverty rates and income inequality, while oil dependence is associated with low spending on health and education (Ross, 2001). Perhaps for these reasons, export of natural resource wealth has seldom translated into improved livelihoods for the poor in resource-rich developing countries.

8. The softness of data on fisheries resources was exposed in a 2001 article in *Nature* that rocked the fisheries world. By modeling expected catches in different zones, Watson and Pauly (2001) determined that China had been systematically over-reporting its catch by almost 100 percent, thereby masking an overall decline in global fisheries catch over the last decade in official FAO statistics.

9. In contrast, an alternative argument suggests that foreign direct investment leads to pollution "halos" as multinational corporations bring industrialized country production standards with them to developing countries.

10. However, typical positions are reversed in the case of fisheries subsidies described above, in which environmental advocates are seeking to use trade disciplines to remove environmentally perverse subsidies, while trading interests (such as Japan) are calling for the matter to be dealt with by a sectorally competent body such as the FAO (WTO, 2002b).

References

Acheampong, Anthony. (1997). "Coherence Between EU Fisheries Agreements and EU Development Cooperation: The Case of West Africa." European Center for Development Policy Management (ECDPM) Working Paper No. 52. Maastricht: ECDPM.

Adriaanse, A. et al. (1997). *Material Flows: The Material Basis of Industrial Economies*. A joint publication of the World Resources Institute (WRI), the Wuppertal Institute, the Netherlands Ministry of Housing, Spatial Planning, and the Environment, and the National Institute for Environmental Studies. Washington, DC: WRI.

Agarwal, Anil, Sunita Narain, and Anju Sharma, eds. (1999). *Green Politics*. New Delhi: Center for Science and Environment.

Agarwal, Anil et al., eds. (2001). *Poles Apart*. New Delhi: Center for Science and Environment.

Anderson, J. W. (2002). "US Has No Role in U.N. Treaty Process." *Resources* (Summer): 12-17.

Andersson, Thomas. (1997). "The Tropical Forests as a Global Resource: Impacts of Trade-related Policy." Working Paper Series in Economics and Finance No. 187. Stockholm: Stockholm School of Economics.

Asian Development Bank. (2000). *Vanuatu: Agriculture and Fisheries Sector Review 2000*. Manila: Asian Development Bank.

Atuna. (2002). "Mexican Tuna Industry Sues US Brand Leaders for $1 Billion." Atuna (17 October). Online at: http://www.atuna.com/markt/News%20Articles/Mexican_tuna_industry.htm (17 December 2002).

Austin, Duncan, and Amanda Sauer. (2002). *Changing Oil: Emerging Environmental Risks and Shareholder Value in the Oil and Gas Industry.* Washington, DC: World Resources Institute.

Baumert, Kevin. (2002a). Personal communication (December).

Baumert, Kevin, ed. (2002b). *Building on the Kyoto Protocol: Options for Protecting the Climate.* Washington, DC: World Resources Institute.

Baumert, Kevin and Nancy Kete. (2002). "Introduction: An Architecture for Climate Protection." In Kevin Baumert et al.,eds., *Building on the Kyoto Protocol: Options for Protecting the Climate.* Washington, DC: World Resources Institute. Online at: http://pdf.wri.org/opc_full.pdf (4 December 2002).

Benedick, Richard E. (1991). *Ozone Diplomacy: New Directions in Safeguarding the Planet.* Cambridge, MA: Harvard University Press.

Brown, DeNeen L. (2002). "Canadian House Approves Kyoto Accord: Legislators Disagree on Whether Pact is Environmental Boon or Economic Trap." *Washington Post* Foreign Service (11 December): A30.

Brown, Lester. (2001). "World Grain Harvest Falling Short by 54 Million Tons." Earth Policy Institute. Online at: http://www.earth-policy.org/Updates/Update3.htm (13 December 2002).

Carpentier, Cline et al. (2002). "Understanding and Anticipating Environmental Change in North America: Building Blocks for Better Public Policy." Environment, Economy, and Trade Program Area, Commission for Environmental Cooperation.

Center for Science and Environment. (2002). "You Don't Take Friends to Court." Equity Watch Special Edition #5. New Delhi: Center for Science and Environment (CSE).

Chartered Insurance Institute. (2001). *Climate Change and Insurance.* London: Chartered Insurance Institute.

Crucible II Group. (2000). *Seeding Solutions. Volume 1. Policy Options for Genetic Resources: People, Plants and Patents Revisited.* Rome: International Development Research Center/International Plant Genetic Resources Institute/Dag Hammarskjöld Foundation.

Daly, Herman E. (1994). "Farewell Lecture to the World Bank." In John Cavanaugh, Daphne Wysham, and Marcos Arruda, eds., *Beyond Bretton Woods: Alternatives to the Global Economic Order.* London: Pluto Press.

Dernbach, John C. ed. (2002). *Stumbling Toward Sustainability.* Washington, DC: Environmental Law Institute.

Dooley, J. J., and P. J. Runci. (1999). "Adopting a Long View to Energy R&D and Global Climate Change." Report by Pacific Norwest National Laboratory operated by Battelle Memorial Institute for the U.S. Department of Energy. Online at: http://energytrends.pnl.gov/integrat/documents/pnnl-12115.pdf (17 December 2002).

Dubash, Navroz. (2002). Personal communication (December).

Dubash, Navroz, Mairi Dupar, Smitu Kothari, and Tundu Lissu. (2001). *A Watershed in Global Governance? An Independent Assessment of the World Commission on Dams.* New Delhi: WRI/Lokayan/LEAT.

E/Environmental Magazine. (2002). "Global Climate Change Threatens the Insurance Industry." (27 August). Online at: http://www.enn.com/extras/printer-friendly.asp?storyid=47833 (17 December 2002).

The Ecologist and Friends of the Earth. (2001). "Keeping Score: Which Countries are the Most Sustainable?" *The Ecologist* 31, (3): 44. Online at: http://www.theecologist.co.uk/archive_article.html?article=243 (3 December 2002).

European Union. (2002). "Environment Commissioner Wallstrom Welcomes Progress on EU Emissions Trading Directive." European Union News Release. No 68/02 (10 December). Online at: http://www.eurunion.org/news/press/2002/2002068.htm (13 December 2002).

Faeth, Paul, and Suzie Greenhalgh. (2000)."A Climate and Environmental Strategy for U.S. Agriculture." World Resources Institute Climate Note (November). Online at: http://www.wri.org/wri/sustag/break_green.html (4 December 2002).

Food and Agriculture Organization of the United Nations. (2000). *The States of World Fisheries and Aquaculture 2000.* Rome: United Nations. Online at: http://www.fao.org/DOCREP/003/X8002E/x8002e00.htm#TopOfPage (12 December 2002).

Gómez-Echeverri, Luis. (2000). "Most Developing Countries Are Neither Prepared to Address nor Interested in Climate Change." In *Climate Change and Development.* Edited by Luis Gómez-Echeverri. New Haven: Yale School of Forestry and Environmental Studies. Online at: http://www.yale.edu/environment/publications/climate/contents.htm (3 December 2002).

_____. (2001). *Conference Proceedings: The State of Food and Agriculture.* Rome, Italy, 2-13 November.

Grote, U. (2002). "Environmental Standards in Developing Countries." In F. Brouwer and D. Ervin, eds., *Public Concerns, Environmental Standards and Agricultural Trade.* Oxon: CABI Publishing.

Grynberg, Roman. (2002). "Fisheries Subsidies: Casting a Net Too Small." *Bridges Monthly Review* Yr. 6 (7). Online at: http://www.ictsd.org/monthly/bridges/BRIDGES6-7.pdf (12 December 2002).

Gupta, Joyeeta. (1997). *The Climate Change Convention and Developing Countries: From Consensus to Conflict?* Dordrecht: Kluwer Academic Publishers.

Hales, David, and Robert Prescott-Alenn. (2002). "Flying Blind: Assessing Progress Toward Sustainability." In Daniel C. Esty and Maria H. Ivanova, eds., *Global Environmental Governance: Options and Opportunities.* Pre-publication draft. New Haven: Yale Center for Environmental Law and Policy.

Houghton, J. T. et al. (2001). *Climate Change 2001: The Scientific Basis.* Contribution of Working Group I to the third assessment report of the Intergovernmental Panel on Climate Change. Cambridge: Cambridge University Press. Online at: http://www.grida.no/climate/ipcc_tar/wg1/index.htm (3 December 2002)

International Center for Trade and Sustainable Development. (2002a). "WTO Group on Rules Discusses Negotiating Agenda, Fisheries Subsidies." *Bridges Weekly Trade News Digest* 6 (5 March). Online at: http://www.ictsd.org/weekly/02-03-05/story1.htm (12 December 2002).

_____. (2002b). "Fisheries Subsidies Remain within General Context of Subsidies Talks at WTO." *Bridges Weekly Trade News Digest* 6 (12 March). Online at: http://www.ictsd.org/weekly/02-03-12/index.htm (12 December 2002).

_____. (2002c). "Canada Tables First Negotiating Paper on WTO Trade Remedy Reform." *Bridges Weekly Trade News Digest* 6 (23 April). Online at: http://www.ictsd.org/weekly/02-04-23/wtoinbrief.htm#3 (12 December 2002).

_____. (2002d). "Rules Negotiations: 'Friends of Fish' Call for Altering Subsidies Disciplines." *Bridges Weekly Trade News Digest* 6 (7 May). Online at: http://www.ictsd.org/weekly/02-05-07/index.htm (12 December 2002).

_____. (2002e). "Rules Negotiations: Japan Questions Uniqueness of Fisheries Subsidies." *Bridges Weekly Trade News Digest* 6 (10 July) Online at: http://www.ictsd.org/weekly/02-07-10/story1.htm (12 December 2002).

International Climate Justice Network. (2002). "Bali Principles of Climate Justice." Set of principles adopted at the final preparatory negotiations for the Earth Summit in Bali, June. Online at: http://www.corpwatch.org/campaigns/PCD.jsp?articleid=3748 (4 December 2002).

International Finance Corporation. (2002). *Developing Value: The Business Case for Sustainability in Emerging Markets.* Washington, DC: World Bank.

International Institute for Sustainable Development (IISD). (2002). "The Dashboard of Sustainability." IISDnet Consultative Group on Sustainable Development Indicators. Online at: http://www.iisd.org/cgsdi/dashboard.htm (13 December 2002).

Jobson, Suki. (1999). "Water-stressed Regions: The Middle East & Southern Africa-Global Solutions." Occasional Paper No 16. London: University of London, School of Oriental and African Studies.

Johnston, Denise, Chris Soderquist, and Donella H. Meadows. (2000). *The Shrimp Commodity System: A Sustainability Institute Report.* Hartland Four Corners: Sustainability Institute.

Karlsson, Sylvia. (2002). "The North-South Knowledge Divide; Consequences for Global Environmental Governance." In Daniel C. Esty and Maria H. Ivanova, eds., *Global Environmental Governance: Options and Opportunities.* Pre-publication draft. New Haven: Yale Center for Environmental Law and Policy.

Kwa, Aileen. (2002). *Laying the Groundwork for Cancun: Another Doha "Success"? Focus on the Global South.* Online at: http://www.focusweb.org/publications/2002/laying-the-groundwork-for-cancun.htm (13 December 2002).

Lankester, Kees. (2002). "The EU-Angola Fisheries Agreement and Fisheries in Angola." Background Document. World Wildlife Fund. Online at: http://www.panda.org/downloads/marine/Angola_Fishing_brief.doc (13 December 2002).

La Viña, Antonio G. M. (2002a). Personal communication (December).

_____. (2002b). "The Emerging Global Regime on Genetic Resources: Its Implications for Local Communities." Working paper. World Resources Institute, Washington, DC, Online at: http://governance.wri.org/project_description2.cfm?ProjectID=148 (13 December 2002).

_____. (2002c). "From Doha to Cancun: The WTO Trade Negotiations and Its Implications for Communities." Working paper. World Resources Institute, Washington, DC Online at: http://governance.wri.org/project_description2.cfm?ProjectID=148 (13 December 2002).

_____. (2002d). "From Kyoto to Marrakech: Global Climate Politics and Local Communities." Working paper. World Resources Institute, Washington, DC, Online at: http://governance.wri.org/project_description2.cfm?ProjectID=148 (13 December 2002).

_____. (2002e). "Sixth Meeting of the Conference of the Parties of the Convention on Biological Diversity." Special bulletin. World Resources Institute, Washington, DC, Online at: http://governance.wri.org/project_description2.cfm?ProjectID=148 (13 December 2002).

_____. (2001f). "Meeting of the Working Group on Access and Benefit Sharing of Genetic Resources of the Convention on Biological Diversity." Special bulletin. World Resources Institute, Washington, DC, Online at: http://governance.wri.org/project_description2.cfm?ProjectID=148 (13 December 2002).

_____. (2001g). "Seventh meeting of the Conference of the Parties of the Framework on Convention on Climate Change." Special bulletin. World Resources Institute, Washington, DC, Online at: http://governance.wri.org/project_description2.cfm?ProjectID=148 (13 December 2002).

Lee, James. (2001). *Environment, Statistics and Policy (ESP) project.* Global Environment and Trade Study at Yale University, New Haven. Online at: http://www.american.edu/TED/esp/about.htm (17 December 2002).

Limpitlaw, Erik M. (2001). "Is International Law Waterproof? The Impact of Technology on the Oceans as a Common." *Syracuse Journal of International Law & Commerce* 29:185: 185-206.

Lobstein, Tim. (1999). "Measuring Food by the Mile." *Living Earth and the Food Magazine* (now *Living Earth*). Online at: http://www.mcspotlight.org/media/reports/foodmiles.html (13 December 2002).

Mabey, Nick, and Charles Arden-Clarke. (1999). "Is There Really a North-South Split on Trade and the Environment?" WWF Discussion Paper (November).

Matthews, Emily. 2002. Personal communication (December).

Matthews, E. et al. (2000). *The Weight of Nations: Material Outflows from Industrial Economies.* A joint publication of the World Resources Institute (WRI), the Wuppertal Institute, the National Institute for Environmental Studies, the Institute for Interdisciplinary Studies of Austrian Universities, and the Center of Environmental Science at Leiden University. Washington, DC: World Resources Institute.

Maurer, Crescencia, and Ruchi Bhandari. (2000). "The Climate of Export Credit Agencies." World Resources Institute Climate Notes (May). Online at: http://www.wri.org/wri/governance/eca.html (19 December 2002).

McCarthy, James J. et al. (2001). *Climate Change 2001: Impacts, Adaptation, and Vulnerability.* Contribution of Working Group II to the third assessment report of the Intergovernmental Panel on Climate Change. Cambridge: Cambridge University Press. Online at: http://www.grida.no/climate/ipcc_tar/wg2/index.htm (3 December 2002).

McDowell, Natasha. (2002). "Ecological Footprint Forecasts Face Skeptical Challenge." *Nature* 419 (October 17): 656.

Metz, Bert et al. (2001). *Climate Change 2001: Mitigation.* Contribution of Working Group III to the third assessment report of the Intergovernmental Panel on Climate Change. Cambridge: Cambridge University Press. Online at: http://www.grida.no/climate/ipcc_tar/wg3/index.htm (3 December 2002).

Meyer, Marion. (1997). "The Insurance Industry and Climate Change on the Prairies: A Status Report." Appendix D in Responding to Global Climate Change in the Prairies, Volume III of the Canada Country Study: Climate Impacts and Adaptation, by Herrington, Ross, Brian Johnson, and Fraser Hunter. Environment Canada, Ottawa, Ontario.

Milazzo, Matteo. (1998). *Subsidies in World Fisheries: A Reexamination.* World Bank Technical Paper No. 406: Fisheries Series. Washington, DC: World Bank.

Munasinghe, Mohan. (2000). "Development, Equity and Sustainability (DES)." In R. Pachauri et al., eds., *Guidance Papers on the Cross Cutting Issues of the Third Assessment Report of the IPCC.* Tokyo: Global Industrial and Social Progress Research Institute (GISPRI).

Myers, Norman, and Jennifer Kent. (2001). *Perverse Subsidies: How Tax Dollars Can Undercut the Environment and the Economy.* Washington, DC: Island Press.

National Environmental Trust. (2002). "First in Emissions, Behind in Solutions: Global Warming Pollution from U.S. States Compared to More than 150 Developing Countries." National Environmental Trust, Washington, DC, Online at: http://environet.policy.net/warming/emissions.pdf (17 December 2002).

Nordhaus, William D. (1998). "New Estimates of the Economic Impacts of Climate Change." Unpublished manuscript. Yale University, New Haven. Online at: http://www.econ.yale.edu/~nordhaus/homepage/impact%20text%20122998a.PDF (13 December 2002).

Organization for Economic Co-operation and Development (OECD). (2002). *The DAC Guidelines: Integrating the Rio Conventions into Development Co-operation.* Paris: OECD.

Panayotou, T. (1997). "Environment and Natural Resources." In *Emerging Asia: Changes and Challenges*, Asian Development Bank.

Pauly, Daniel et al. (2002). "Towards Sustainability in World Fisheries." *Nature* 418 (August 8): 689-695.

Pearce, David. (2000). "How Developing Countries Can Benefit from Policies to Control Climate Change." In Luis Gómez-Echeverri, ed., *Climate Change and Development*. New Haven: Yale School of Forestry and Environmental Studies. Online at: http://www.yale.edu/environment/publications/climate/contents.htm (3 December 2002).

Petkova, Elena et al. (2002). *Closing the Gap: Information, Participation and Justice-making for the Environment*. Washington, DC: World Resources Institute.

Pirog, Rich et al. (2001). "Food Fuel and Freeways: An Iowa Perspective on How Far Food Travels, Fuel Usage, and Greenhouse Gas Emissions." Leopold Center for Sustainable Agriculture, Iowa State University. Online at: http://www.leopold.iastate.edu/pubinfo/papersspeeches/food_mil.pdf (13 December 2002).

Porter, Gareth. (2002). *Fisheries and the Environment, Fisheries Subsidies and Over-fishing: Towards a Structured Discussion*. Vol. 1. UNEP. Geneva: United Nations. Online at: http://www.unep.ch/etu/etp/acts/capbld/rdtwo/FE_vol_1.pdf (12 December 2002).

Raghavan, Chakravarthi. (1996). *Third World Network Trade and Development Series: The New Issues and Developing Countries*. Book No. 4. Penang: Third World Network. Online at: http://www.twnside.org.sg/title/rag-cn.htm (13 December 2002).

Redefining Progress. (2002). "Ecological Footprint Accounts: Moving Sustainability from Concept to Measurable Goal." Redefining Progress. Online at: http://www.redefiningprogress.org/programs/sustainability/ef/efbrochure.pdf (20 December 2002).

Repetto, Robert. (1995). *Jobs, Competitiveness and Environmental Regulation: What Are the Real Issues?* Washington, DC: World Resources Institute.

Repetto, Robert, and Duncan Austin. (1997). *The Costs of Climate Protection: A Guide for the Perplexed*. Washington, DC: World Resources Institute.

Riggs, Peter. (2002). Personal communication (December).

Roodman, David M. (1998). *The Natural Wealth of Nations: Harnessing the Market for the Environment*. New York: W.W. Norton & Company.

Ross, Michael. (2001). "Extractive Sectors and the Poor: An Oxfam Report." Oxfam America, MA. Online at: http://www.oxfamamerica.org/pdfs/eireport.pdf (12 December 2002).

Runge, C. Ford, et al. (1997). *Sustainable Trade Expansion in Latin America and the Caribbean: Analysis and Assessment*. Washington, DC: World Resources Institute.

Schiermeier, Quirin. (2000). "How Many More Fish in the Sea?" *Nature* 419 (October 17): 662-665.

Schmidt-Bleek, Friedrich. (2001). "The Story of Factor 10 and MIPS." Factor 10 Institute. Online at: http://www.factor10-institute.org/Mipsstory.htm (3 December 2002).

Schmidt-Bleek, Friedrich, and Ernst Ulrich von Weizsaecker. (2001). "The Development and Promotion of the Ecological Rucksacks and Material Input Per Unit Service (MIPS) Concepts, as Measures of the Ecological Stress of Products and Services." Takeda Award 2001 for World Environmental Well-Being. Takeda Foundation, Tokyo, Japan. Online at: http://www.takeda-foundation.jp/en/award/takeda/2001/fact/03_1.html (13 December 2002).

Schorr, David, ed. (2001). "Hard Facts, Hidden Problems: A Review of Current Data on Fishing Subsidies." World Wildlife Fund. Online at: http://www.worldwildlife.org/oceans/hard_facts.pdf (12 December 2002).

Schorr, David. (1998). "Towards Rational Disciplines on Subsidies to the Fisheries Sector: A Call for New International Rules and Mechanisms." World Wildlife Fund Discussion Paper. (September).

Seymour, Frances. (2002). "Private Finance." In John C. Dernbach, ed., *Stumbling Toward Sustainability*. Washington, DC: Environmental Law Institute.

Slade, Tuiloma, and Jacob Werksman. (2000). "An Examination of the Kyoto Protocol from the Small Island Perspective." In Luis Gómez-Echeverri, ed., *Climate Change and Development*. New Haven: Yale School of Forestry and Environmental Studies. Online at: http://www.yale.edu/environment/publications/climate/contents.htm (3 December 2002).

Sokona, Youba et al. (2002). "Climate Change and Sustainable Development: Views from the South." World Summit on Sustainable Development Briefing Paper. International Institute for Environment and Development and International Networking Group (RING). Online at: http://www.iied.org/pdf/wssd_07_climatechange_long.pdf (13 December 2002).

Sturm, Andreas, Mathis Wackernagel, and Kaspar Müller. (2000). *The Winners and Losers in Global Competition: Why Eco-Efficiency Reinforces Competitiveness: A Study of 44 Nations*. Zürich: Rüegger.

United Nations Conference on Trade and Development (UNCTAD). (2002). "Environment Requirements and International Law." Background Note TD/B/COM.1/EM.19/2. Trade and Development Board. Commission on Trade in Goods and Services, and Commodities. Expert Meeting on Environmental Requirements and International Trade, Geneva, 2-4 October.

United Nations Environment Program (UNEP). (2002). "Fisheries Subsidies and Trade Liberalization." UNEP Briefs on Economics, Trade and Sustainable Development. Geneva: United Nations. Online at: http://www.unep.ch/etu/publications/UNEP_Fisheries.pdf (12 December 2002).

United Nations. (1992). "Rio Declaration on Environment and Development." United Nations Doc. A/CONF.151/26 (vol. I) (1992); 31 ILM. 874 (1992). Online at: http://www.un.org/documents/ga/conf151/aconf15126-1annex1.htm (19 December 2002).

_____. (2002). "Global Trade System Keeps Developing World from Benefiting, Delegate Tells Second Committee as Trade and Development Debate Concludes." United Nations Press Release GA/EF/3021. (11 December). Online at: http://www.un.org/News/Press/docs/2002/GAEF3021.doc.htm (13 December 2002).

_____. (2002a). "Report of the World Summit on Sustainable Development." United Nations Doc. A/CONF.199/20. Online at: http://www.johannesburgsummit.org/html/documents/summit_docs/131302_wssd_report_reissued.pdf (19 December 2002).

Villar, Juan Lopez. (2001). *GMO Contamination Around the World*. Amsterdam: Friends of the Earth International.

Wackernagel, Mathis, and William Rees. (1996). *Our Ecological Footprint: Reducing Human Impact on the Earth*. Philadelphia: New Society Publishers.

Watson, Reg, and Daniel Pauly. (2001). "Systematic Distortions in World Fisheries Catch Trends." *Nature* 414 (November 29): 534.

Werksman, Jacob, Kevin Baumert, and Navroz Dubash. (2001). "Will International Investment Rules Obstruct Climate Protection Policies?" World Resources Institute Climate Note (April). Online at: http://pdf.wri.org/investrules.pdf (20 December 2002).

Wilson, John S., et al. (2002). "Dirty Export and Environmental Regulation: Do Standards Matter to Trade?" Working Paper No. 2806. Environment: Pollution, Biodiversity and Air Quality. Washington, DC, World Bank. Online at: http://econ.worldbank.org/files/13167_wps2806.pdf (13 December 2002).

World Bank. (2000). *Cities, Seas, and Storms: Managing Change in Pacific Island Economies*. Volume 1 Summary Report. (13 November). Washington, DC: World Bank.

_____. (2001a). *Making Sustainability Commitments: An Environment Strategy for the World Bank.* Washington, DC: World Bank.

_____. (2001b). "OED Review of the Bank's Performance on the Environment." Sector and Thematic Evaluation Group. Operations and Evaluations Department. (5 July). World Bank. Online at: http://wbln0018.worldbank.org/oed/oedevent.nsf/ f46f97c4d58ae624852568860054ffbe/77e5ad90ef06cf3c85256a7d006fb06f/$FILE/ OED_environment_review.pdf (20 December 2002).

_____. (2003). *World Development Report 2003: Sustainable Development in a Dynamic World: Transforming Institutions, Growth, and Quality of Life.* Washington, DC: World Bank.

World Commission on Dams. (2000). *Dams and Development: A New Framework for Decision-Making.* London: Earthscan.

World Trade Organization (WTO). (2001). "Ministerial Declaration WT/MIN(01)/DEC/ 1." Ministerial Conference, Fourth Session, Doha. (November).

_____. (2002a). "The Doha Mandate to Address Fisheries Subsidies: Issues." Submission from Australia, Chile, Ecuador, Iceland, New Zealand, Peru, Philippines, and the United States. WTO Negotiating Group on Rules. TN/RL/W/3 (24 April). Online at: http://www.mft.govt.nz/foreign/tnd/wtonegotiations/fishsubsidiesprop.html (13 December 2002).

_____.(2002b). "Japan's Basic Position on the Fisheries Subsidies Issue." WTO Negotiating Group on Rules. TN/RL/W/11. (2 July). Online at: http://www.jmcti.org/ 2000round/com/doha/tn/tn_rl_w_011.pdf (17 December 2002).

World Wildlife Fund. (1999). *Underwriting Overfishing.* No. 1 (September). Online at: http://www.panda.org/resources/publications/water/overfishing/Issuesum.pdf (12 December 2002).

World Wide Fund for Nature (WWF International). (2000). "Integrating Biodiversity and EU Fisheries Policy" Workshop 2: Subsidies and Financial Incentives. Presented at the WWF-UK workshop on Subsidies and Financial Incentives, London.

_____. (2002a). *Turning the Tide on Fishing Subsidies: Can the World Trade Organization Play a Positive Role?* WWF Issue Brief (October). Online at: http://www.panda.org/ downloads/policy/turning_tide_on_fishing_subsidies.pdf (13 December 2002).

_____. (2002b). *Living Planet Report.* Gland: World Wide Fund for Nature (WWF-International). Online at: http://www.panda.org/downloads/general/LPR_2002.pdf (12 December 2002).

_____. (2002c). "EU Takes the Lead on Implementing Kyoto Climate Treaty." U.S. Newswire (10 December). Online at: http://www.usnewswire.com/topnews/prime/ 1210-109.html (13 December 2002).

Yale Center for Environmental Law and Policy. (2002). *2002 Environmental Sustainability Index: An Initiative of the Global Leaders of Tomorrow Environment Task Force.* World Economic Forum Annual Meeting. New Haven: Yale University.

Zarsky, Lyuba. (1997). "Stuck in the Mud? Nation-states, Globalization and the Environment." Globalization and Environment Study. OECD Economics Division. The Hague, The Netherlands.

_____. (1999). "Havens, Halos and Spaghetti: Untangling the Evidence about Foreign Direct Investment and the Environment." Paper presented at OECD Emerging Market Forum, Conference on Foreign Direct Investment and the Environment, The Hague, The Netherlands, 28-29 January.

9

Some Observations on the Question of Coherence and Development

Yilmaz Akyüz[1]

In a closely integrated world economy, no country should be expected to be able to put its house in order independently of what is happening elsewhere. This is true for all countries, including the most advanced, but above all for developing countries. The issue of coherence should accordingly be formulated not just in terms of the impact of rich countries' policies on the poor, but also of the repercussions for multilateral rules and practices for development.

Thus, we have three sets of overlapping influences on development:

- Multilateral rules and practices (including those of the World Trade Organization, the Bretton Woods Institutions, and the United Nations). Clearly a few major industrial countries exert an undue influence on the shaping of the global institutional framework.
- Policies in the major industrial countries. In principle, these should be subject to the same set of multilateral rules and surveillance as the policies of other countries. But in practice, constraints imposed on the policies of industrial countries are significantly less than those on developing countries, and industrial countries enjoy considerably greater policy autonomy and greater scope for unilateral action than developing countries.
- Policies in developing countries. Many of these countries perhaps have more policy space than they effectively use to promote development and determine the pattern of integration into the world economy, but policy autonomy in developing countries is in general highly circumscribed, not only by multilateral rules and practices (including

271

WTO rules and IMF/WB conditionality), but also because of the sheer unilateral pressure of some industrial countries as well as financial markets.

A comprehensive study of coherence should focus on all three areas. One should start with a conceptual framework rather than with a piecemeal approach to the impact of this or that policy or practice on development. To be sure, advocacy is as important as research. But if one believes that efforts to influence national and global policies and practices of industrial countries are unlikely to bear fruit (that is, if the global environment cannot be made more development friendly), then one should enquire into how to survive in such an environment, seeking to reduce external vulnerability and increase self-reliance. Such a mood increasingly dominates the thinking of policymakers in developing countries, notably those in some Latin American countries, who realize that following an externally oriented pattern of development, and particularly catching up with the rich, is becoming more and more difficult.

What I would call "systemic coherence" could thus focus on whether or not multilateral rules and practices, and policies in industrial countries and developing countries in the areas of trade, investment, finance, debt, labor and so forth reinforce each other in support of economic growth and development. What is at stake here is not just whether policies and practices in each of these are individually supportive of development, but also whether they reinforce or work against each other. A partial approach to any one of these areas of influence, including the impact of rich countries' policies on development, would mean ignoring such linkages. In the case of trade, this was explicitly recognized in the WTO's Marrakech Declaration, which states: "Ministers recognize...that difficulties the origins of which lie outside the trade field cannot be redressed through measures taken in the trade field alone. This underscores the importance of efforts to improve other elements of global economic policymaking to complement the effective implementation of the results achieved in the Uruguay Round."[2]

"Systemic coherence" was the fundamental question that preoccupied the architects of the post-World War II international economic system in the Bretton Woods and Havana Conferences. Their goal was to establish a global system that would prevent the problems that were encountered in the interwar period, including financial crises, deflationary macroeconomic pressures, the collapse of primary commodity prices, leading to ad hoc restrictions over trade and capital flows, and beggar-thy-neighbor exchange rate policies. Their proposed solution was to be based on four pillars, explicitly stated among the objectives of the International Monetary Fund and in the charter of the proposed International Trade Organization:

- Full employment policies as a basis for trade expansion and liberalization and greater integration—thus putting jobs and growth in front of trade.
- Exchange rate and commodity price stability to ensure a predictable and stable trading environment and steady expansion of trade. Exchange rate stability was to be attained in conditions of strictly limited private international capital flows, which had proved excessively damaging in the interwar period. Commodity stability was to be secured by establishing an International Commodity Stabilization Fund to create buffer stocks.
- Provision of international liquidity for countries facing short-term payments imbalances in order to avoid deflationary macroeconomic policies and destabilizing currency adjustments.
- Provision of long-term finance for war-torn European countries to address their problems of structural trade imbalances and resource gaps.

The initiative was only partially successful in putting in place the institutional arrangements needed, and these arrangements functioned effectively for less than three decades, the so-called "golden age."

The International Trade Organization was intended to provide a rules-based framework for a multilateral trading system as well as to coordinate national policies to insure adequate levels of global demand and employment, but it was not created. The WTO that was finally established in the 1990s is based in principle on a single-tier system of rights and obligations for industrial countries and developing countries alike, and has placed trade liberalization in front of expansion of economic growth and full employment, thereby rekindling mercantilist agendas.

The proposed International Commodity Stabilization Fund never came into existence either. In the absence of global arrangements, industrial countries, notably the United States and the members of the European Union, resorted to unilateral protectionist schemes in order to provide stability to primary commodity prices and earnings for their producers. A Compensatory Financing Facility was established in 1963 at the IMF to deal with the consequences of commodity price fluctuations for developing countries, but this scheme eventually became ineffective.

Controls over international private capital flows were gradually lifted starting in the 1960s because they became ineffective as a result of inconsistent policies in the major industrial countries. The system of fixed but multilaterally negotiated adjustable exchange rates broke down in the early 1970s for the same reason. The United States, as the main reserve currency country capable of borrowing in its own currency, chose a benign neglect of the exchange rates of its currency. Europeans never opted for free floating against each other and chose to stabilize intra-European currencies within narrow bands, supported by effective institutional arrangements. These protected particularly the smaller European countries, which lost autonomy against Germany and gained autonomy vis-à-vis international financial markets and the International Monetary Fund (none of them has resorted to IMF borrowing since the 1970s). Again, developing countries were left alone to find unilateral solutions to the problem of managing their currencies.

Contrary to its original mandate, the International Monetary Fund has become an institution promoting deflationary adjustment to external shocks in developing countries, rather than providing international liquidity to prevent the need for such an adjustment. Recently, with increased capital account liberalization and recurrent financial crises in emerging markets, it has shown greater proclivity for financial bailout operations than for current account financing to countries facing temporary export shortfalls or rapid increases in import costs.

The specific problems of developing countries regarding long-term financing were not discussed in the Bretton Woods Conference but added only as an afterthought, with the emergence of the World Bank for multilateral development financing. However, the World Bank's resources and lending lagged considerably behind the growing needs of developing countries and, starting in the 1970s, increased emphasis has been placed on private capital flows for financing development.

Thus, in direct contrast to the arrangements that were originally thought necessary to promote coherence and global welfare, current arrangements favor private capital flows over official flows, exchange rate flexibility over stability, deflationary adjustment over financing, and the interests of creditors over debtors. The Bretton Woods/Havana arrangements were founded on the belief that adverse influences emanating from trade, finance, and debt should be countered through measures to preserve growth and development. But under present arrangements and policies, developing countries almost invariably find themselves obliged to adjust to international imbalances through domestic retrenchment. It is thus not surprising that once again the question has been raised whether developing countries' participation in the system is compatible with their development objectives.

Research Priorities

The current research on coherence concentrates on individual areas of policy and neglects, in large part, the question of consistency across the different realms of policy. More importantly, in so doing it focuses primarily on trade, and emphasizes the adverse impact of trade restrictions and lack of liberalization in industrial countries on development, including protection in agriculture, textiles, and clothing; agricultural subsidies; restrictions on transfer of technology (TRIPs); or labor mobility. In this sense, it is quite consistent with the current ideological rhetoric on the virtues of liberalization, adopted by the very same governments practicing such restrictions. Certainly, such a line can generate a broad alliance and can be potentially effective. However, the flip side of the coin is often neglected: that is, the adverse impact of the excessive and premature liberalization forced on many developing countries by the Bretton Woods Institutions or industrial countries in the context of WTO negotiations. For instance, there is very little in the literature on the impact of import liberalization on jobs, wages, and wage differentials, on government revenues and social spending, or on prices and incomes received by agricultural producers.

This point is also relevant for attempts to compartmentalize the economic and social aspects of development challenges, which criticize the Washington Consensus only for leaving out the latter from its agenda. Here the question that needs to be asked is whether social objectives could simply be added to the agenda of liberalization and privatization to form a coherent program.

To illustrate the inconsistencies that may result from partial and piecemeal approaches to coherence, one can look at the agricultural trade policies in the North. As noted above, various stabilization/intervention/subsidy schemes were originally introduced in response to the failure to deal with the global commodity problem in the post-war period. Now the agenda is to dismantle these while leaving the commodity problem outside the international agenda. Clearly, this does not make sense and it is not politically sensible to expect the governments in industrial countries to leave their commodity producers to the vagaries of markets in the same way that producers in Africa and elsewhere have been left. Thus, any realistic agenda for agricultural trade liberalization should bring the commodity issue back to the global agenda. Perhaps this explains the recent French interest in global commodity issues.

In addressing the possible benefits for developing countries of liberalization in trade-related matters by the North, it is also important to take into account reciprocity and single undertakings that govern the negotiations in the WTO. These mean that any trade concessions given by the industrial countries to developing countries are likely to be matched by concessions in the same or other areas of negotiation.[3] Thus, the benefits of the package as a whole, rather than that of increased mobility of labor, would need to be assessed.

Despite recurrent financial crises in developing countries, with their devastating consequences for poverty and development, the impact of global financial arrangements and financial and macro-economic policies in industrial countries on development has not received as much attention as trade-related issues. This is quite surprising, given that for most developing countries the financial shocks resulting from volatile capital flows and sudden changes in the terms and conditions of external financing have become a much more important source of disruption to development than trade shocks. The cost of financial instability and crises to developing countries may be at least as high as the potential benefits of liberalization in trade-related areas.

The greater vulnerability of developing countries to external financial shocks arises from a number of structural factors including their external indebtedness, the denomination of their external debt in foreign currencies, a higher degree of dollarization, the small size of their financial markets, and their underdeveloped institutions and practices for financial regulation and control. These factors magnify the adverse impact of destabilizing financial impulses from the major industrial countries, including changes in their monetary conditions, macroeconomic policies, interest rates, and exchange rates. Just as the sharp rise in United States interest rates and the appreciation of the dollar was a major factor in the debt crisis of the 1980s, likewise the swings in exchange rates and monetary conditions in the major industrial countries were major influences on both the surge in capital inflows and the subsequent outflows associated with the East Asian crisis. And shifts in monetary conditions in the United States have played a large role in the fluctuations in private external financing for Latin American countries. The instability of G3 exchange rates poses serious difficulties for developing countries, which typically link their exchange rates to major reserve currencies. It is indeed open to question whether emerging markets can attain exchange rate stability when the currencies of the major industrial countries are subject to large gyrations. Indeed, many observers (including Volcker and Soros) have suggested that the global economy will not achieve greater systemic stability without some reform of the G3 exchange rate regime, and that emerging markets will remain vulnerable to currency and financial crises as long as the major reserve currencies remain highly unstable.

The International Monetary Fund conducts bilateral surveillance of individual countries' policies through annual Article IV consultations, and multilateral surveillance through periodic reviews of global economic conditions in the context of the *World Economic Outlook*. So far, IMF surveillance has not succeeded in ensuring stable and properly aligned exchange rates among the three major currencies, or protecting weaker and smaller economies against adverse impulses originating from monetary and financial policies in the major industrial countries. This failure is due to the unbalanced nature of its surveillance procedures, which give too little recognition to the disproportionately large global impact of monetary policies in major industrial countries.

Given the degree of global interdependence, a stable system of exchange rates and payments positions calls for a minimum degree of coherence among the macroeconomic policies of major industrial countries—subject to the proviso that this quest should not lead to a deflationary bias in policies, since, as stated by IMF Article IV, the ultimate objective of policy is to foster "orderly economic growth with reasonable price stability." The existing modalities of IMF surveillance do not include ways of attaining such coherence or dealing with unidirectional impulses resulting from changes in the monetary and exchange-rate policies of the United States and other major OECD countries. Without incentives and enforcement procedures linked to the process of peer review under IMF surveillance, other countries in the world economy lack mechanisms under the existing system of global economic governance for redress or dispute settlement regarding these impulses. In this respect, governance in macroeconomic and financial policies lags behind that for international trade, where such mechanisms are part of the WTO regime, even though macroeconomic and financial policies have much greater impact on the economic performance of developing countries by influencing private capital flows, exchange rates, and the terms and conditions of their external debt.

Notes

1. The author is the former director, Globalization and Development, United Nations Conference on Trade and Development, Geneva. This chapter is based on remarks prepared for the seminar on "The Coherence and Impact of Rich Countries' Policies on Developing Countries" OECD Development Center, Paris, 23-24 June 2003. The opinions expressed here are those of the author and do not necessarily reflect the views of the UNCTAD Secretariat.
2. World Trade Organization (1994), "On the Contribution of the World Trade Organization to Achieving Greater Coherence in Global Economic Policymaking," Declaration of the World Trade Organization, 15 April 1994, Marrakech, paragraph 4.
3. For instance, in negotiations on trade in services, this could mean having a package combining, for example, Mode 4 of movements of natural persons with trade in financial services.

10

Linking Research, Monitoring, and Advocacy: Worlds Together or Worlds Apart?

Keith A. Bezanson[1]

One of the recent mantras in social policy research pays homage to the links between researchers and policymakers. A variant on the mantra places advocacy as an intermediary link in the chain, responsible for forcing the pace of policy change by using the results of research as leverage on those who take decisions. The vocabulary of policy research has shifted accordingly and embraces terms such as "networked global knowledge systems," "ex ante linkages with policy makers," "collaborative agenda setting," "continuous feedback," and so on. The mantra and the vocabulary notwithstanding, there is much to suggest that the reality is quite different and the policy researchers and policymakers remain more "worlds apart" than "worlds together."

In its 1998 *World Development Report*, the World Bank reaffirmed the centrality of knowledge (and research as an essential component of knowledge) to the development prospects of nations. The Bank's assessment of this centrality was unequivocal:

...the balance between knowledge and resources has become perhaps the most important factor determining...standard of living.... Forty years ago, Ghana and the Republic of Korea had virtually the same income per capita. By the early 1990s Korea's income per capita was six times higher than Ghana's...half of the difference is due to Korea's greater success in acquiring and using knowledge.[2]

In most respects, this view from the World Bank is entirely unsurprising. From the dawn of time, knowledge, research, and technology have been key elements in the growth and development of societies. Entire eras are named for the levels of their research and technological sophistication: the Stone Age; the Bronze Age; the Iron Age; the Age of Sail; the Age of Steam; the Jet Age; the Computer Age. But the links between knowledge and development are much more than jets and computers. They involve a combination of knowledge, techniques, and concepts; of tools, machines, farms, and factories; of organization, processes, people; and decisions by policymakers. The cultural, historical, and organizational context in which knowledge is generated and applied is the key to its success or failure. In short, the key to the value of new knowledge and of research is found in the science and the art of getting things done through their application.

Yet the history of advance through new knowledge and new technologies is not only a matter of successful strategies, plans, or knowledge management systems, important as these are. The history of development breakthroughs by way of new knowledge and new technologies has been far more one of surprises and of unpredicted shifts. We need only recall that in the early years of the twentieth century, the Annual Report of Western Union (the large American telegraph company) announced to shareholders that the newly invented telephone was an "interesting but limited" piece of equipment that would prove of "little consequence to the economy." We are also reminded that, some thirty years later, Thomas Watson, founder of IBM, wrote that the computer would have only very few commercial applications.

It is obvious, therefore, that attempts to craft and apply longer-term arrangements linking research systems to policy systems are complicated and fraught with dangers. This would appear to be more so today than ever before. Ours is a hybrid era, one caught somewhere between bronze and computers, between sail and jet engines, one in which quality has become confused with quantity, and means with ends. For poorer countries, it is a time of immense technological opportunity and optimism. It is also a period when the world confronts the continuation of unimaginable poverty and hopelessness. It is a time of unprecedented flows of information and of speed of technological change. And it is unlike any other period in history; for today, the direction of new knowledge and of technology is influenced and fashioned not only by artisans and artists, farmers, machinists, and dreamers, but also by politicians, bureaucrats, economists, far-away corporate planners, aid agencies, and charities. Never before in history have so many non-technical people exerted so much influence on the advancement, retardation, and movement of science and technology.

The Role of National Policy Sciences

This context has led to an increasing emphasis on what Yehezkiel Dror,[3] writing in the 1970s, termed "policy sciences"—arrangements, structures, and methodologies whose principal aim is to embed research into policy and policymaking into research. Throughout the world, the 1960s and 1970s witnessed a virtual explosion in the number of research units and institutes constructed on the policy sciences model. The vast majority of these focused specifically on economic and social policy through research.

In recent years the success and the value of these policy science institutes has been the subject of contentious debate and vastly divergent views. Matters are complicated by the fact that the impacts of policy research have always been especially difficult to measure and causal linkages almost impossible to establish. But these debates are really a subset of a much larger debate on the value of *national* policy research systems in economics, science, and technology. The argument goes this way: national policy research systems are designed to provide advantage to a national economy by creating and facilitating a competitive edge for the goods and services produced within the nation's borders. A globalized trading arrangement means not only that goods, business, and finance move in an unrestricted manner across national borders, but that the products of R&D, in the form of ideas, systems, skills, science, and technology, will increasingly move in the very same manner. In a globalized world, the argument continues, national policies for science and technology are doomed because any possible benefits will quickly move, or "leak," out of the individual country.

In its extreme form, the argument against national policy and policy research systems goes further. It grants as desirable national policies for macroeconomic stability (for example exchange rate policies, fiscal balance measures). Beyond such fundamentals, however, the extreme argument holds that effective economic decisions can only be made at the level of the individual company or firm. Finally, the argument holds that rapid technological change calls for fully flexible approaches to policy and that national (i.e., government) policies are necessarily rigid and run counter to the interests of development.

This argument against national research and policy systems in economics, science, and technology dominated the debate over most of the past fifteen years. More recently, however, strong arguments have emerged in support of the role that the policy sciences can play in national economic development.

First and perhaps most significantly, the argument against national systems is itself being modified as a result of new evidence. For example, in its 1997 *World Development Report*, the World Bank, following extensive examination, concluded that the role of national economic, industrial, technological, and social policy is critical to establishing conditions for development that go beyond those that the market itself is likely to create. In arriving at this conclusion, the Bank was explicit on the policy imperative for poorer countries to fine-tune the complex relationship between the market and society. In this regard, the Bank observed that the experience of the East Asian tigers as well as the failures of national efforts elsewhere lend strong support to the need for appropriate instruments of modernization, including national science policy instruments.

Second, the investments by firms and companies that go with globalization have been shown to be targeted to locations whose comparative advantage is not only low-cost labor but the particular strengths of a healthy, educated, and technically skilled population. Long-term national economic, social, and human resources policies have been shown, particularly in Southeast Asia, to be critical in attracting and retaining such investments.

Third and of great significance is the finding that—if the strength of globalization lies in its wealth-creating capacity—its weakness— if undirected and uncontrolled—lies in its disregard for and damage to the environment and its exacerbation of gross inequalities both within and between nations. In Japan, such negative consequences are increasingly defined as "evidence of market failure," as they affect deleteriously such "national purposes" as social cohesion, reasonable equity, access to public goods, and political stability. These debates on national science policy systems appear to be becoming less polarized. Especially for developing countries, the main issue today is less whether such systems are or can be of value to national development and more whether individual countries can establish institutional arrangements that will provide a satisfactory cost-benefit return. An important question here is what linkages can best serve the production of new knowledge by social researchers and the application of that knowledge by policymakers.

Researcher and Policymaker: The Linear Model

The general view that research is important to good decisions goes back a long way. In Western societies it dates at least to the Enlightenment period in the eighteenth century, when reason and science rather than religion were affirmed as the basis for human progress. Over the past 300 years, societies have accepted, and most often supported enthusiastically, the notion of a productive relationship between the producers of knowledge (researchers) and the consumers of knowledge (decision-makers). There have been, of course, exceptions when decision-makers closed universities, ordered the burning of books, and attacked, imprisoned, or killed intellectuals and social theorists. But for the most part, a defining feature of Western society since the eighteenth century has been a general belief in "the inevitability of progress through the accumulation of knowledge."[4] Hence, research in general has tended to be regarded as a good thing. Policymakers have most often been inclined to provide, encourage, or even champion support to researchers.

A second characteristic that has been important to the relationship between research and policymaking has been an assumption that knowledge proceeds to policy in a linear manner.[5] This assumption may be seen in the social sciences though it has perhaps been clearest in the physical sciences, where the general practice was to leave decisions on research to scientific researchers, usually working in universities or specialized research laboratories. Applied research was essentially treated as a separate function and assigned to specialized units, departments, or institutes staffed by engineers, designers, and technicians. The job of applied research was to convert scientific research into prototypes of utilitarian products and processes. These, in turn, would go to the production/application lines of producers and manufacturers. The essential task of the policymaker was to ensure that the separate components of the linear system were all in place, and that they were adequately staffed and funded.

Things were, of course, seldom quite this simple or sharply differentiated, but the broad outlines do generally reflect the relationship between university research and manufacturing, the structure of large-scale manufacturing, and the role of policymakers.

Decline of the Linear Model

Since the 1970s, this linear model of knowledge has been increasingly abandoned, initially as a consequence of changes in the industrial sector. The relationship between the production of new knowledge and its application has been experiencing its most profound transformation since the eighteenth century. The viewpoint of international firms is that they need immediate access to research and knowledge that will allow them to deliver low-priced goods and services of greater quality and diversity. This, they have concluded, cannot be achieved without *integrating research, industrial design, and production and ensuring continuous innovation and improvements.* Throughout the world, firms have abolished their departments of research, applied research, engineering, and strategic planning and have integrated their functions fully into their production departments.

This same trend is now occurring in public institutions. Decision-makers in governments in much of the world are, in effect, challenging the linear model. To some extent, the trend is being driven by purely financial considerations, but it is also motivated by the considerations reached by the industrial sector, that is, that much of research should be demand-driven; that major benefits result from a tighter integration of the functions of research, design, and production, and that continuous innovation is essential. The results are that government research facilities in North America, Europe, and in much of the developing world have been or are being "privatized." Universities throughout the world are being required to compete for and raise by themselves the funds required for research.

The Drivers of the Change

The initial impetus to a social reordering of the linkages between knowledge production and knowledge application came from the severe economic slowdown that occurred in the 1970s in most industrialized economies.[6] Though severe and extended, the slowdown reversed by the early 1990s, but the social reordering of knowledge production and application has continued. Thus, the slowdown alone does not adequately explain the extent to which subsequent industrial restructuring eliminated the linear model. Nor does it explain at all well the widespread public institutional changes that are similarly reordering the structural characteristics of a knowledge system that had powered Western progress for more than three centuries.

The dramatic shifts in the characteristics of the relationship between researchers who produce knowledge and policymakers, including business managers, who use that knowledge, are, in fact, the result of a much deeper set of changes that is occurring in policymaking itself and in the conduct of research. Let us consider some of these changes first from the perspective of policymaking and second from the perspective of research.

Changes in Policymaking and the Demand for Research

The relationship between decision-makers and knowledge systems has undergone major change over the past several decades. The metaphor of a tidal wave has been used to characterize the enormous amount of data that was being put at the disposal of managers, government officers, executives, and policymakers everywhere.[7] Although surprise is expressed at this situation, it is not one that came about suddenly. Rather, it evolved steadily over the last eighty years, though the scale and momentum of change have grown exponentially over the past few years. The evolution has had three distinct stages:

First Era: Easy Information

In the first stage, which may be dated up to the Second World War, information sources were relatively few. Although scattered, they were rather easy to identify, and—if resources were sufficient—to access. Sources had few interconnections and information gathering and processing operated as an "iterated system"[8] in which the various interactions between the system and its environment (between knowledge production and decision-making) could be dealt with independently from one another. At this stage, the structure of the web of information sources would correspond to what Emery and Trist called "the placid-clustered"[9] environment for an organization, in which it is possible to ignore the interconnections within the environment of a system.

Thus, at this stage an organization's capacity to process and use information would probably exceed the capacity of the environment to generate it, and information gathering and decision-making would be more sequential than synonymous processes. The decision-maker in this era would have adequate personal connections to information sources, would use a high degree of personal judgment to assess the validity and relevance of information, and would not use technical gadgets.

Second Era: Managed Information

The second stage (after 1945) saw a substantive increase in the generation of information, a multiplication of data sources, and rapid growth in the amount of information provided to policymakers, planners, and decision-makers. Special efforts were required to follow the evolution and characteristics of information sources. The performance of an organization would have been governed to a large extent by the advantages gained through access to privileged information and by the capacity to acquire and process reliable information from specialized services.

In these circumstances, strategies to gain access to information and to manage secrecy (by selective withholding of data, protection of information sources, etc.) become crucial aspects of competitive strategies. The increased speed of information transmission makes it necessary for organizations to develop short reaction times, which, in turn, require vastly increased and specialized information processing capabilities—the use of computer processing, mathematical models, telecommunication facilities, and the establishment of specialized information processing units. This is the era of management information systems and of computer data networks in which there are many interconnections among the components of the environment and the system. The decision-maker in this era would rely on specialists to access and assess the validity of information through management and computer data systems, would seek to react quickly to unforeseen situations using the information provided, and would use some technical gadgets.

Third Era: Information Overload

We are now in the tidal wave era of vast information overload from a constantly multiplying number of sources. The technologies that accompany this third stage, however, are also allowing a synthesis of stages one and two by making it relatively easy once again to identify and access information sources (again, resources permitting).

Today there are many sources for each unit of information and a large amount of redundancy and interconnection in the networks and channels. There is no longer a need to devise sophisticated strategies for gaining access to data and for preserving secrecy. With such overload and richly interconnected information networks, there are ample opportunities to contrast different sources of information, checking them against each other. The management of secrecy has generally been replaced by a need to devise strategies for competing in a transparent information environment. In organizational theory terms, this new situation would correspond to what Emery and Trist have called "the turbulent environment,"[10] in which the main task of a system is to maintain an unstable equilibrium and to develop organizational response capabilities. The decision-maker in this era needs specific information to respond to a specific need, is able to assess the importance of data, can function in terms of large scenarios while facing an information overload, and can deal with constant shifts in knowledge that create a climate of policy turbulence.

Let us examine in a little more detail the context for decision-making in this third era. Some of the main features seem to be:

Knowledge is being created at unprecedented speed. A universal complaint of policymakers today is that they are faced with information overload. As David Linowes points out, knowledge has been growing at an astonishing pace:

It took from the time of Christ to the mid-eighteenth century for knowledge to double. It doubled again 150 years later, and then again in only 50 years. Today it doubles every 4 or 5 years. More new information has been produced in the last 30 years than in the previous 5,000.[11]

This is not surprising. Scientific advances and technological innovations are at the root of the complex transformations that have taken place during the last half-century. Increasingly, the products of research in the forms of science and technology have become deeply enmeshed in all aspects of human activity, to the extent that it has now become commonplace to speak of "knowledge societies" as the key to future success. Most observers agree that this has profound implications for the organization of human activities and for all aspects of social policy.[12]

Networks have become the organizational basis for policymaking. By their very nature, networks require the integration of inputs and actors into the process of decision-making. The commercial linkages between transnational corporations now cover manufacturing, finance, trade, and services. Strategic alliances between corporations in pre-competitive research and development, coupled with fierce competition in final-product markets, demand new corporate and national strategies. A significant shift is taking place in the organization of productive and serviced activities in the globalized segments of the world economy. The economic unit is no longer the enterprise, whether local, international, or transnational, but a specific *network* created for a particular purpose at a particular time, that operates in large part independently of the various enterprises that established it. As Castells points out, "...organizational arrangements...are all based on networks. Networks are the fundamental stuff of which new organizations are and will be made."[13]

Policymaking has become more complex and difficult. This is especially true in the public domain where an increasing number of issues interact with each other, more actors are involved, time has accelerated, and second-order effects have become more important. There is a need to consider not only domestic issues, but an important range of external factors. This is the case not only for economic and business decisions but also for social decisions. According to some observers,[14] strictly domestic policies hardly exist any more. The policymaker, therefore, has been internationalized and must articulate a range of external and internal factors and does not have the luxury of focusing only on domestic constituencies.

The process of policy implementation has also become more complex. Policy instruments, which include legal devices, organizational structures, and operational mechanisms, must contend with multiple perspectives and a growing variety of interest groups, many of which focus only on a single issue. This requires that many more issues be taken into consideration in the implementation of policies.

Institutions now matter much more than in the past and there are many more of them. In parallel with (and perhaps because of) the impetus towards globalization has been a dramatic rise in institutions at the local level. More broadly, there has been a worldwide "explosion"[15] in civil society and voluntary organizations. Because of this, anticipation, foresight, and strategic planning aimed at defining both priorities and sequences have acquired greater importance for policymakers.

Public goods are becoming less local and more regional and global. A public good is a commodity, service, or resource whose benefits, if they are available at all, are available to everyone, so that consumption by one individual does not detract from its consumption by another. If the benefit of the public good is limited geographically, it is a local or national public good, but if benefits accrue across all or many countries it is a global or regional public good. In practice, most public goods relevant to development are not "pure" but "mixed" public goods—in the sense that they provide individual, local, or national benefits but increasingly have spillover effects of importance to other countries. The World Bank has provided the following working definition of global public goods:

...commodities, resources, services—and also systems of rules or policy regimes with substantial cross-border externalities that are important for development and poverty reduction, and that can be produced in sufficient supply only through cooperation and collective action by developed and developing countries.[16]

The increasing integration and interdependence of nations is converting a broad range of what used to be regarded as purely local or national public goods into goods whose benefits (and costs) spill over into other countries. This trend was first recognized in the 1970s and the 1980s with respect to the environment and the associated implications for conserving biodiversity, reducing deforestation, managing water resources, and curtailing desertification, among other goals. Other global public goods (and global public "bads") that have been explicitly recognized as such by multilateral organizations such as the World Bank now include peace building and reconstruction efforts, which have increased with the demise of the Cold War; interventions to forestall health epidemics, particularly the spread of AIDS/HIV in Sub-Saharan Africa; environmentally induced public health problems; corruption; money laundering; drug-trafficking; and human rights abuses.

The increasingly regional and global character of public goods raises thorny questions of the appropriate division of labor among communities, states, and international organizations and about who should pay for these goods.

These factors outline the dramatically changed and continuously shifting context in which decision-makers find themselves today. The same factors also suggest that, if the needs of decision-makers are to be served, significant changes must occur in the pattern and content of research provided to them. The conduct of research itself (especially social science research) has, however, also experienced major changes that affect the relationship between research and decision-making. Let us now turn briefly to these.

Research and Its Implications for Policy

Social science research has made important strides during the last decades and has become more and more intertwined with policy and decision-making. Much of this trend has been demand-led and has resulted from shifts over the past twenty years in public support for social science research. Public authorities in much of the world have increasingly linked public support for social science research to public policy concerns. While many social researchers have opposed and lamented this trend on the grounds that it overemphasizes utilitarianism, many other researchers have welcomed the change as an incentive to demonstrating the relevance of scholarship to public benefit.

The number of social science publications aimed specifically at decision-makers has increased significantly, but it is the new information technologies that have afforded an especially powerful tool for social scientists to communicate policy-relevant knowledge directly to policymakers. As knowledge about social interactions, human activities, and decision-making has increased, the capacity of social science research to synthesize has become more important.

Monitoring in real time the way in which institutions, enterprises, agencies, and individuals behave and make decisions has become much more important. This has led to new indicators and methods of research, which respond to the need for more accurate, speedy, and reliable sources of information. In particular, social science research has focused on the development of new indicators (such as the human development index, freedom index, corruption index, environmental indicators, gender indicators, and so on) to better portray a more complex and messy reality, and to trace the impact of changes in policies and decisions.

At the same time, there are new social science research methods at our disposal. Polling techniques have improved considerably, and now include "deliberative polling" as a way to overcome the difficulties associated with the lack of information by those persons being polled. Focus groups are now extensively used to test the acceptability of proposed policies, as well as the reactions of the man and woman in the street to ideas and viewpoints posited by high-level policy and decision-makers. Search conferences and similar group-dynamic techniques are now being used to explore issues in depth and to forge consensus among the main actors in policy and decision-making. These were not widely available just a few years ago and provide new means to "verify" the content and relevance of policies.

As regards new methods of social science research of particular relevance to poorer countries and poorer populations within countries, there has been a growing emphasis on participatory poverty assessments (PPAs). These have shown that poor people throughout the world emphasize different dimensions of poverty than those typically used in policy analysis and by policymakers. For many years, poverty assessments have used income and consumption indicators, education levels, and health status to determine levels of poverty, such data being derived from household surveys. PPAs have begun to sharpen the diagnosis of poverty by applying methods that aim to understand poverty from the perspective of the poor. The method elicits both quantitative and qualitative data on broader indicators of poverty and aims directly at influencing policymaking.

The Internet now provides access to a huge amount of information of all types, from archival records to up-to-date statistics, and to a wide variety of views and opinions. The possibility of organizing consultation processes using the Internet has also altered the way in which policies are made.

The cycle between theory formulation and verification has been shortened considerably, and it is now necessary to continuously adjust theories and conceptual frameworks. The overabundance of information makes theory all the more important, for it provides a way of filtering what is important and what is not, of focusing attention, and of guiding the search for relevant information. Imagination and creativity acquire greater importance, and it is better to have the capacity to interpret and assess information about policies and decisions than to have access to that information.

This new context for policymaking places extraordinary demands on the capacity to exercise power and authority legitimately, fairly, and effectively. At the national level, governance has become an exceedingly difficult process of mediation among interests and aspirations that have their roots both within and outside a country. New global and international phenomena have appeared in full view, and for many of these phenomena there is no precedent to which to refer in arriving at decisions. Networks have become the organizational unit for decision-making.[17] In this context, social research is challenged as never before to provide timely and valuable inputs.

Differences in Culture and Rewards between Policymakers and Social Researchers

The interests of policymakers and social researchers may now overlap more than in the past, but large gaps still exist in both culture and reward systems. Some of the goals and values of social researchers differ quite widely from those of policymakers. Economists, for example, emphasize efficiency, whereas policymakers tend to emphasize winners and losers (i.e., distributional concerns). Policymakers often express goals in rather arbitrary quantitative terms (for example, "to extend comprehensive education to 95 percent of the population") whereas social scientists might speak of investing in basic education services to the point that marginal returns equal marginal costs.

Policymakers and social researchers also differ in how they measure the achievement of goals. For policymakers, success in terms of costs and benefits is a matter of the number of people affected, whereas social researchers in economics measure financial costs and benefits. A policymaker, therefore, might measure health performance in terms of the number of new hospital beds, whereas a social researcher would seek to measure improvements in health.

Policymakers also employ different decision-making criteria from those suggested by social researchers. An economist, for example, would emphasis the future cost of any potential project, whereas policymakers would tend to attach high importance to sunk costs in order to justify further investments. From the perspective of the policymaker, this is entirely logical as it reflects the amount of credibility that the policymaker has already invested, as well as the size of the project's constituency and its expectations.

A further issue is that of compensation. For the policymaker this is usually a critical factor. For the social researcher, especially for economists, it is usually an afterthought. Economists tend to find a solution satisfactory if, in theory, the losers *could* be compensated. For policymakers, the credibility of a new policy of project usually depends on mechanisms that guarantee that losers *will* be compensated.

Reward systems also often establish major gaps between policymakers and social researchers. An example of this comes from recent experience at the Institute of Development Studies. The Institute has been working for some years on a very large policy research program on access to education, especially for girls, in several African countries. This also involves working directly with the Forum for African Women's Education (FAWE), which is made up of African ministers of education and senior African educators. About two years ago, the members of FAWE and the social researchers were asked to rank the outputs they desired from the program. The results testified just how far apart the world of researchers can be from the world of policymakers. The rankings are shown in Table 10.1.

Much can be done to increase the relevance and value of social research to policymakers, but a good deal of university research will almost certainly remain unsuitable for use by policymakers. There are several reasons for this:

- Researchers often take much longer to produce results than policymakers with short deadlines can tolerate. The time needed for solid and serious research is often at irreconcilable variance with the time allowed to a policymaker.
- Social researchers often produce results that are highly critical of policy, without offering positive suggestions for action. This may be in keeping with the critical role of scholarship, but it often avoids simple recommendations that could be acted upon. Further, the tendency of some researchers is to learn tools and techniques and then to search for problems to which they can be applied. Streeten calls this "the law of the hammer according to which a boy, given a hammer, finds everything worth pounding, not only nails but also Ming vases."[18]
- The state of social science research is such that consensus is rare. Academic excellence is determined by success in questioning and in overthrowing existing theories and in replacing them with new ones. Thus, a state of conflicting views and information is normal. But this can undermine the confidence of policymakers when they realize that every study presented to them has a counterpart that provides opposite conclusions. Under such circumstances, policymakers are right to conclude that research is more likely to complicate matters than resolve them and that research may even serve to delay badly needed action because of conflicting advice.[19]

Table 10.1
Desired Outputs: Rankings by Policymakers and Researchers

FAWE		Researchers
1	Capacity building in planning and policy analysis	5
2	Endorsement of findings by government	4
3	Policy reform	3
4	High quality research and analytical inputs	2
5	Longer-term fundamental contribution to knowledge	1

Bringing Together the Worlds of Policymakers and Social Researchers

It has become almost a mantra for governments, international organizations, and research institutions to advocate stronger ties, partnerships, and "mutual learning." The writings of many social researchers urge that linkages between research and policymaking be established at the time of research design. Many authors have made suggestions about the design and dissemination of social research to make it more likely that the results will be applied. Some have discussed the conditions under which results are most likely to be used. Others have made very specific recommendations. There is, however, no magic formula or "one- size-fits-all" solution. The recommendations and writings on the subject would all flow logically from the issues, context, and experiences outlined in previous sections of this chapter.

For social researchers who want their scholarship to influence the decisions of policymakers, there are perhaps no better guiding principles than the "ten commandments" presented in a paper written almost twenty years ago.[20] These "commandments" were aimed specifically at economists but could apply more generally to all social researchers who wish their work to impact on policy:

1. Learn about the history of an issue. By researching previous arguments, the analyst can identify key interest groups, areas of disagreement, and data gaps, as well as changes in context that may influence future bargaining.
2. Find out who will be making the decision. Target the recommendations to those groups and present them in a form appropriate to the audience.
3. Timing is critical. Recommendations should be presented when they are most likely to receive attention. Generally, it is best to get into the debate before positions harden.
4. Learn about everyone's interests and arguments.
5. It's OK to think like an economist but don't write like one. Emphasize the decision at hand, the underlying problem, and options to solve it. Minimize descriptions of methodology, jargon, and equations.
6. Keep it simple. Where it is essential to explain complete features of an issue, illustrate them simply, using examples where possible.
7. Policymakers care more about distribution than efficiency. Explain what groups will be affected by the proposed measures, avoiding general references to "welfare losses for the economy."
8. Take implementation and administration into account. Don't propose measures that are technically optimal but too complex or costly for an agency to administer.
9. Emphasize a few crucial and striking numbers. Use statistics that emphasize the number of people affected, rather than aggregate dollar figures.
10. Read the newspapers. More generally, try to gain access to the same sources of general information as the policymaker, since these sources influence their perceptions.

These ten commandments may seem to suggest that the principal aim of research should be to satisfy policymakers and that all other purposes should be traded off in order to achieve that aim.

This would be a totally wrong conclusion. It is very often the case that the best and most appreciated research serves to challenge existing assumptions, ways of doing things, and previous decisions by policymakers.[21] No other factor is more important to the longer-term relationship between social research and policymaking than the quality of scholarship. The strongest and most consistent conclusion in independent assessments explaining the impact of policy research institutes is that the key factors are the quality of the research and the reliability of its methodology.

Notes

1. The author is director of the Institute of Development Studies, UK.
2. World Bank (1998).
3. Cited in Sagasti (1983).
4. Heller (1981).
5. Freeman (1991).
6. The "contagion" of this slowdown was to have particularly adverse effects on much of the developing world in the 1980s and 1990s.
7. Sagasti (1983).
8. Ashby (1996).
9. Cited in Sagasti (1983).
10. Cited in Sagasti (1983).
11. Cited in Sagasti (1999).
12. Drucker (1968).
13. Castells (1996).
14. See, for example, Deacon (1998).
15. Salamon (1994), pp. 109-122.
16. Development Committee (2000), p. 2.
17. Falk (1995).
18. Streeten (1988), pp. 9-40.
19. Aaron (1978).
20. Verdier (1984), pp. 373-384.
21. Weiss and Bucavalas (1977).

References

Aaron, Henry. (1978). *Politics and Professors: The Great Society in Perspective.* Washington DC: Brookings Institution.

Ashby, Ross. (1996). *Design for a Brain.* London: Science Paperbacks.

Castells, M. (1996). *The Rise of the Network Society.* Cambridge, MA: Blackwell Publishing, Inc.

Deacon, Bob. (1998). "The Prospects for Global Social Policy." In B. Deacon, M. Koivusalo, and P. Stubbs, eds., *Aspects of Global Social Policy Analysis.* Helsinki: Stakes.

Development Committee. (2000). "Poverty Reduction and Global Public Goods: Issues for the World Bank in Supporting Global Collective Action." Document DC/2000-16. Washington DC: World Bank (6 September).

Drucker, Peter (1968). *The Age of Discontinuity.* New York: Harper and Row.

Falk, R. (1995). *On Humane Governance: Toward a New Global Politics*. University Park: Pennsylvania State University Press.

Freeman, Christopher. (1991). *The Economics of Hope*. London: Pinter Publishers.

Heller, A. (1981). *Renaissance Man*. New York: Schocken Books.

Sagasti, Francisco. (1983). *Techno-economic Intelligence for Development*, IFDA Dossier (May/June).

_____. (1999). *Development Cooperation in a Fractured Global Order*. Ottawa: IDRC Books.

Salamon, Lester. (1994). "The Rise of the Nonprofit Sector." *Foreign Affairs* (July/August).

Streeten, Paul. (1988). "Reflections on the Role of the University and the Developing Countries." *World Development* 10, 6.

Verdier, James. (1984). "Advising Congressional Decision-makers: Guidelines for Economists." *Journal of Policy Analysis and Management* 3, 3.

Weiss, Carol, and Michael Bucavalas. (1977). "The Challenge of Social Research to Decision-making." In C. Weiss, ed., *Using Social Research in Policy Making*. Lexington, MA: Lexington Books.

World Bank. (1998). *Knowledge for Development*. Washington DC: World Bank and Oxford University Press.

11

Security and Development

Robert Picciotto[1]

The development endeavor is a creation of the second half of the twentieth century. Continuous reconsideration of concepts, processes, and instruments has been its hallmark. But the original vision of its pioneers has endured. The intellectual framework for a global enterprise grounded in shared objectives and buttressed by international cooperation was constructed in the 1950s. For more than fifty years, change and diversity have characterized development operations in response to dynamic technological change, market integration, geopolitical fragmentation, and the enduring attachment of peoples everywhere to their distinctive cultures.

But the noble aspiration of a world free of poverty, ignorance, and disease is the golden thread that runs through the troubled times of the past six decades. As early as 1941, President Franklin Roosevelt had made a commitment to bring the four universal freedoms (freedom of speech and expression, freedom of worship, freedom from fear, and freedom from want) to the four corners of the world. By 1998, we had come full circle when Amartya Sen, the Nobel laureate, identified freedom as the overarching end as well as the most effective means of development.

Spirited controversies about priorities, programs, and policies have characterized the development business. They have been informed by a peculiar compulsion for critical self-examination. Again, and again, development priorities (some label them fads) have shifted direction. A bewildering diversity of aid agencies and voluntary groups has emerged at national, regional, and global levels. The highly differentiated cultures, concerns, and aspirations of peoples and nations have elicited tailor-made policies and programs. A volatile operating environment has favored adaptive strategies.

The basic concepts of the development business emerged out of the ruins of World War II. They reflected the "can do" technocratic credo of the times as well as the demise of colonialism and the ascent of national self-determination. A universal declaration of human rights was adopted by the United Nations General Assembly in 1948 to give equal regard to all races and peoples. By turning swords into ploughshares, the international community made visible its continued adherence to the common values of freedom and decency that had motivated the allied forces in their successful war against tyranny. Then as now, the development enterprise was conceived in global terms and motivated by a universal yearning for peace and prosperity.

Whereas war had repressed the hopes and aspirations of humanity, the new development endeavor offered scope for people of goodwill to gather their scattered energies and skills toward a better and more secure world. But the Cold War intervened, and it inevitably re-shaped the volume and direction of development activities. More recently, the escalation in the number and severity of civil wars at the periphery (as well as the emerging global threat of terrorism) have cast a long shadow over the ideals of peaceful development cooperation.

Deep public concerns about personal safety and national security dominate the public discourse, with far-reaching implications for development. The legitimate security concerns of rich and poor countries will have to be heeded. But what is the meaning of security today, and how does security interact with development? How is freedom from fear connected with freedom from want?

Recent Trends

Only six months after the savage attacks on the twin towers of the World Trade Center, the United Nations Financing for Development Conference in Monterrey achieved its historic development consensus. The reciprocal obligations embedded in the Monterrey compact, combined with the unanimous endorsement of precise performance indicators by all members of the United Nations, have enhanced the public image of development. For the first time in a decade, aid levels are rising.

A major transformation of development policy is underway. The role of development assistance is likely to escalate in importance in the wake of the geopolitical turmoil triggered by the rising terrorist threat. The tensions between Europe and the United States should abate since the industrial democracies share fundamental security interests. The potential costs of continued division among them are unacceptably high and the need for enhanced multilateral action in reconstruction of war-torn countries is self-evident.

Aid flows expanded during the Cold War. They stagnated and eventually slumped after the fall of the Berlin wall and the demise of the Soviet Union. The trend was reversed and a recovery began soon after the United States announced its determination to fight terrorism around the world. Given that the emerging security threats are unlikely to be swept away any time soon, and considering that the chaotic conditions that breed terrorism are anchored in social and structural dysfunctions that cannot be remedied in the short run, aid should continue to rise from its current low levels.

Development theory and practice have evolved to reflect the changing structures of the integrating global economy, the disappointing economic and social performance of all developing regions outside of East Asia, and the resulting stresses for societies and the physical environment. By now there is little debate about the fundamentals of sound economic management. Endogenous growth models have incorporated the contribution of science and technology to wealth creation. Environmentally and socially sustainable development principles have broadened the development consensus. Development research has yielded valuable knowledge about the policies and capacities that are needed to make effective use of the rising international trade and cross-border capital flows associated with globalization.

Policy adjustment and institution building have replaced asset creation as the central focus of development assistance. Human capital, natural capital, and social capital—along with physical and financial capital—are now widely acknowledged as critical determinants of national competitiveness. Principles of effective aid have been endorsed by the Development Assistance Committee of the OECD to emphasize a holistic approach to development, ownership of policy reforms, partnership among governments, the civil society, and the private sector as well as a focus on results. The notion of concentrating aid resources on countries that take responsibility for their development has gained considerable currency. Looking ahead, more attention is likely to be devoted to security concerns and to the dilemma of states characterized by failed or failing governance.

Security and Development

The postwar rituals associated with rehabilitation and reconciliation give victorious powers an opportunity to promote their vision of international order and security. Emma Rothschild's finding that "all great postwar settlements of modern times have been accompanied...by new principles of international security" is illustrated by the centrality of the security deliberations at the San Francisco Conference that created the United Nations in 1945. Similarly, the founding fathers of the international financial system at Bretton Woods saw fit to frame the articles of agreement of the World Bank around the twin themes of reconstruction and development.

A long twilight struggle against the chaos of poverty, despair, and terror lies ahead and no grand design for a new international security framework is expected to emerge any time soon. Instead, gradual reform of existing international institutions lies in store. It will give more weight to human security because of the rising threats to peace and stability and also because the security of citizens is the main object of the nation state as well as the overarching goal of international relations.

Since the pioneering days of development, the promotion of economic and social welfare and the prevention of conflict have been conceived as complementary goals. While the financing of development and the promotion of peace making and peacekeeping were assigned to different parts of the international system, the overall architecture of the United Nations emerged as a coherent whole. Its foundations were laid on the bedrock of an expanded notion of international security that embraces individuals and groups as well as states. Whereas military security issues that involve relations among states were assigned to the Security Council, social and economic security issues that impact on individuals and groups were allocated to specialized agencies.

Prior to the postwar reconstruction of countries and institutions devastated by World War II, the notion of security as an individual good (rather than only a collective or state good) had been in decline. But its origins are deeply rooted in Western culture, and it is again on the rise. Cicero defined security as "the absence of anxiety upon which the happy life depends." Adam Smith defined it as "freedom from the prospect of a sudden or violent attack on one's person or property." Montesquieu described political freedom as "the opinion that one has of one's security." Tom Paine listed security (along with liberty, property, and resistance of oppression) among the protections offered by the Declaration of the Rights of Man.

Of course, the liberal ideas of the enlightenment philosophers have always been contested. The Universal Declaration of Human Rights presaged the elevation of individual and group security as the major aim of international relations. But the artful language of the Declaration, forged by compromise, is not binding under international law. The collective security doctrine on which the United Nations still relies is anchored in the sovereign nation state. Two detailed covenants (one devoted to civil and political rights; the other to social, economic, and cultural rights) were not approved until 1966. It took another ten years to secure enough signatures for their ratification. In 1977, the General Assembly adopted a resolution stating that political and civil rights are mutually interrelated and inseparable from social, economic, and cultural rights. Finally, the right to development was proclaimed by the United Nations General Assembly in 1986.

All of these proclamations conceal sharp ideological differences among member states. They are rooted in history. For example, the framers of the United States constitution were committed to the proposition that citizens have a natural right to pursue their own individuality in an open society. The French Revolution, by contrast, was dedicated to the premise that liberty is best achieved through individual participation in collective decisions. Communitarian, corporatist, and authoritarian regimes throughout history have tended to subordinate individual rights to the interests of the group, the party, or the nation. Both World War II and the Cold War were contests between competing views of security that pitted a liberal view of public legitimacy grounded in individual sovereignty against a monolithic concept grounded in the primacy of a state or an ideology. Similarly, rather than a clash of civilizations, the global war on terror today is the latest incarnation of the same contest. Hence, it is not altogether surprising that France, Germany, and Russia wished to "contain" Iraq instead of "liberating it" as the United States and the United Kingdom eventually proceeded to do.

The notion that democratic governments are above all instituted to secure individual human rights enjoys wide public appeal. Even the most authoritarian states label themselves democratic. But not all democracies are liberal, and not all liberal governments are democratic. The original concept of security as an individual good conceived by the enlightened philosophers eroded, and was swiftly reinterpreted as a collective good to be ensured by diplomatic or military means during the later phases of the French Revolution and throughout the Napoleonic wars. Subsequently, the state-centered notion of security became dominant and it achieved its most extreme form in totalitarian Nazi Germany and the authoritarian Soviet Union. In response, the industrial democracies followed suit and chose to emphasize state security—if only to mobilize the allied nations for the struggle, and to give the ideal of individual freedom a chance ultimately to prevail.

Recently, in the wake of the global terrorist threat, the United States has taken unprecedented steps to protect the security of its homeland. Legitimate public concerns have arisen about the potential erosion of individual rights in the very country that has spilled so much blood and treasure to protect them. Equally the doctrine of preemptive intervention announced by the United States, its unrivalled military superiority, and its renewed readiness to engage in conflict have created a great deal of unease in the international community. At the same time, as Leslie H. Gelb and Justine A. Rosenthal have remarked, "something quite important has happened in American foreign policymaking with little notice or digestion of its meaning. Morality, values, ethics, universal principles—the whole panoply of ideals in international affairs that were once the exclusive domain of preachers and scholars—have taken root in the hearts, or at least in the minds, of the American foreign policy community...the ethical agenda has at its core the rights of the individual."

Nor is the rise of ethics in foreign policy limited to the United States. The international civil society has made major progress in sensitizing public opinion in all countries to the outrages of genocide, ethnic cleansing, torture, genital mutilation, human trafficking, and corruption. The protection of human rights is no longer considered irrelevant as a rationale for humanitarian intervention. Fundamentally for the future of freedom, an entirely different security challenge prevails today, and it is bringing forth a concerted international response that transcends the traditional national security agenda. It has become crystal clear that the security threat posed by terrorism cannot be handled through traditional means since it is hidden, diffuse, elusive, and global in character.

State-centered security doctrines are still relevant vis à vis rogue states that provide platforms for deadly attacks against the industrial democracies and their partners. Specifically, once traditional diplomatic efforts have been exhausted, the awesome means of modern warfare available to the United States can be used to defeat states that fund or sponsor terror. But this approach cannot tackle flexible global networks that rely on a deadly mix of fanatical dedication, cheap and lethal technologies, and modern communications. Such networks are embedded in societies that are mired in stagnation, disconnected from the dynamic global economy, and overwhelmed by a demographic wave of unemployed young men who are seeking outlets for their anger and frustration. Only broad-based development strategies and a resolute tilt of global policies to favor the developing world can provide durable solutions to the basic security problems of the world community in this millennium.

According to a worldwide poll commissioned by the World Bank, an overwhelming majority of opinion leaders, especially those in the poorest countries, agree that fighting poverty is key to achieving world peace and lowering global tensions. Large majorities of opinion leaders in every region point to poverty reduction as critical to achieving peace. That sentiment is especially strong in Sub-Saharan Africa (91 percent), South Asia (87 percent) and the Middle East and North Africa (79 percent). But support for this proposition is also high in rich countries, where seven in ten opinion leaders strongly believe that fighting poverty is the path to peace.[2]

Consequences for the Development Agenda

The evolution of development priorities has always mirrored the ebb and flow of international security concepts. To be sure, the comprehensive concept of security held by most Western powers was not asserted decisively until after the Cold War had been waged and won. Specifically, the euphoria of the postwar reconstruction era was short-lived, as tensions between centrally planned countries and market-oriented democracies quickly arose and the Cold War began. The ideological confrontation yielded a development doctrine that emphasized infrastructure development in the public sector as the foundation of development. The policy made sense because of the pent-up demand for such investments throughout the developing world. It was convenient because it facilitated needed resource transfers through projects that could be effectively managed from afar. Most importantly, it was politically realistic since it represented a workable compromise between two competing notions of security, pitting the industrial democracies against the centrally planned economies.

The Cold War was waged not only through military and diplomatic means but also in the development arena. By the time the Soviet Union unexpectedly dissolved, following the fall of the Berlin wall in 1989, the development consensus had gradually moved toward a concept of economic security that transcended the state-centered view and reached downward to groups and individuals as well as upward to the global international system and even the biosphere itself. Thus, the peaceful velvet revolution led by Vaclav Havel in Czechoslovakia was explicitly motivated by the revival of the Enlightenment notion that individuals and the civil society are the only legitimate foundations of political legitimacy. In parallel, socially oriented nongovernmental organizations pressed the case for global poverty reduction, while worldwide environmental activism succeeded in bringing the interest of future generations to bear on the politics of the day.

In parallel, the share of the world's population living in electoral democracies rose, and the expansion of the concept of security accelerated during and after the Cold War. A comprehensive definition of security that incorporates individuals, groups, and the global environment germinated and flowered. This explains why the mix of development operations that was financed during the past decade gradually evolved from infrastructure projects and policy adjustment operations (designed to connect developing countries to the mighty engine of the global economy) toward social sectors and pluralistic interventions that tackle improved governance in the public sector, civil society participation, and the financing of private enterprises (including small and micro-enterprises), as well as the initiation of collaborative programs designed to fight infectious diseases, facilitate knowledge dissemination across borders, and protect the fragile global ecosystem.

Mirroring the extension of the security concept vertically as well as horizontally, the 1990s witnessed increased development assistance to the private sector as well as more reliance on small projects implemented by grassroots-oriented organizations, social funds, and community-based organizations. In parallel, multi-country collaborative alliances were assembled to strengthen the delivery of global public goods and promote the protection of the global commons. By 2000-01, the conceptual linkage between the expanded notion of international security and the comprehensive approach to development was consecrated by the specific inclusion of individual and family security (along with opportunity and empowerment) as one of the three main drivers of poverty reduction in the World Bank's landmark *World Development Report.*

Needless to say, extraordinary complexity in development programs resulted from the shift from macroeconomic policy adjustment (geared to reforming the state and accommodating global market forces) to a holistic and comprehensive development strategy that puts human development at the center of public policy and seeks to deal with all social and structural constraints on equitable and sustainable growth. Inevitably, the gap widened between these extraordinarily ambitious goals and the available financial resources and skills. The new paradigm induced inevitable inefficiencies as well as cynicism and resistance—among practitioners who still yearn for the simpler days when public sector projects were favored, and among market fundamentalists who rely on the providential workings of the hidden hand. Modest action toward specialization of functions within the development system, improved aid quality, and reduced transaction costs have resulted. But the pluralistic and liberal paradigm of development conceived as a social transformation process centered on individuals, groups, and future generations had largely triumphed when terrorists crashed planes on the twin towers of the World Trade Center.

Consequences for Policy Research

The expansion of the development agenda and the diversification of development activities have had major consequences for policy research. To appreciate how changing security considerations will influence policy research, it is necessary to bring in the concept of risk. Security is the antidote to risk; security policy is closely connected to risk-management theory, and policy research has to do with the objective assessment of public policies and programs.

Praise of individual risk taking is a characteristic of market societies. The myth of the frontier and the heroism of the entrepreneur resonate in the popular mind. By contrast, liberal democracies display extraordinary aversion to collective risk taking in the public sector. For any OECD politician, imposing any risks on citizens without their explicit consent is a career buster. Hence, a double asymmetry (the primacy of the individual over the society, and the equation of risk with danger if not catastrophe) motivates policymaking, and this is why policy research will increasingly be called upon to assess impacts. Precise identification of winners and losers has become an essential component of impact assessment. It will not be enough to concentrate on averages.

Nor is probabilistic thinking very influential in policy making. The Hippocratic oath ("first, do no harm") rather than the pursuit of the aggregate welfare dominates public policy. Hunger kills eight times as many people every day as died in the attacks of September 11, yet the resources allocated to development aid by the United States are only 3 percent of those allocated to the military. Clearly, different attitudes to risk prevail in different public policy domains.

In the most contested policy areas, tolerance of risk is low since decision makers must grapple with absolutist notions of what constitutes public policy success. Such an asymmetrical focus on failure rests on the urge to combine collective action with continuous accountability to local communities as well as to future generations. From this perspective, the public defines risk strictly in terms of negative outcomes, and risk management in the public sector is conceived as a set of constraints on public policy that is achieved through regulation, legislation, judicial processes, independent verification, and autonomous enforcement.

This means that Pareto-optimality is a political imperative in pluralistic societies. Any negative externality is perceived as an abuse of power requiring retribution. Any claim about uncertainty is interpreted as an excuse to escape responsibility. Risk assessment becomes a weapon to fight if not demonize authority, and consultation processes turn into obstacle courses for the sponsors of any intervention that causes environmental damage, social dislocation, or private discomfort—irrespective of its merits to the overall society.

The high transaction costs as well as the hidden costs of stagnation associated with total risk aversion are rarely recognized when policy decisions are made. Yet few worthwhile development ventures or policy adjustments make everyone better off; there are inevitably winners and losers. This means that leadership is critical to achieve the common good and compensation arrangements are essential to achieve sustainable policy reform.

At the global level, hierarchy is weak and reform hard to achieve. For example, OECD agricultural subsidies amount to $311 billion, compared to $52 billion in aid annually (2001). These subsidies benefit very few, and relatively prosperous, farmers and agro-industrial firms. They encourage intensive agriculture with negative consequences for the environment. They support uneconomic production of meat, dairy products, sugar, rice, cotton, and other crops that can be produced at a fraction of the cost in developing countries. The cost of these policy distortions is borne by consumers and taxpayers in OECD countries, and by poor farmers in the developing world.

Similarly, the highest tariffs on industrial goods imposed by rich countries affect products that are critical to the economic prospects of developing countries—steel, textiles, clothing, leather—and are consumed by relatively low-income consumers in OECD countries. But how will farmers in rich countries, and the communities they live in, be affected by agricultural trade liberalization? What compensation arrangements are needed to make a socially acceptable transition? What domestic coalitions of consumers and taxpayers can be assembled to change the political dynamics and achieve sustainable reform?

From a development perspective, how will reduced agricultural subsidies actually affect food-deficit countries suddenly faced with a larger import bill? Will a cut in milk subsidies benefit poor farmers in poor countries or large farmers in Australia, and New Zealand? How will a cut in sugar subsidies affect the former European colonies of the 18 ACP countries? Should agricultural policy reform, improved support services, and strengthened farm associations in poor countries precede agricultural trade liberalization in order to facilitate the transition and trigger a supply response? What would be the production and poverty impact of relaxing import restrictions on processed foods derived from such products as coffee, cotton, or cocoa? Isn't lack of competitiveness, and monopoly power in the highly concentrated agro-industries sector, a major constraint on reform? Would a gradual and comprehensive liberalization strategy in agriculture, manufactures, and services, combined with redirected aid, induce less dislocation and deliver more poverty reduction than a single-track focus on agricultural trade liberalization?

Striking the right balance between the protection of minorities and the interest of the majority is no easy task. When vested interests are tightly organized they tend to have disproportionate influence, and, as a result, they often capture social and governmental processes unless checked by the civil society. The single-issues constituencies that dominate the civil society draw their authority from the claim that they represent weak and neglected groups. But just as governments need the oversight of independent authorities, the legitimacy of voluntary agencies cannot be taken for granted. Their influence needs to be balanced by a hierarchy of democratically elected leaders that are accountable to the broader electorate and operate within the constraints of laws that promote the public interest.

This is where policy research comes in. By bringing objective evidence to bear, it informs policy debates and enhances public accountability. By facilitating mediation between the interests of individuals, groups, and the state, it contributes to the general welfare. By providing fair assessments of the performance of public, private, and voluntary agencies, it helps to adjudicate between their competing claims. This kind of role is needed especially in pluralistic and open societies. The development, democratization, and devolution process associated with globalization underlies the growing demand for policy research worldwide.

The New Security Equation

The current global security equation incorporates individuals as well as states because peace and development concerns are converging. At the recent Evian summit of the G8, adherence to the

Millennium Development Goals was reaffirmed, and the agenda put equal emphasis on development and security issues. Famine, water, health, e-government, illegal logging, the marine environment, science and technology, trade, debt sustainability, and financing for development were discussed along with the fight against terrorism, nonproliferation of weapons of mass destruction, and small arms trade.

Even from a narrow national security perspective, it no longer makes sense to concentrate solely on preventing and resolving international conflict. The capacity to engage in humanitarian interventions should be added to the arsenal of the international community. Civil wars are far more numerous, lengthy, and deadly than international wars. They induce large-scale displacement of people. They are a major factor in the growing flow of illegal trade in arms, drugs, diamonds, and people. They create failed states, and havens for terrorist movements and international criminal organizations. They provide breeding grounds for further international conflict by spilling over national borders and creating far-flung networks specialized in violence. These networks make use of modern communications and anonymous financial channels to generate huge illicit profits and to invest in the perpetuation of civil and international strife.

The ready availability of small arms has made civil wars increasingly lethal and lengthy. Countries where governance is weak, dependence on primary commodities is high, and income inequality is prevalent are especially at risk. High population growth, lack of employment opportunities, and social fragmentation create a favorable breeding ground for extremist propaganda and violent behavior, and facilitate recruitment by criminal and terrorist networks. Leaders of rebel groups and terrorist movements capture natural resources and exploit them for their private benefit and for the recruitment of mercenaries, disaffected youth, and abandoned children. Frequently, neighboring countries enter the fray and seek to gain control of territory and resources.

In many countries, the chaos of poverty and despair is almost indistinguishable from the chaos of war. Over the past decade, 10-15 percent of countries have been involved in civil wars. About 35 million people have been driven from their homes by conflict and repression. The World Bank estimates that more than a billion people live in countries that lack the policies or the capacities needed to sustain development without special support. Their economies are in decline; their governments are incompetent, and their unemployed youths are vulnerable to the lure of illegal profit and radical ideology. Some of these poor countries are already in the throes of conflict. Others are seeking to emerge from a conflict trap. Still others are teetering on the brink, and could be pushed into civil war by economic crisis, social fragmentation, or corrupt leadership. Recent trends suggest that civil war could become a chronic feature of the international environment, with substantial risks of spillover into rich countries through the lethal transmission belts of infectious disease, terrorism, and illegal trade in deadly weapons.

Thus, the economics of international security resemble the economics of public health. The risk of contagion is such that prevention is cheaper than cure. For countries vulnerable to conflict, well-targeted and competently managed conflict-resolution mechanisms, combined with generous development assistance, are the appropriate remedies. Thus, to contain the coming anarchy vividly described by Robert Kaplan, it would be prudent for the international community to equip itself, and make sufficient resources available to resolve the numerous conflicts that still rage in the developing world. The task is demanding and multifaceted. It involves mediation or military intervention. It requires breaking the iron triangle of poverty, violence, and isolation in which countries vulnerable to conflict are currently imprisoned. It calls for precautionary measures to protect neighboring countries from the contagion of unrest and violence.

Just as public health policy goes beyond medical attention, security policy extends to the enabling environment within which violence breeds. The task is global. The vectors on which conflict depends for its dissemination must be destroyed. The behaviors that encourage its spread must be discouraged. The root causes of social anomie must be addressed through the provision of economic opportunity, social safety nets, infrastructure investments, public education, and civil society empowerment. In sum, conflict prevention is just another term for broad-based development.

In time, based on rational analysis, defense analysts will recommend adjustments in the strategic plans of rich countries, greater reliance on multilateral conflict management measures, and a shift in resources from military to aid budgets. This is the logical thing to do, but logic does not always drive policy where risk is concerned. Currently, it is the public perception of danger rather than dispassionate risk analysis that drives resource allocations. Reliable surveys have established that actual knowledge about relative dangers from alternative sources has a minimal relationship with risk perception.

Nor are psychological profiles decisive in shaping risk perceptions. Appreciation of a particular risk is more often colored by ideology and personal experience. Attitudes toward authority and political orientation are equally influential. Rather than knowledge per se, it is the confidence that people place in the credibility of the institution that provides the information or formulates the policy (as well as the general worldview of the respondent) that seems to matter. Thus, credible evaluation, public advocacy, and political involvement hold the key to changes in security policy, and in development policy as well.

New Development Emphases

What do the foregoing observations imply for the future development agenda? First and foremost, the comprehensive concept of security is likely to prevail, and greater attention will be given to the security of groups and individuals in resource allocations. This will give a fillip to a reinvigorated and comprehensive development agenda that will gradually tackle the unfairness of global rules of the game that currently govern aid, trade, foreign investment, migration, intellectual property, and the environment. In time, the eighth Millennium Development Goal will be adjusted and monitored as systematically as the other seven goals. Aid alone will not do the trick.

Second, aid flows will continue to recover, making the achievement of the Millennium Development Goals more likely, with positive spillovers on the security environment. Aid will continue to address the main drivers of poverty reduction because they are almost the same as those that affect security, and will help to build goodwill. Aid policy reform will focus more deliberately on reducing transaction costs; untying aid; reforming technical assistance; harmonizing procurement, disbursement, and fiduciary practices; streamlining and effectively monitoring safeguard policies; consolidating aid delivery channels; and coordinating aid.

Third, the naivety of aid allocation policies that are driven by simplistic proxy indicators of a country's policy and institutional environment will be widely recognized. The methodological limitations of the static analyses and simplifying assumptions that underlie strict performance-based allocation doctrines have already been exposed. The current consensus of expert opinion is that aid can work in poor policy environments and that absorptive capacity and vulnerability conditions matter to aid effectiveness. Appropriate selection and sequencing are critical to the sustainability of security and development interventions. Too much aid too early in a failed state or a conflict-ridden country does not work. But scarce post-conflict aid does not work either.

Fourth, development will have to move further toward the front lines of conflict. Risks will undoubtedly be high, but the astronomical economic benefits of successful conflict-prevention and resolution would amply justify increased and proactive assistance for security and development in conflict-prone countries—using multilateral pressure and resources to impose mediated or externally imposed solutions on internal factions, followed by substantial and extended rehabilitation and reconstruction assistance, involving private sector agents and voluntary agencies as vehicles for aid delivery. In conflict-prone areas, transparency in royalty payments for extractive industries projects must be mandated; non-fungible contributions to special funds targeted toward poverty reduction activities must be provided; tight fiduciary, environmental, and social safeguards backed up by independent verification arrangements for enclave projects of strategic significance (for example in the energy sector) must be imposed, and output-based aid delivery mechanisms must be put in place.

Fifth, anti-capitalist protests will gradually abate as nongovernmental organizations find productive outlets for their idealism and join development advocacy groups in pressing politicians to adopt coherent policies toward the developing world. New and unexpected development coalitions will be forged between nongovernmental organizations, private industry associations, and private foundations. The delivery of key public goods that affect the welfare and security of the entire planet (prevention of HIV/AIDS and other infectious diseases; environmental protection programs; water supply) will be strengthened through global funding. Systematic creation of global issues networks involving governments, the private sector, and the civil society will define voluntary standards of corporate behavior that will secure broad public support by ensuring sustainability and equity without the need for regulations.

Implications for Policy Research

Creating knowledge is only one aspect of policy research. Delivering the right knowledge at the right time to the right individuals so that they take the right decisions that will affect people's lives is the other critical aspect. Policy research lies at the intersection of the social sciences and politics. Its function has forensic content[3] since the policy process in a democracy is fundamentally a debate about accountability.

During the Watergate hearings, Senator Howard Baker asked: "What did he know? and When did he know it?" Both questions arise every time a policymaker makes a decision that directly or indirectly affects public welfare.[4] Congruence between what a decision-maker knows and what he/she does is critical to his/her credibility. Policy research, provided it is transparent, strengthens the link of accountability between those who govern and those who are governed. It helps to protect the many against the abuses of power of the few.

A related benefit of policy research is that it shatters ill-founded dogmas and self-serving policy assumptions. Joseph Conrad called action "the enemy of thought and the friend of flattering illusion." This is why policy research is a target for capture by policymakers who want to maximize their room for maneuver. Speaking truth to power makes authority responsible by clarifying options and drawing the implications of policy decisions. But it is not welcomed when it challenges the prevailing consensus.

Finally, policy research has to do with learning. It provides evidence that helps to distinguish between good and bad decisions. This benefit is tapped through good communication between researchers and practitioners. Independence without isolation is a characteristic of good policy research.

Policy coherence is likely to become a growth area for development research. In physics, the meaning of coherence is precision— either the viscosity of a substance or the constant phase relationship of waves. Not so in the social sciences, where common usage prevails, and where, according to the dictionary, coherence connotes holding firmly together, being consistent, avoiding self-contradiction, or minimizing change over time.[5]

In public affairs, coherence thus defined is critical to credibility since the lack of it connotes political indecision, factional strife, or unprincipled behavior. Yet representative government must take account of divergent interests before reaching decisions so as to achieve workable compromises and get things done. Equally, changing circumstances, unexpected obstruction from third parties, and external contingencies ("acts of god") often intervene and justify shifts in government positions.

Only absolute and competent dictatorships operating in stable environments can be expected to achieve full coherence all of the time. The more complex and volatile the operating environment and the more open and diverse the society, the greater the chances that many goals must be pursued simultaneously to satisfy diverse constituencies, and trade-offs among them may be needed to achieve a consensus. Inevitably, the coherence of policies among sovereign political entities coherence is especially elusive. This is the thrust of Kenneth Arrow's Impossibility Theorem.

Against this background, four dimensions of coherence in development can be distinguished. They are closely interrelated since decisions that affect coherence along one dimension may have implications for coherence in another. Together, they summarize the global development challenge:

- *internal or policy design coherence:* defined as the consistent alignment between the objectives, modalities, and protocols of an individual policy carried out by a national government.
- *intra-country or policy agenda coherence:* the consistency among the policies of a particular country in terms of a specified objective (e.g., development).
- *inter-donor development policy coherence:* the consistency of policies across countries from a development perspective.
- *donor-recipient policy coherence:* the consistency of policies between rich and poor countries to achieve a given set of development objectives (such as the MDGs).

Much of the aid effectiveness literature has focused on the first kind of coherence—the alignment of means with goals. Only recently have other dimensions of policy coherence appeared on the radar screen of research analysts and decision-makers. Trade-offs and synergies exist both in the formulation of policy agendas and in the design of individual policies at the country, regional, and global levels.

Unintended incoherence may arise because of factors outside the control of policymakers. Incoherence may also be intended, and even necessary, to achieve acceptable outcomes, for example where tradeoffs must be made to accommodate conflicting goals. But there is no excuse for intended and unnecessary incoherence. That occurs all too frequently and delivers outcomes that are inefficient from an aggregate welfare perspective even though more acceptable outcomes would have been feasible.

Such incoherence may result from corruption or from unequal power relationships, which lead to outcomes that benefit the few at the expense of the many. Or it may be linked to bad luck or interference from outside parties. The search for coherence seeks to minimize unnecessary incoherence (whether intended or not) through good policy design, effective governance, shrewd negotiating skills, and good risk management. Good research on policy coherence is badly needed.

A related research challenge raised by the new development agenda involves replacing the current explanatory framework that ascribes all country development results to the performance of aid agencies and their developing-country partners. New research should broaden the scope of these assessments to encompass the rules of the game that poor countries must contend with. Doing so would be consistent with the agreed development partnership paradigm that takes account of the distinct accountabilities and obligations that rich countries owe to poor countries. Comparative research on the development coherence and impact of rich countries' policy reforms (in aid, trade, foreign investment, migration, intellectual property, and the environment) has high priority. After all, it is the combination of a range of policies in developed countries and in developing countries, rather than aid, that determines the scale of global poverty reduction at the periphery:

- *Trade:* research models[6] estimate the welfare benefits of trade liberalization in agriculture and manufactures to range anywhere from $108 billion to $760 billion for developing countries. Models including liberalization of trade in services raise the benefits by a factor of four to five.[7]

- *Private capital flows* are four times larger than aid flows.
- *Migration*: aid contributed about $49 billion in net official financing to developing countries in 2002 while migrants' remittances to developing countries were estimated to be at least $80 billion.
- *Intellectual property:* without free access to knowledge and technology, developing countries will remain marginalized in the global economy.
- *Environmental policies:* developing countries are highly dependent on natural resources for their livelihood; they will suffer disproportionately from global warming, from the depletion of the world's fisheries, and from the rising pressures on scarce land and water resources.
- *Security policies* need objective assessment. Bono, the music star, points out that international terrorists took refuge in Afghanistan, and that there may be ten Afghanistans in Africa. Even in strict security terms, does it make sense for the world to spend more than $830 billion on arms every year, and only $50 billion in aid, when an extra $24 billion would provide reproductive heath care for all women and another $19 billion would eliminate starvation and malnutrition?

Hence, the final challenge has to do with carrying out policy research focused on the costs of war, the benefits of conflict prevention and resolution, and the relative returns on development and military expenditures, in terms of the security benefits secured per dollar invested. The United States spends more than $300 billion annually on the military and about $10 billion in aid. Does this allocation make sense even from the standpoint of national security? What about the $900 billion of military expenditures in comparison with about $50 billion in aid?

Conclusion

Development has less to do with charity than with security. The comprehensive, holistic approach to development is well adapted to the long-term security strategy that is needed to deal with terrorism and civil wars. In conjunction with anti-terrorism precautions, diplomatic skills, and military initiatives geared to the prevention, mediation, and resolution of conflicts will be required, along with more and better aid, as well as a global policy framework that is friendlier to developing countries' efforts to help themselves. This is simply because tough governance issues, social problems, and economic policy dysfunctions lie at the source of the new security threats. Throwing the light of reason and bringing the weight of evidence to bear on the management of security and development risks constitutes the new policy research agenda. It is hoped that this volume will offer encouragement to social scientists to join together, explore new frontiers of peace and prosperity, and promote comprehensive reforms of development policies in rich and poor countries alike.

Notes

1. The author is managing director of the Global Policy Project and former director general, Operations Evaluation of the World Bank Group.
2. See http://web.worldbank.org/WBSITE/EXTERNAL/NEWS/0,,contentMDK: 20114427~menuPK:34458~pagePK:34370-
3. Webster's dictionary defines forensic as "characteristic of, or suitable for, a law court or public debate." Policy research is endowed with all three characteristics: publicness, contestability, and compliance with agreed standards of evidence.
4. The ongoing controversy about the intelligence available about weapons of mass destruction prior to the decision that led to British participation in the Iraq war illustrates this principle.
5. Hoebink (2001).
6. The high end of the range is drawn from Dessus et al. (1999) and is based on a dynamic model with productivity growth. The low end of the range is by Anderson et al. (2000) and is based on a static steady state model.
7. World Bank (2002).

References

Anderson, K., et al. (2000). *Potential Gains from Trade Reform in the New Millennium*. Paper presented to the Third Annual Conference on Global Economic Analysis, held at Monash University, Melbourne.

Dessus, Sebastien, K. Fukasaku, and R. Safadi. (1999). *Multilateral Tariff Liberalization and the Developing Countries*. OECD Development Center Brief No. 18. Paris.

Hoebink, Paul. (2001). *Evaluating Maastricht's Triple C: The C of Coherence*. Working Document, Policy, and Operations Evaluation Department, Ministry of Foreign Affairs, The Netherlands.

World Bank. (2002). *Global Economic Prospects and the Developing Countries*. Washington, DC.